JOURNAL · OF
M · O · R · A · L
THEOLOGY

VOLUME 7, NUMBER 1
JANUARY 2018

CHILDREN AND YOUTH:
FORMING THE MORAL LIFE

Edited by Mary M. Doyle Roche

JOURNAL · OF MORAL THEOLOGY

Journal of Moral Theology is published semiannually, with regular issues in January and June. Our mission is to publish scholarly articles in the field of Catholic moral theology, as well as theological treatments of related topics in philosophy, economics, political philosophy, and psychology.

Articles published in the *Journal of Moral Theology* undergo at least two double blind peer reviews. Authors are asked to submit articles electronically to jmt@msmary.edu. Submissions should be prepared for blind review. Microsoft Word format preferred. The editors assume that submissions are not being simultaneously considered for publication in another venue.

Journal of Moral Theology is available full text in the *ATLA Religion Database with ATLASerials®* (RDB®), a product of the American Theological Library Association.
Email: atla@atla.com, www: http://www.atla.com.
ISSN 2166-2851 (print)
ISSN 2166-2118 (online)

Journal of Moral Theology is published by Mount St. Mary's University, 16300 Old Emmitsburg Road, Emmitsburg, MD 21727.

Copyright© 2018 individual authors and Mount St. Mary's University. All rights reserved.

Except for brief quotations in critical publications or reviews, no part of this book may be reproduced in any manner without prior written permission from the publisher. Write: Permissions. Wipf and Stock Publishers, 199 W. 8th Ave., Suite 3, Eugene, OR 97401.

Pickwick Publications, An Imprint of Wipf and Stock Publishers, 199 W. 8th Ave., Suite 3, Eugene, OR 97401. www.wipfandstock.com. ISBN 13: 978-1-5326-4838-0

JOURNAL · OF
M · O · R · A · L
THEOLOGY

EDITOR EMERITUS AND UNIVERSITY LIAISON
David M. McCarthy, *Mount St. Mary's University*

EDITOR
Jason King, *Saint Vincent College*

ASSOCIATE EDITOR
William J. Collinge, *Mount St. Mary's University*

MANAGING EDITOR
Kathy Criasia, *Mount St. Mary's University*

EDITORIAL BOARD
Melanie Barrett, *University of St. Mary of the Lake/Mundelein Seminary*
Jana M. Bennett, *University of Dayton*
Mara Brecht, *St. Norbert College*
Jim Caccamo, *St. Joseph's University*
Meghan Clark, *St. John's University*
David Cloutier, *The Catholic University of America*
Christopher Denny, *St. John's University*
John J. Fitzgerald, *St. John's University*
Mari Rapela Heidt, *Waukesha, Wisconsin*
Kelly Johnson, *University of Dayton*
Warren Kinghorn, *Duke University*
Kent Lasnoski, *Quincy University*
John Love, *Mount St. Mary's Seminary*
Ramon Luzarraga, *Benedictine University, Mesa*
M. Therese Lysaught, *Loyola University Chicago*
William C. Mattison III, *University of Notre Dame*
Christopher McMahon, *Saint Vincent College*
Joel Shuman, *Kings College*
Matthew Shadle, *Marymount University*
Msgr. Stuart Swetland, *Donnelly College*
Christopher P. Vogt, *St. John's University*
Brian Volck, *University of Cincinnati College of Medicine*
Paul Wadell, *St. Norbert College*
Greg Zuschlag, *Oblate School of Theology*

JOURNAL OF MORAL THEOLOGY
VOLUME 7, NUMBER 1
JANUARY 2018

CONTENTS

Children and Youth: Forming the Moral Life
   Mary M. Doyle Roche 1

The Vice of "Virtue": Teaching Consumer Practice
   in an Unjust World
   Cristina L.H. Traina 13

Families in Crisis and the Need for Mercy
   Marcus Mescher 28

Transgender Bodies, Catholic Schools, and a Queer Natural Law
   Theology of Exploration
   Craig A. Ford, Jr. 70

Hooking Up, Contraception Scripts, and Catholic Social Teaching
   Kari-Shane Davis Zimmerman and Jason King 99

Youth, Leisure, and Discernment in an Overscheduled Age
   Timothy P. Muldoon and Suzanne M. Muldoon 112

Children's Right to Play
   Mary M. Doyle Roche 124

Review Essay
Exclusion, Fragmentation, and Theft: A Survey and Synthesis of
   Moral Approaches to Economic Inequality
   David Cloutier 141

Contributors 173

Children and Youth: Forming the Moral Life

Mary M. Doyle Roche

THERE ARE PLENTY OF AUTHORS MAKING THE best seller lists and the rounds on morning television news magazines talking about childhood. A number of popular books are shaping the public debate to which theologians and ethicists are endeavoring to contribute.[1] Many of the titles play on and stoke parental anxieties. A "crisis" gets attention and sells books: Robert Putnam's *Our Kids: The American Dream in Crisis*, U.S. Senator Ben Sasse's *The Vanishing American Adult: Our Coming-of-Age Crisis—and How to Rebuild and Culture of Self-Reliance*, and Leonard Sax's *Boys Adrift: The Five Factors Driving the Growing Epidemic of Unmotivated Boys and Underachieving Young Men*, *Girls on the Edge: The Four Factors Driving the New Crisis for Girls*, and *The Collapse of Parenting: How We Hurt Our Kids When We Treat Them Like Grown-Ups – Three Things You Must Do to Help Your Child or Teen Become

---

[1] There are a number of volumes that have explored various historical periods, religious traditions, and theological contributions and potential resources for a theology of childhood in the Christian tradition. They approach questions from the perspectives of systematic theology, ethics, practical theology, history, ecclesiology, law, and biblical studies. These include: Martha Bunge, ed., *The Child in Christian Thought* (Grand Rapids: Wm. B. Eerdmans Publishing Co., 2001), *The Child in the Bible* (Grand Rapids: Wm. B. Eerdmans Publishing Co., 2008), and *Children, Adults, and Shared Responsibilities* (New York: Cambridge University Press, 2012); Bonnie J. Miller-McLemore, *Let the Children Come: Reimagining Childhood from a Christian Perspective* (San Francisco: Jossey-Bass, 2003) and *In the Midst of Chaos: Caring for Children as Spiritual Practice* (San Francisco: Jossey-Bass, 2007); Don S. Browning, *Equality and the Family: A Fundamental, Practical Theology of Children, Mothers, and Fathers in Modern Societies* (Grand Rapids: Wm. B. Eerdmans Publishing Co., 2007); Joyce Ann Mercer, *Welcoming Children: A Practical Theology of Childhood* (Saint Louis: Chalice Press, 2005); Martin E. Marty, *The Mystery of the Child* (Grand Rapids: Wm. B. Eerdmans Publishing Co., 2007); David H. Jensen, *Graced Vulnerability: A Theology of Childhood* (Cleveland: The Pilgrim Press, 2005); Jerome W. Berryman, *Children and the Theologians: Clearing the Way for Grace* (New York: Morehouse Publishing, 2009); Patrick McKinley Brennan, ed., *The Vocation of the Child* (Grand Rapids: Wm. B. Eerdmans Publishing Co., 2008); Timothy P. Jackson, ed., *The Best Love of the Child* (Grand Rapids: Wm. B. Eerdmans Publishing Co., 2011); Annemie Dillen and Didier Pollefeyt, ed., *Children's Voices: Children's Perspectives in Ethics* (Leuven, Belgium: Peeters, 2010)*, Theology and Religious Education*; and John Wall, *Ethics in Light of Childhood* (Washington, DC: Georgetown University Press, 2010).

a Fulfilled Adult are just a few. Sounding an alarm is not new. In 1982, Neil Postman wrote *The Disappearance of Childhood* which highlighted how media is pressuring children to adopt adult patterns of dress and behavior. Jonathan Kozol has been writing for decades about the experiences of children who face racism and poverty in our nation's schools.[2]

The development of character, in the form of self-reliance and perseverance is prominent in the conversation. Angela Duckworth's best seller, *Grit: The Power of Passion and Perseverance* (along with her popular TED Talk) highlights the importance of the ability to stay with a task or committed to a goal even in the face of challenge and adversity. Paul Tough's *How Children Succeed: Grit, Curiosity, and the Hidden Power of Character* is another title in this genre. Building on this are the parental self-help selections like Lisa Damour's *Untangled: Guiding Teenage Girls Through the Seven Transitions into Adulthood*, Julie Lythcott-Haims' *How to Raise an Adult: Break Free of the Overparenting Trap and Prepare Your Kid for Success*, Jessica Lahey's *The Gift of Failure: How the Best Parents Learn to Let Go So Their Children Can Succeed*, and Lenore Skenazy's *Free Range Kids: How to Raise Safe, Self-Reliant Children (Without Going Nuts with Worry)*. Finally, there is the wildly controversial memoir promoting a mix of perseverance and over- (or better yet, hyper-) parenting, *Battle Hymn of the Tiger Mother* by Amy Chua.[3]

Though these authors differ on what precisely is the root cause of the current "crisis" and how adults (parents in particular) should respond, a number of common themes emerge. With the exception of Putnam and Kozol, who stand out for their attention to social systems and structures of injustice that impact children's well-being, most of

---

[2] See, for example, Jonathan Kozol, *Savage Inequalities: Children in America's School* (New York: Random House, Inc., 1991) and *Amazing Grace: The Lives of Children and the Conscience of a Nation* (New York: Random House, Inc., 1995).

[3] Amy Chua, *Battle Hymn of the Tiger Mother* (New York: Penguin Press, 2011); Lisa Damour, *Untangled: Guiding Teenage Girls Through the Seven Transitions into Adulthood* (New York; Ballantine Books, 2016); Jessica Lahey, *The Gift of Failure: How the Best Parents Learn to Let Go So Their Children Can Succeed* (New York: HarperCollins Publishers, 2015); Julie Lythcott-Haims, *How to Raise an Adult: Break Free of the Overparenting Trap and Prepare Your Kid for Success* (New York: St. Martin's Press, 2015); Ben Sasse, *The Vanishing American Adult: Our Coming Of Age Crisis and How to Rebuild a Culture of Self-Reliance* (New York: St. Martin's Press, 2017); Leonard Sax, *Boys Adrift: The Five Factors Driving the Growing Epidemic of Unmotivated Boys and Underachieving Young Men* (New York: Basic Books, 2007), *Girls on the Edge: The Four Factors Driving the New Crisis for Girls* (New York: Basic Books, 2010), and *The Collapse of Parenting: How We Hurt Our Kids When We Treat Them Like Grown-Ups – Three Things You Must Do to Help Your Child or Teen Become a Fulfilled Adult* (New York: Basic Books, 2016); Lenore Skenazy, *Free Range Kids: How to Raise Safe, Self-Reliant Children (Without Going Nuts with Worry)* (San Francisco: Jossey-Bass, 2009).

these authors focus on the importance of *personal responsibility*, on the part of parents and young people alike, for moral formation and growth in virtue. The target audience for these books are parents and families who enjoy some privilege in the culture whether it be based on race, gender, class, education level, or some combination of these. These are parents who can make choices about school environments (or who can demand, with some expectation of success, a say in how their schools work) and recreational activities, who can assume a certain degree of security in their homes and neighborhoods (though as Skenazy points out, these families tend to be risk averse in many ways and overestimate the kind and number of dangers their children face every day). The flip side of personal responsibility for success is individual blame for failure to achieve and succeed. The call to any social or communal responsibility ebbs.

Related to personal responsibility is the importance of *character and the cultivation of virtue*, but not just any virtue. Temperance as self-control makes a comeback as Sax advises, "The job of the parent is to teach self-control. To explain what is and is not acceptable. To establish boundaries and enforce consequences."[4] Amy Chua's children were required to practice musical instruments for hours on end and forgo other activities like sports, sleepovers, and the like. Obedience, on the part of children and young people, is the key to establishing right relationships between the generations. Lamenting the current state of affairs as he sees it, Sax writes, "Over the past three decades, there has been a massive transfer of authority from parents to kids. Along with that transfer of authority has come a change in the valuation of kids' opinions and preferences. In many families, what kids think and what kids like and what kids want now matters as much as, or more than, what their parents think and like and want."[5] Sasse advocates work (in addition to other enriching activities) as a vital pathway to the cultivation of virtue, though he clearly imagines work that is safe and done in the context of family and community. Sasse is also highly critical of "bureaucratized" education systems in the U.S. and, though he recognizes value in schools, advocates homeschooling as an option that allows for greater flexibility for children and freedom on the part of adults to pass along important values and ideas. The risk here is an even further entrenched tiered system of education than is already the case, in which some children receive training in a bureaucratic setting and others a more expansive experience that builds both intellectual and social capital (often building on the financial, intellectual, and social capital of their parents).

Linked to the cultivation of virtue and character among children is the set of required virtues for effective and, some would argue, loving

---

[4] Sax, *The Collapse of Parenting*, 50.
[5] Sax, *The Collapse of Parenting*, 7.

parenting. Though none of the authors would dispute that children need affection and support, Sax attempts to balance children's need for unconditional love with a more authoritative parenting style, and Chua maintains a more authoritarian posture and claims that successful Chinese parents "never compliment their children in public" and always side with other adults when there is a disagreement between their child and that adult.[6] Parenting is about power. Skenazy adopts a more "hands-off approach" to child-rearing but the aims are similar: strong, and resilient children who can withstand what many see as an epidemic of "fragility" among young people. Duckworth suggests that there is a "sweet spot" to be found between having high expectations and excessive permissiveness—ethicists might call this prudence.

Underlying much of this discussion about the state of children and childhood today is an atmosphere of *conflict and competition*. Some of this is evident on the face of things. Fretting over the period of adolescence arises in part because of conflicts between teens and their parents, that while infuriating, seem also to be a "normal" part of the developmental process. The "tiger mother" is all about competition and status. Her children must be the best at whatever they do (though the "whatever they do" is decided by the parent and must be something akin to classical piano rather than something like bowling). She is herself in a competition to be the best and most successful parent and relies on her children to give her this status. Parents also need to maximize the advantage that their children have over other children in order to be successful and "success" is only loosely tethered, if at all, to making a genuine contribution to the common good.

The conflicts and competitions run even deeper. Sax, for example is highly critical of peer culture. Parents and the family in general are in a battle for the hearts and minds of their children. Other children and adolescents are, then, the enemy, the obstacle, the "bad influence." The problem with this view, of course, is that it is always someone else's children who pose the threat. The family stands apart from the culture, and there is little critical reflection about how these very same families can play a role in shaping and benefitting from the culture they fear. Sasse's keys to successful parenting and raising responsible adults are: overcome peer culture, work hard, resist consumption, travel to experience the difference between need and want, and become truly literate.[7] The family is either set in opposition to the culture or at least carefully curates the culture. There is an operating system of value that at first glance appears worthwhile but can subtly run the risk of denying the value and dignity of other children and families.

This is the field on which discussions about the moral development of children and youth unfold. On the one hand, there is concern that

---

[6] Chua, *Battle Hymn of the Tiger Mother*, 5.
[7] Sasse, *The Vanishing American Adult*, 8-10.

children need to be protected and even insulated from a culture that undermines the values of family and parental authority. On the other hand, overprotection has also insulated some children from responsibility and the risk of failure that could play a role in developing the resilience that is required in adulthood. Children are either growing up too fast or they are "failing to launch." The weight of responsibility falls on parents to pass on key values of personal responsibility, obedience to parental authority, and perseverance through hard work. While most of the authors resist the extremes of the tiger mother who sees the success of her children, in competition with other children, as a zero-sum game with one winner and the rest losers, there is an unavoidable air of conflict and competition rather than cooperation, shared risk, and solidarity. Children are the objects in the process of moral development rather than its subjects, and adults take much of the credit and the blame.

It is here that ethicists and moral theologians are poised to make a crucial contribution to conversations *about and with* children and young people. They also provide a rich vision of moral development that resists the binary and linear models that have dominated the discourse in favor of the development of intergenerational moral communities marked by solidarity in the process of moral development for everyone, attention to the experiences of those who are poor, vulnerable and otherwise marginalized, and a pursuit of virtue that is inextricably bound to the common good.

MORAL AGENCY, SOLIDARITY, AND PARTICIPATION: THE CONTRIBUTION OF CHRISTIAN ETHICS

Catechists and youth ministers have long been concerned with the moral formation and religious education of children and young people. They have attended to children's experiences and developed creative pedagogical models of instruction to deepen the life of faith and service to others. Ethicists and moral theologians have joined the conversation about children's spirituality and have been making important contributions that expand the range of issues with which Christian communities must wrestle.

Scholars including Jennifer Beste and Annemie Dillen have constructed important bridges between children's spirituality, practical theology, and moral theology – or perhaps it is better to say that they have made the boundaries between these approaches more porous and the intersections more dynamic. To the trajectory influenced by Bonnie Miller-McLemore, who articulated a vision of the care of children as a spiritual and morally enriching practice, Beste and Dillen have brought the distinctive lens of Catholic moral theology. Beste explores children's status in the church and their moral agency in sacramental preparation.[8] Her ethnographic research confirmed that children are "social actors simultaneously influencing and being influenced by their social context." She finds a strong link between children's experience of agency and their experience of sacramental life in the Church, "a correlation between children's perceived sense of agency (or lack thereof) and (1) their affective response, (2) whether the sacrament is personally meaningful, and (3) its impact on their relationship with God and others."[9]

Dillen has called for approaches grounded in both care and liberation for children and young people and critiqued simplistic and sometimes romantic pastoral practices that use children's presence as a sign of parish vitality.[10] Operating out of an asset- rather than a deficit-based view of religious education she writes, "Children and parents are each competent in specific aspects of this process. However, the learning process is not totally dependent of the competences of the partners in the dialogue." Dillen notes that "revelation also occurs through the learning process, when there is respect for each partner." Of the hermeneutical-communicative model of religious education she advocates, Dillen claims, "Hermeneutics refers to searching for, but also to finding one's own interpretations, and this finding is always a heteronomous process, whereby people 'receive' from each other and even from God new interpretations, new ideas, and even, potentially, new life."[11]

Cristina L. H. Traina (a contributor to this volume) has explored the moral agency of children (and the factors that limit or undermine agency) in contexts of injustice.[12] Beginning with the experiences of children living in poverty and multiple forms of insecurity, and drawing on themes in Catholic Social Teaching and liberation theology,

---

[8] Jennifer Beste, "Children Speak: Catholic Second Graders' Agency and Experiences in the Sacrament of Reconciliation," *Sociology of Religion*, 72 no. 3 (2011): 327-350; "The Status of Children within the Roman Catholic Church," *Children and Childhood in American Religions*, Don S. Browning and Bonnie J. Miller-McLemore, ed. (New Brunswick: Rutgers 2009): 56-70.

[9] Beste, "Children Speak," 347.

[10] Annemie Dillen, "Children Between Liberation and Care: Ethical Perspectives on the Rights of Children and Parent-Child Relationships," *International Journal of Children's Spirituality*, 11, no. 2 (2006): 237-250; "The Resiliency of Children and Spirituality: a Practical Theological Reflection," *International Journal of Children's Spirituality* 17, no. 1 (2012): 61–75; "Religious Participation of Children as Active Subjects: Toward a Hermeneutical-Communicative Model of Religious Education in Families with Young Children," *International Journal of Children's Spirituality* 12, no. 1 (2007): 37–49.

[11] Dillen, "Religious Participation of Children as Active Subjects," 46.

[12] Cristina L.H. Traina, "Children and Moral Agency," *Journal of the Society of Christian Ethics* 29, no. 2 (2009): 19-37; "Children's Situated Right to Work" *Journal of the Society of Christian Ethics* 31, no. 2 (2011): 151-167.

Traina presses the commitment to children's intrinsic dignity as persons in God's image and likeness, "If children are full persons, not persons-in-the-making, then adult advocacy for them must arise from solidarity with them."[13] Working to overcome unjust conditions for children requires a spirit of genuine "collaboration" even as adults must live up to their distinctive responsibilities; "Critical solidarity privileges children's accounts without taking them at face value, and it is attentive to power dynamics of which children may be only vaguely aware, especially to forms of exploitation that prey on their particular vulnerabilities."[14] In the complex context of child work, Traina deftly holds together legitimate concerns about the protection of children and their human rights to participation in society: "As full persons participating in interdependent human society, children have a situated right to appropriate, meaningful work that precedes and grounds their right to protection from harmful work and to protection from exploitation."[15] Making an option for children working out of necessity for themselves and their families leads to a more nuanced vision of moral agency and moral development. Even work by children and young people, which is central to the character building programs in the popular literature, is given richer meaning beyond a pedagogical tool used by adults to foster virtue. Their work often *arises from* the virtues of fidelity, solidarity, and self-care (which includes but is not limited to personal responsibility) on the part of young people and can prompt adults to pursue justice for all people.

The commitment to children's rights is also taken up by John Wall in his recent book *Children's Rights: Today's Global Challenge*. He calls for a view of rights as crucial tools not merely for saving children from inhuman conditions but more importantly for child empowerment. This emphasis on empowerment implies that "children's rights are founded on a deeper respect for children as equally important contributors to societies" and that "in whatever new and imaginative ways would be necessary, children need and deserve to be included as fully empowered members of the human rights community."[16] Wall explores the implications for children's protection and participation in education, new forms of child slavery, and political participation through voting. In contrast to the fears about shifts in power and authority from parents to children, Wall, like Traina, attends to issues of power and the very real and concrete responsibilities of parents and other adults but opts to imagine the possibilities for the shared power

---

[13] Traina, "Children's Situated Right to Work," 154.
[14] Traina, "Right to Work," 154.
[15] Traina, "Right to Work," 152.
[16] John Wall, *Children's Rights: Today's Global Challenge* (Lanham: Rowman & Littlefield, 2017), 4.

and responsibility that make embracing creative tensions (as opposed to conflict and stalemate) possible.

The contributions of ethicists and moral theologians are striking for their deliberate attention to children living in unjust social conditions at the intersections of poverty, racism, sex and gender discrimination, religious discrimination, and multiple forms of violence and insecurity. They are also particularly concerned, even and perhaps especially when considering the rights of children, to focus on the family as a vital context for welcoming children. However, this particular focus on family, while it recognizes the proper responsibilities of families for children informed by the principle of subsidiarity, emphasizes the interrelatedness and interdependence among families and other institutions of civil society. Families are not isolated and autonomous (even when families with privilege claim to be taking care of their own on their own) but rather require a constellation of social supports and rely on access to and participation in the common good in order to flourish. Julie Hanlon Rubio's *Family Ethics: Practices for Christians* serves as one key example. While not about children per se, Rubio's work on the "social mission of the family" takes children seriously as full members of families with rights and responsibilities to act for the good of the family and society, and in service to the most vulnerable and marginalized. For example, the family meal, touted by the popular literature and parenting self-help resources as central to raising children who do well in school, resist illicit drugs and alcohol, and delay sexual debut, becomes a site of hospitality to neighbor, stranger, and enemy and an opportunity to consume more justly and in solidarity with those who grow, harvest, transport, and sell the food families enjoy. Children are active participants in this gospel witness.[17]

Even as pundits are lamenting "adultish" children and childish adults, the assumption is that parents already know, by virtue of being adults, what it means to be just and faithful and children have yet to learn. Experience does teach important lessons with time and age, but it is also true to say that children's presence in family and communal life, proximity to children, brings important lessons about justice and fidelity that are learned from and with children and youth. Children are not only agents in their own moral development but in the moral development of the adults in their families and communities. They ask, sometimes over and over again, challenging questions about how and why things are the way they are. They sometimes refuse to settle for the answers they get. They try and fail and try again (if they are encouraged to). They push buttons and boundaries that reveal as much about parents' disordered values and desires as they do about a "culture of disrespect" among young people. This interdependent process

---

[17] Julie Hanlon Rubio, *Family Ethics: Practices for Christians* (Washington, DC: Georgetown University Press, 2010).

of moral growth is not about relinquishing power, as some commentators fear, it is about sharing a journey with siblings in Christ, being disciples together.

IN THIS ISSUE

Essays in this volume certainly address the role that adults play in the moral lives of children, but they are also keenly attuned to the ways in which the presence of children, proximity to children,[18] and children's experiences are vital to the moral development of individual adults, families, communities, and the Church. Adults have distinct responsibilities to be sure, whether they are in relationships with particular children or not, and knowing how to fulfill those responsibilities with prudence requires attending to the experiences, insights, and vulnerabilities of children they know and those they don't.

Essays by Cristina L.H. Traina and Marcus Mescher wrestle with moral formation in the context of market influences and consumerism. Traina explores virtue in the context of consumerism and conspicuous consumption and challenges the simplistic advice to "change your motives; restrain your desires; consider function over status, form, and novelty; be willing to run against the grain; consider the future (both yours and others') and the common good." Looking more carefully at the impact of race and class in patterns of consumption, she is able to highlight virtuous motives in the choices of families with fewer means who engage in conspicuous consumption, choices that are often frequently attributed uncritically to vice by families of privilege. Traina explores "the ways in which consumer 'virtue' among the affluent and 'vice' among other groups issue from, support, and replicate unjust social structures" and argues for moral formation around consumption that models both personal reflection on complicity in injustice and structural change that makes striving in virtue possible for all families.

Mescher takes up the work of Robert Putnam in *Our Kids: The American Dream in Crisis* which exposes the impact of economic class inequality on access to and realization of the American dream of security and affluence. Mescher proposes Pope Francis's call to mercy as a particularly fruitful way to think about pursuing flourishing for children, families, and communities. It is the family's vocation in the church and the world to "incarnate God's infinite love and tenderness." He claims that, "To say that families are in crisis is to say that families are in need of mercy." This is mercy that includes but is not limited to forgiveness and charity. Mercy here is much more expansive and sits at the foundation of moral formation and the cultivation of virtues, "Practicing mercy should inspire an emboldened moral im-

---

[18] This insight about "proximity" is credited to Bryan Stevenson, *Just Mercy: A Story About Justice and Redemption* (New York: Spiegel and Grau, 2014).

agination that stretches the boundaries of what is possible for the parents, children, relatives, and friends who belong to and build up families."

Articles by Craig Ford and Jason King with Kari-Shane Davis Zimmerman explore resources for sexual ethics for young people and frameworks for moral formation in this aspect of their development and growth. Ford explores the possibilities for natural law theory to inform a sexual ethic that disrupts heteronormative assumptions in the current teachings of the Catholic Church. Ford attends to the experiences of queer and transgender young people in particular and argues that the church and its institutions, particularly its schools, can more authentically honor the intrinsic dignity of LGBTQ young people and adults in their practices around hiring and facility accommodations. The article exposes the magisterium's failure to offer a "substantive account" of what people who disagree with the current teaching (particularly LGTBQ persons) actually believe about sex, gender, gender identity and roles, etc. Ford challenges both gender complementarity and gender essentialism and the binary thinking that reinforces these concepts. He offers an ethic of exploration as both consistent with natural law and truer to the lived experiences and moral strivings of LGBTQ young people that continues "the counterhegemonic tradition of queer thought by pointing a beam of hospitality towards that which is unknown, towards that which is potentially strange and unsettling."

King and Davis Zimmerman take the experiences of many students they encounter in the classroom of liberal arts Catholic colleges as the starting point for an ethic that responds to the challenges of the hookup culture that dominates life on many campuses. They note that students perceive and participate in (or opt out of) this culture in a variety of ways. There are "scripts" that shape the parameters of their decisions about sexual relationships and contraception. King and Davis Zimmerman advocate a nuanced use of Natural Family Planning in their pedagogical approach to teaching about sex. NFP challenges the "abbreviated anthropology" that caters to the presumed interests of privileged, white, male students and can foster critical conversations about intrinsic human dignity and solidarity with and among students. They note that dignity and solidarity "help illuminate the dynamics of power and privilege, as well as weakness and vulnerability" and can inform prudential decisions about intimate relationships, sexual activity, and the use of contraception.

Tim and Sue Muldoon and Mary Roche look at leisure and recreation and the challenges to thinking about time and place with children and young people. The Muldoons ask, "How ought parents and other caregivers of children respond to the time pressures that affect childhood?" They respond to a context in which children are "overscheduled" with school, sports, and activities which "must be ordered toward some other end—winning or working towards a scholarship, internship or job." The result is a dramatic reduction in the leisure time to use their imaginations, engage in free play, and cultivate habits of discernment required for the life of discipleship. A turn to Aristotle and traditions in Christian theology encourages a view of the intrinsic value of leisure as "a state which allows for contemplation and resting in the existential good of life itself." The life of worship can provide an alternative imaginary that can sustain familial practices as well as prompt work for social and organizational changes that promote leisure and play.

Roche returns to the framework of children's rights to explore play and recreation as basic needs to be protected and provided for by both individual adults and social institutions as well as vital means of children's participation in the common good. Roche argues, "Thinking about play as a form of participation in the common good and playfulness as a virtue may enhance child well-being *and* adult flourishing." Participation in the common good as the context for the exercise of human rights allows Christian communities to think about both rights and responsibilities as shared by everyone at every stage in life. Noting a cultural ambivalence about play and echoing the Muldoon's assessment about its instrumentalization, Roche pursues Susan Linn's insight that play requires "time, space, and silence." She argues, "Cultivating a habit of playfulness and being attuned to the very practical play requirements of time, space, silence, props, and partners could open a way to imagine and re-create new, more welcoming, more just, and more compassionate ways of living."

HOME BY ANOTHER WAY

Where can the conversation go from here? Where and how is the conscience of Christian communities calling us to grow in our moral formation with children and young people? This issue of the *Journal of Moral Theology* was being "put to bed" during the Advent and Christmas seasons (with visions of sugar plums no less). The gospel accounts of the Annunciation, the birth of Jesus, the first visitors to the manger, the presentation in the Temple, the machinations of Herod, the flight into Egypt, the slaughter of innocents, and Jesus's early life provide rich fruit for reflection on relationships and experiences with children in communities that are familial, communal, religious, national, and global. Though the Christian commitment to the dignity of children as gifts from God remains steadfast, the arrival of children can be occasion for joy, awe at the mystery of life and God's goodness but also trepidation, anxiety, and fear. Jesus's birth was a sign of God's promises for Simeon and Anna, a threat to a tyrant like Herod, and a source of wonder and confusion for Mary and Joseph. Each year, the Church's journey in formation comes back around to these stories and with God's grace, like the Magi, Christians go home by another way, one that makes it possible for children to survive, thrive, and transform the world. Moral formation is a complex, dynamic, and lifelong process for Christians and the Church itself. Children and young people receive important values and habits, but they also force the reevaluation of long-held values and shake up habits and routines for the good of us all.

The work in this volume joins that of other scholars who focus on the global migration of children, children living with the uncertainty of "undocumented" status, children in armed conflict, children sold in sex trafficking and other forms of modern slavery, children dying of preventable illness and disease, and children experiencing domestic violence. Any proposal for Christian moral development must account first for these children, for the moral decisions they make in virtue (however "burdened" these virtues might be), and for the social conditions that both limit authentic agency and impose unjust responsibility too early in life. As Ethna Regan claims, "Children have become a new measure of justice for the church *ad intra*, a measure that will determine our credibility to speak on matters of justice for children, born and unborn, in a world where poor children continue to suffer from having too much to bear and from being given too little to develop properly."[19] So long as children do not have what they need for moral formation, no one will.

Editor's note: I am profoundly thankful to the editors and peer reviewers at JMT and in particular, to the contributors to this volume. I read each essay eagerly as a scholar, teacher of young people, and parent. Each one had something valuable to teach me about my relationships with children and young people as I strive to live well in these vocations. I am hopeful that JMT readers will find the same.

---

[19] Ethna Regan, "Barely Visible: The Child in Catholic Social Teaching," *Heythrop Journal* 55, no. 6 (2014): 1021-1032, 1030.

The Vice of "Virtue": Teaching Consumer Practice in an Unjust World[1]

Cristina L. H. Traina

IN THE EARLY TWENTY-FIRST CENTURY, teaching children consumer virtue is often portrayed as inculcating habits of resisting commercial consumer media, limiting conspicuous consumption, delaying gratification, and preferring lasting, often intangible goods. The argument is usually made by white, upper-middle- and upper-class moralists, among whom I count myself. It is premised on the moral theological assumption that habits that are good for the soul, all things being equal, are also good for society. But if this assumption is incorrect, what then? This article lays out the classical consumer virtue argument and then questions the connection between personal virtue and the social good. First, it reflects on race and class variations in consumption patterns, exploring some of the circumstances and motives that lie behind differences. Then, engaging Lisa Tessman's work on burdened virtues, it asks what happens to virtue and its assumed connection to personal and public flourishing in structurally unjust situations. Next, it argues that this question shifts our focus from simply promoting virtue to also overcoming the structural injustice that stunts and contorts virtue and severs its connections to flourishing. Finally, it recommends a socially critical approach to modeling virtuous consumption, one that focuses as much on justice and social change as on personal practice. In the background lies one uncomfortable assumption: in the world we know, it is not possible to consume in a way that perfectly supports classical understandings of virtue as well as true, holistic personal and communal flourishing. We must hold impeccable standards, but we will not meet them.

I. THE INNOCENT CHILD IN THE BIG BAD WORLD: ASSUMPTIONS ABOUT VIRTUOUS CONSUMPTION

Early twenty-first-century literature on parenting and new media seems to have reached a consensus: an evil, newly predatory culture of consumption, supported by ubiquitous, media-savvy marketing, en-

---

[1] Helpful suggestions from the anonymous reviewer from the *Journal of Moral Theology* improved this essay. All remaining flaws in the argument are mine.

dangers vulnerable children by forming them into mindless consumers. On this view, parents raised in the post-baby-boom ethos of accepting differences in values and behavior, children with rising disposable incomes, and ever-present media poised to target their spending converge to create a toxic market in which anything, especially obscenity and violence, can be sold directly to children while adults stand by helplessly if not exactly haplessly.[2] Even when they try to avoid the worst appeals, parents and their children fall victim to "the siren song" of commercial marketing aimed at "good" parenting of "successful" children.[3] Even children's spirituality is a marketing opportunity.[4]

The result of these trends, according to this argument, is self-centered consumers who focus on private benefit. Worst of all, Benjamin Barber adds, the effect is lasting and fatal: market-driven consumer habituation stunts moral maturity, creating infantilized adults who not only consume mindlessly but become incapable of effective democratic participation.[5] Contemporary market capitalism's uncontested, steady aim at vulnerable child consumers will be the downfall of society and therefore of the common good.

This argument translates easily into the language of moral theology. For example, Chad Engelland and Brian Engelland point to a failure "to distinguish needs from wants" that leads to "splurging" and "wasteful spending."[6] Consequent vices like a desire to "keep up with the Joneses," with its tendency to "sacrifice long-term goods for short-term satisfactions," are responsible for the ills of a market that has

---

[2] Diane Ravitch and Joseph P. Viteritti, "Toxic Lessons: Children and Popular Culture," in *Kid Stuff: Marketing Sex and Violence to America's Children*, ed. Diane Ravitch and Joseph P. Viteritti (Baltimore: Johns Hopkins, 2003), 1-18, at 3-4. See also Teresa Malcolm, "Hard to find sanctuary from $17 billion in marketing to kids," *National Catholic Reporter*, Nov. 16, 2007, 5a; Ellen T. Charry, "Countering a Malforming Culture: Christian Theological Formation of Adolescents in North America," in *Nurturing Child and Adolescent Spirituality: Perspectives from the World's Religious Traditions*, ed. Karen Marie Yust, Aostre N. Johnson, Sandy Eisenberg Sasso, and Eugene C. Roelkepartain (Lanham: Rowman and Littlefield, 2006), 437-448. For a more balanced approach in this latter volume, see Joyce Ann Mercer, "Spiritual Economies of Childhood: Christian Perspectives on Global Market Forces and Young People's Spirituality," 458-471.
[3] Valerie Weaver-Zercher, "Buy, Buy Baby," *Sojourners*, January 2009, 38-39, 41-43.
[4] Joyce Ann Mercer, "Capitalizing on Children's Spirituality: Parental Anxiety, Children as Consumers, and the Marketing of Spirituality," *International Journal of Children's Spirituality* 11, no. 1 (2006): 23–33.
[5] Benjamin R. Barber, *Con$umed: How Markets Corrupt Children, Infantilize Adults, and Swallow Citizens Whole* (New York: Norton, 2007).
[6] Chad Engelland and Brian Engelland, "Consumerism, Marketing, and the Cardinal Virtues," *Journal of Markets and Morality* 19, no. 2 (2016): 304.

converted private property from an engine for communal flourishing to an item for individualist accumulation and enjoyment.[7]

A significant proportion of this literature also agrees on the solution to the problem. It argues that if we raise children to become virtuous consumers who can resist the ubiquitous cultural force of media-driven marketing, we will promote the common good in three ways: people will become morally virtuous, with respect to both their consumption and their concern for the social whole; both individuals and society will flourish materially because people will spend mindfully rather than wastefully; and the main instigator of vice, the overwhelming media marketing giant, will wither for lack of an audience. For instance, the Engellands promote the four cardinal virtues, "habits that enable us to act well in four aspects of life," for both consumers and marketers: "moderation regarding pleasure, courage regarding pain, justice regarding people, and prudence regarding truth and goodness."[8] Small changes on the individual level will add up to social transformation.

> We wish to curb frivolous consumption for the sake of the person and encourage consumers to weigh more heavily long-term value into their purchase calculus. Doing so will free up resources that can be directed toward the poor and the environment, and these are good reasons to pursue the virtues.[9]

In short, the diagnosis of the consumption problem is personal vice, and the recommendations for curing it boil down to virtue both for consumers and for producers and advertisers: change your motives; restrain your desires; consider function over status, form, and novelty; be willing to run against the grain; consider the future (both yours and others') and the common good.

While the interdependent system of consumption, production, and marketing vices is certainly responsible for exacerbating social ills, not to mention encouraging personal sinfulness in children, the argument that market-driven consumption is the product purely of individual vice and is the font of all American social ills is overly simplistic. Richard Reeves's *Dream Hoarders* and Elizabeth Currid-Halkett's *The Sum of Small Things* argue that, in the context of current structural injustice and social inequality, the classical virtuous consumption patterns usually embraced in arguments that adopt a white, upper-middle class perspective reinscribe and harden race and class stratification: "virtue" works against the common good. Conversely, I argue, many

---

[7] Engelland and Engelland, "Consumerism," 298, 310.
[8] Engelland and Engelland, "Consumerism," 301.
[9] Engelland and Engellend, "Consumerism," 299.

so-called "irresponsible" patterns of consumption often attached pejoratively to the bottom 80% and to people of color are driven by virtuous motives. If we wish to engage children on the ethics of consumption, then, we need to explore the nuances of virtue, holistic flourishing, the common good, justice, and the often uncertain connection among them.

II. RACE, CLASS, AND CONSUMPTION: COMPLICATING THE STORY

Recent research has illuminated important differences in American consumption patterns. Broadly speaking, US African Americans and Latinxs spend about 30 percent more of their incomes on visible goods than whites with similar incomes but much less than whites on less visible goods like education, entertainment, and health care.[10] Currid-Halkett expands this less visible category—which she calls inconspicuous consumption—to include services like house cleaning that make life simpler, investments like 401K plans, and higher-status, more expensive versions of ordinary items. In this last case, one might substitute children's hockey for basketball, organic for conventional food, or elite private for public universities.[11] What she calls "the aspirational class"—defined by valuing "smart" consumption informed by superior, intangible, socially current knowledge over conspicuous consumption—emphasizes inconspicuous consumption at all income levels.[12] It invests in goods, experiences, communities, and activities that will advantage their children with good connections and socially valued knowledge later, and, when possible, in services to free up the parental time needed to pursue those activities and earn the income that supports them. Currid-Halkett finds racial differences, too: whites devote comparatively more of their spending to this socially advantageous inconspicuous consumption than other groups.[13] Reeves emphasizes the cumulative impact even of apparently less significant practices. For instance, "Take Your Daughters (and Sons) to Work Day" works out very differently for children of parents who are professionals, blue-collar workers, and jobless.[14] Children in the top 20 percent get training in professional workplace interaction and strong, implied messages about the rewards of gratification delayed by investment in education. Children of blue-collar workers may sense, and possess, the

---

[10] Kerwin Kofi Charles, Erik Hurst and Nikolai Roussanov, "Conspicuous Consumption and Race," *The Quarterly Journal of Economics* 124, no. 2 (2009): 443.
[11] Elizabeth Currid-Halkett, *The Sum of Small Things: A Theory of the Aspirational Class* (Princeton: Princeton University Press, 2017), 21-22, 36-37.
[12] Currid-Halkett, *Sum of Small Things*, 17-20.
[13] Currid-Halkett, *Sum of Small Things*, 38.
[14] Richard V. Reeves, *Dream Hoarders: How the American Upper Middle Class is Leaving Everyone Else in the Dust, Why That is a Problem, and What to Do about It* (Washington, DC: Brookings Institution Press, 2017), 114.

ambivalence of pride in work well done and embarrassed disappointment in the increasingly meager rewards of a job that may not require specialized training. Children of the jobless receive no clear picture of connections between thoughtful consumption and a holistically good life.

The virtuous consumption argument would seem to applaud the spending habits of whites and the top 20 percent: delay gratification by avoiding imprudent conspicuous consumption, with its immediate rewards, and investing in education, health, and other items that secure one's welfare in the long run. But Currid-Halkett and Reeves do not award gold stars for consumer virtue to the groups at the tops of the various charts—whites, aspirationals, top 20 percenters—for their preference for inconspicuous consumption. Instead, both implicitly make benefit to the common good a test for moral virtue. They insist that inconspicuous consumption by the better-off harms the common good by perpetuating and exaggerating class difference and is therefore morally problematic. Currid-Halkett argues that "aspirational," inconspicuous consumption is actually a new form of status-seeking that, "veiled in morality" of healthful and wise parenting choices, serves up children whose access to non-material advantages (like elite education and its intangible social benefits) reproduces the status of their parents and ossifies class.[15] Reeves, also worried about class rigidity, calls upon the top 20 percent to check their privilege, accept policy changes that will undo structural inequalities that perpetuate wealth disparities, and prepare to embrace some relative downward mobility in the interest of the social good.[16]

Reeves and Currid-Halkett explode the apparent virtue of inconspicuous consumption, but they do not spend much time arguing the converse: that in our current social, economic, and racial circumstances, the more conspicuous consumption patterns of less-advantaged parents have moral weight. For instance, some people of color try strategically to deflect micro-aggressions by spending money on goods that indicate status.[17] The lesson taught to children here is clear: identifiably prestigious clothing, accessories, and cars are armor

---

[15] Currid-Halkett, *Sum of Small Things,* 196.
[16] From the title of chapter 8 in Reeves, *Dream Hoarders.*
[17] For a discussion of this literature, see Raphaël Charron-Chénier, Joshua J. Fink, and Lisa A. Keister, "Race and Consumption: Black and White Disparities in Household Spending," *Sociology of Race and Ethnicity* 3, no. 1 (2017): 51. In Charles et al., "Conspicuous Consumption and Race," 457-58, the authors agree but argue that this effect generally holds for publically visible consumption, not necessarily within social groups or households. Cassi Pittman argues that African Americans see the likely incremental increase in respect that dressing well brings as often not worth the effort; they would rather risk stigma (say, when running to the grocery store) than change clothes. See Cassi Louise Pittman, "Race, Social Context, and Consumption: How Race Structures the Consumption Preferences and Practices of Middle and Working-Class Blacks" (Ph.D. Dissertation, Harvard University, 2012), 172.

against a dangerous world. They protect dignity and life. Cassi Pittman suggests a double financial jeopardy: items African Americans buy to "fit in" with white professional culture and signal status do not necessarily reflect their own tastes and preferences. If they wish to express these in the company of household and friends, they need to buy additional goods.[18] This sort of code switching, which preserves both public dignity and group identity, is expensive. In addition, although Latinx and African American families carry no more debt than white families, their lower levels of household wealth (in 2013, the average white household held thirteen times as much in assets as the average African American household and ten times as much as the average Latinx household) probably lead to prudent avoidance of the risk of taking on debt for expensive "inconspicuous" consumption like private university education.[19]

Dignity, identity, and prudent weighing of risk figure strongly in Allison Pugh's research on children as well. African-American parents and children whom she studied in Oakland, California, were sensitive to ways in which particular goods eased children's status and dignity within their groups, moving them from marginalization to belonging. In Pugh's study, both children and parents valued the social access—significantly, not social superiority—that came with possessing certain consumer goods. Pugh also noted that African-American families who could afford to move their children to mixed neighborhoods with higher-performing schools—the sort of "pathway" (Pugh) or "aspirational" (Currid-Halkett) decision that an ethic of virtuous consumption might praise as a self-sacrificing investment in children—often chose not to do so. They valued the dignity and belonging their children found in Oakland's majority African-American schools and feared the effects of the racism, rejection, and marginalization they might encounter elsewhere. That is, they judged that their children could flourish more holistically in a community where they had unproblematic access to affirmation and status rather than in one where they did not.[20] They made a self-conscious choice to promote

---

[18] See Pittman, "Race, Social Context, and Consumption," 167-71.
[19] In 2012, low-to-middle income white families had more credit card debt than either African American or Latinx families; the average overall was $7145. See Amy Traub and Catherine Ruetschlin, "The Plastic Safety Net: Findings from the 2012 National Survey on Credit Card Debt of Low- and Middle-Income Households," *Dēmos*, www.demos.org/publication/plastic-safety-net. On wealth, see Rakesh Kochhar and Richard Fry, "Wealth Inequality Has Widened along Racial, Ethnic Lines since End of Great Recession," *Pew Research Center Fact Tank*, www.pewresearch.org/fact-tank/2014/12/12/racial-wealth-gaps-great-recession/.
[20] Allison J. Pugh, *Longing and Belonging: Parents, Children, and Consumer Culture* (Berkeley: University of California Press, 2009), 125-26. All citations of this book in this article are made to the Adobe Digital Editions electronic version. Pugh notes (134, 139) that affluent African-American parents often do send their children to such "uncomfortable" schools to expose them to dominant white culture but then find extra-

their children's good by *not* consuming housing in a "better" neighborhood.

In Oakland and the nearby area, then, Pugh found not mindless consumerism driven by children's uncensored access to predatory media but a sophisticated culture of parental care mediated in part by access to consumer goods. She argues that "children's desires for things stem less from individual vice, a lack of self-control, or a particular vulnerability to persuasion than from the emotional connection that possession has come to promise" in an "economy of dignity" focused on social belonging.[21] Their desires are a product of a culture—"a patterned, collective process by which people attach personal, emotional significance to their world, indeed, as a sort of dynamic, two-way bridge between the social and the psychological"—that in our case has inscribed consumption as an essential element of children's social belonging and therefore of parental care.[22]

Why goods have come to mediate children's desires and status is a complicated question. Although she dislikes the media market machine, Pugh tentatively traces the cause to a paradoxical combination: public disinvestment from children at the very moment when they replaced women as symbols of the home has landed strategic investment in children's futures in the laps of their households rather than of the larger community. She argues that the conspicuous goods many children receive are either bets that their families place on safety and access in the larger culture or tickets to belonging in household and community, and that sometimes guaranteed belonging at these more intimate levels seems a better investment risk than merely possible belonging in wider society. In other words, when they are aimed at children's holistic flourishing in particular social contexts, the more conspicuous consumption patterns of persons of color, "non-aspirationals," and lower 80 percenters signal virtue: behavior consonant with care and flourishing. Context cues these families, just as it cues Currid-Halkett's "aspirationals."

However, it is essential to recall that the context from which these cues arise is toxic. Protection against racism underlies many choices about what to consume and where to consume it. Barriers like safety considerations often block access to inconspicuous goods that parents of color can afford. Even worse, despite African-American households' comparatively high level of conspicuous consumption, African Americans at all income levels spend less money overall than whites

---

curricular activities for them in African American and lower-class contexts. This practice prepares them to code switch, valuing both cultural identity and access to upper-class and white culture.

[21] Pugh, *Longing and Belonging,* 146, 15.
[22] Pugh, *Longing and Belonging,* 24-25.

of similar income. The reasons for this difference are external, cultural, and systemic: poor credit access, retail and service desertification, and consumer discrimination. Higher income softens the credit blow but does little to counteract desertification and discrimination.[23] Consequently, African-American households who might want to spend more on health care, music lessons, after-school tutoring, and other "pathway" goods for their children—not to mention high-quality rental and purchased housing—may simply be unable to do so without exerting impractical amounts of time and energy. In addition, much of the consumption that these inequities drive damages the common good: proportional overconsumption of inconspicuous goods tilts the playing field toward the children of those who can afford them, and proportional overconsumption of conspicuous goods tilts it away from children whose parents cannot make the kinds of inconspicuous purchases that have currency beyond household and close community.

Consequently, there is a disconnect between what has been called virtue (and might still be called that in a just society) and holistic flourishing at all scales from the individual to the national. Parents rightly act to promote their children's good. Consumption that makes sense to parents of means advantages their children to the detriment of others in ways that are hard to reverse. Consumption that makes sense to lower-income parents, especially parents of color, protects their children from harm in ways that necessarily disadvantage their long-term holistic flourishing in comparison to children of parents of means. Both patterns tend to reinforce and perpetuate the class differences that produce them. As Pugh argues, when "social conditions that imbue commercialized goods with powerful meanings like belonging and care, harnessing them to the market" shape parental consumption and modeling, they reconfirm "the powerful asymmetries that order our experience."[24] How do we think of classically-informed consumer virtue when it does not deliver on its promise to benefit the common good?

III. WHEN VIRTUE DOES NOT PROMOTE FLOURISHING: BURDENED VIRTUES

Classical virtue theory assumes that acting virtuously creates constructive resonance in self and society: the virtues support each other, the good society promotes virtue in its members, and what is good for

---

[23] Charron-Chénier et al., "Race and Consumption," 51. Recent research shows that higher-income African Americans are *more* likely than lower-income African Americans to encounter slurs, negative assumptions and comments, and people acting afraid of them. See National Public Radio, the Robert Wood Johnson Foundation, and Harvard T. H. Chan School of Public Health, "Discrimination in America: Experiences and Views of African Americans," www.npr.org/assets/img/2017/10/23/discriminationpoll-african-americans.pdf.

[24] Pugh, *Longing and Belonging,* 146, 25.

my soul generally leads to holistic flourishing for me, for those close to me, and for my community. However, as the philosopher Lisa Tessman has argued, structural injustice gives the lie to these assumptions. By disconnecting virtue from its salutary consequences, injustice raises the cost of virtuous behavior for victims of injustice by making them, and those for whom they care, worse off rather than better, creating what Tessman calls "burdened virtues." For instance, the courage to run against costly norms of children's dress leads to children's marginalization in some neighborhoods but to physical danger, even loss of life, in others. The consequence is that the burden of some families' temperate behavior (saving money on clothing to spend on other developmental goods) is greater for them and for their children than it is for more affluent households. Another way to describe this dilemma is that prudence with regard to one important dimension of a child's well-being (dignity, social acceptance, and safety) and prudence with regard to another (access to elite knowledge) may be mutually exclusive. In both of these ways, injustice stymies both virtue and holistic flourishing.

Although unjustly privileged people are relatively immune to the burdens of the disconnection between virtue and holistic flourishing, Tessman is quick to point out that they flourish by embracing vices of domination that parade as virtues. Among the well-off, what seems virtuous behavior—prudently providing for one's children's future well-being by strategizing their access to elite knowledge—interacts in predictable and unpredictable ways with unjust structures to perpetuate inequality in society at large. For instance, it gives children access to top-tier school systems, and then top-tier universities, then well-connected internship programs, and then influential recommendations and elite hiring fairs, not to mention the lessons learned at all levels about how to conduct oneself in the professions. An acquaintance described the schedule of his retreat-style training at a major financial consulting firm as, more than anything, messaging about the firm's work culture: work eight hours, break for dinner, return to the office for two hours, break for drinks with colleagues, repeat. A consultant who wanted to guarantee [at that time] his children's continued access to social advantages had to adhere to these norms.

Tessman admits that Aristotle would not have viewed social inequality generally as unjust because he limited the pursuit of virtue, including mutually-regarding virtues based in equality, to a male elite. Justice as right relationship among unequals did not imply justice as equality. But, she argues, in a society that regards all persons as deserving of the same levels of flourishing, both moral and holistic, habits that perpetuate structural inequalities that prevent broad flourishing are unacceptable. In these circumstances affluent parents' habits like uncritical planfulness, thrift, self-denial, and delayed self-gratification wound objective justice by hoarding the privilege they already possess. Widespread agreement about these virtues among unjustly privileged people allows them to read others' suffering as the product of those others' own failures of virtue, and this reading encourages indifference to suffering.[25] Thus, privileged "virtues" model the vices of injustice and indifference to children under the guise of prudence and temperance.

In addition to the question whether elite consumer virtues are truly vices, there is the question whether poor and working-class consumer vices are truly virtues. Tessman chooses a third path. She is neither rigorist—condemning victims of injustice for their inescapable inability to be virtuous and succeed in caring well—nor defeatist—allowing people to throw up their hands hopelessly and stop attempting to act well. She argues that redefining virtue to embrace "the best that is possible under oppressive conditions" as truly morally good is morally troubling: it would lessen our obligation to eradicate systemic injustice by denying the fact that systemic injustice makes not just material suffering, but also true moral failure, inevitable for its victims. On the contrary, oppression is evil because it *does not* lessen victims' mutually unfulfillable moral obligations to virtue and to persons.[26] Her point is especially important for moral theology, a tradition in which virtue is first among the goods that make up flourishing. Lowering the bar of virtue from the ideal to "the best that is possible" would be the easy way out; instead Tessman maintains our obligation to accomplish the holistic justice under which the ideal truly becomes practicable for all. That is, to rephrase a popular dictum, if you want virtue, work for justice.

What broad lessons can we draw for modeling and instilling consumer virtue? First, we need to see our own and others' problematic patterns of consumption not merely as the products of individual vices like greed but also as the shapes that the desire to be virtuous takes when it is presented with a systematically unjust society and a culture that ties care and belonging to the possession of "insider" goods and knowledge. Allison Pugh defends children and parents against simplistic accusations of greed and insists that they are not advertisers' puppets. Still, she insists, "The hidden crisis of consumption emanates from the social conditions that imbue commercialized goods with powerful meanings like belonging and care, harnessing them to the

---

[25] Lisa Tessman, *Burdened Virtues: Virtue Ethics for Liberatory Struggles* (New York: Oxford, 2007), 75-80.
[26] Lisa Tessman, "Idealizing Morality," *Hypatia* 25, no. 4 (2010): 798. For Tessman's later elaboration of the ethics of moral failure, see Lisa Tessman, *Moral Failure: On the Impossible Demands of Morality* (New York: Oxford, 2014).

market" and inevitably reproducing social position.[27] The harm is moral, not just material.

Second, although Tessman is a moral philosopher, her perspective carries deep analogies to Christian theologies of sin and the reign of God. According to Tessman, perfect virtue and perfect justice are impossible to accomplish, either corporately or individually, in concrete human life, but they are obligatory aspirations: "One should live aiming at an unattainable ideal—flourishing in a fully human way and thus exercising the virtues—but with no expectation for 'success' given the unconducive conditions in which one must strive."[28] Perfection is impossible to human beings; in Christian terms, sin is inevitable. But to give up the struggle to accomplish either personal moral virtue or the just, flourishing society in which virtue is truly possible is to give up the struggle to be ethical, and to believe that virtue and justice are incompatible is to declare human life essentially rather than temporarily absurd. It is to decide that virtue and justice have no connection at all.[29] In Christian terms, to give up either virtue or justice is to give up belief in the goodness of creation and hope in God's redemption and grace. We must strive for both virtue and objective justice, despite lack of concrete evidence of either here and now.

Third, "virtue" among the relatively powerful often contradicts the common good, and "vice" among the relatively powerless often protects them from the attacks of an unjust society. Both are adaptations to oppressive cultural systems. Tessman reminds us to always see warped virtues and apparent vices as symptoms of the moral damage that larger social ills create *in addition to social and material suffering*: burdened virtues, which demand supererogatory commitment and contravene care, and moral failure, which is also destructive to moral virtue.[30] The theological analogy is that oppression damages moral and spiritual goods, not just material ones. If more is at stake than "mere" bodily suffering then even traditions that generally value moral over physical flourishing should see analysis and eradication of social injustice as a moral, spiritual priority.

Fourth, although Tessman refuses to loosen her standards for the virtues—they are mandatory aspirations incompatible with personal and communal flourishing in an unjust world—she does argue that we must revise them after communal critical analysis of their effects in

---

[27] Pugh, *Longing and Belonging,* 146.
[28] Lisa Tessman, "Feminist Eudaimonism: Eudaimonism as Non-Ideal Theory," in *Feminist Ethics and Social and Political Philosophy: Theorizing the Non-Ideal,* ed. Lisa Tessman (New York: Springer, 2009), 56.
[29] Tessman, "Feminist Eudaimonism," 55-56.
[30] For instance, see Christine Koggel, "Burdening the Burdened Virtues," *Hypatia* 23, no. 3 (2008): 197-204, at 198.

the social order and in the context of our other firmly held moral commitments.[31] In Tessman's case, this practice of critical revision tends to make a virtue more, not less, rigorous because it is more, not less, skeptical of the motives of the powerful classes who hold that virtue. Her expansion of Aristotle's vision of a mutually regarding, just social order from a small, leisured male elite to all of humanity is a case in point. Justice is about equal relations among billions, not among a few persons at the top of the race, class, and gender pyramid. Currid-Halkett's aspirationals and Reeves's top 20 percent are the contemporary versions of Aristotle's tiny, self-serving circle with its limited vision of justice. Temperance, prudence, justice, and fortitude are indeed true virtues, but, if the use society is making of them does not support holistic—including moral—flourishing at all levels from the individual to the global, their definitions demand revision.

Finally, Tessman's insistence on critical revision also implies that the contents of virtue and morality are not naturally, in the sense of originally, given once for all, but that they are natural in the sense that the social process of critical discernment is natural to human beings.[32] Virtue is empty without it. How can we instill this habit in children, with regard to consumption?

IV. RAISING CHILD CONSUMERS: AWARENESS AND JUSTICE

Just as we cannot stop eating, we cannot stop consuming. However, we can use consumption to instill the virtue of critical discernment. Certainly, we can teach children to be critical and skeptical of advertising, but, as the discussion above illustrates, this is only the beginning. We can demonstrate more clearly how cultural expectations, time, finances, class, family and neighborhood context, and availability and unavailability of goods affect our considerations about purchases. The more social power we have, the more deeply we should model querying the virtue of our own consumption habits and our children's and the more thoroughly we should model revisiting our unspoken assumptions about the questionability of others' purchasing decisions. We can also embrace the passion and non-perfectionism of Tessman's apparently paradoxical advice: We must both strive uncompromisingly for virtue and justice and realize that we will never accomplish either. All of our consumption will have conflicting implications and contradictory motives as long as it is set in the framework of an unjust society that ties care and belonging to costly goods; teaching children to both rue and accept this fact will help them to develop the non-perfectionistic, socially passionate self-critical skills that keep their understanding of virtue fresh.

---

[31] Lisa Tessman, "Reply to Critics," *Hypatia* 23, no. 3 (2008): 210.
[32] Tessman, "Reply," 209-10.

What does this mean in the concrete? As Currid-Halkett implies, our habits of consumption are the sum of many small decisions. We can begin by being conscious of the monologues and dialogues we already carry out in front of children. We can encourage children to wonder aloud about why they want things, and we can model this habit by doing so ourselves, regularly. What does it mean to buy belonging?

We can also discuss the specific conflicts of virtues and values that purchase decisions impose on us. If we live in a relative food desert, do we shop locally, buying increased family time with higher cost and lower food quality, or do we take a few busses to a more distant chain store, lowering costs and increasing food quality but losing family time and moving profits out of our immediate community? All parents can illuminate motives, social cues, and social effects of children's consumer decisions as well. Teens can be asked to be honest about whether they volunteer as homework tutors with the intent of bolstering their college applications or of helping younger children with their writing and algebra, and they can be asked to think about the differential impacts of privileged inconspicuous consumption—like club sports or college exam tutoring classes—on college access. Children can receive gifts of branded basketball shoes in the spirit of keeping up with the Joneses or in a sense of pride for playing on their middle school team, and they can be asked to think about the commercial drivers for shoe sales and about who benefits from the profits. Above all, as perfect consumer virtue is impossible, parents can model asking the questions that help children to understand the contradictory implications of their buying and to decide which ones to weight more heavily.

To be sure, individual purchasing choices can model consumer virtue and even have some positive effects on the market. Many readers of this article probably buy organic produce on the principle that creating demand will prime supply, which in turn will lower costs, which will put healthful and environmentally sound organic produce within the reach of all. There is some merit to this argument: the discount grocery retailer Aldi would not have been able to choose to purchase and offer economically-priced organic products if there were no demand for them.[33] But the market forces that get organic products into discount grocery stores do not get discount grocery stores into food deserts. There is a limit to what collective individual decisions, even on a large scale, can do to rectify structural injustices in the marketplace.

Allison Pugh agrees that families' practices of instilling deeply critical consumer virtue in their children, even on a large scale, cannot

---

[33] Hayley Peterson, "Aldi is fixing its biggest weakness, and that should terrify Whole Foods," *Business Insider*, January 23, 2016, www.businessinsider.com/aldi-is-fixing-is-biggest-weakness-and-that-should-terrify-whole-foods-2016-1.

dislodge a culture that ties children's dignity and belonging to commodities. An effective response must also be cultural in scale, spanning neighborhood, school, and even nation. School uniform policies, mandatory school lunches, and other leveling practices reduce the salience of difference at school, even though they do not eliminate it outside of educational hours. Training teachers in perceiving classroom culture sensitively, recognizing and resolving conflicts at early stages, and modeling constructive responses to differences of all kinds would do more. Parents can band together to examine and recalibrate their own, and their children's, cultures of consumption.[34]

Yet the most important lesson parents can teach children about virtue and consumption is not about consumption at all. As Pugh implies, real change in the culture that pegs belonging and dignity to commodity ownership ultimately requires disrupting the class and income gap, the gap that Reeves and Currid-Halkett argue is growing both more extreme and more intractable because it is more tied to intangible, inconspicuous goods that reproduce advantage for some and exclusion for others. As Reeves insists, these differences are rooted not in personal behavior but in structural injustice, which demands change in law, policy, and institutional practice that transcends individual and even community-level decisions. Reeves urges that better access to contraception, home visiting for all new parents, provision of the best teachers to the worst-off children, fairer college funding (with fewer tax advantages to the best-off), zoning changes, ending legacy college admissions, better regulation of internships, and correcting regressive taxing policies would do much to reduce inequality and encourage mobility.[35] We could expand the list by drawing on the work of Raphaël Charron-Chénier and his colleagues: changing lending policies to increase credit access and adjusting tax and business loan policies to overcome desertification.

These structural suggestions merely scratch the surface of the changes genuine justice requires. Some of them will turn out to be insignificant and even counterproductive. But they are the product of a habit of critical discernment turned outward to the structures that shape our possibilities for practicing consumer virtue, and thus critical discernment is an essential element of consumer virtue. In Tessman's terms, we must expand our vision of virtuous consumption to include both critique of structural injustice and, for those of us with the power to do so, the political effort to repair it. Children need training in structural critique as much as they do in self-critique and cultural critique. To give them less is to limit consumer virtue to rearranging the produce bins at the supermarket.

---

[34] Pugh, *Longing and Belonging*, 146-48.
[35] Reeves, *Dream Hoarders*, 123-52.

We are only beginning to understand the ways in which consumer "virtue" among the affluent and "vice" among other groups issue from, support, and replicate unjust social structures. Future social research will reveal gaps, and even errors, in the tentative suggestions offered here. Although our responsibilities for structural change differ with the degree of social power that we wield, we can all model for children the most important virtues of all: a dedication to truth—critical analysis of the interdependence between consumption habits and social injustice—and a hopeful commitment to the holistic common good, to a just society in which consumer virtue is truly possible. M

Families in Crisis and the Need for Mercy

Marcus Mescher

MORE THAN TWENTY FIVE YEARS ago, the University of Chicago's Religion, Culture, and Family Project proclaimed that families in North America "are in crisis." This project highlighted the instability produced by family breakdown, paying special attention to the effects on children and the decline in shared stability and prosperity.[1] Robert Putnam's recent work in *Our Kids: The American Dream in Crisis* provides even more recent corroborating evidence for the claim that families in the United States are in crisis. He argues that this trend has been exacerbated by a "nationwide increase in class inequality" that jeopardizes equal opportunities and social mobility.[2] Moreover, Putnam argues, this "ballooning economic gap has been accompanied by growing de facto segregation of Americans along class lines" reinforced by neighborhood, education, and marriage.[3] As families continue to struggle, our social fabric frays and pulls apart; the parts and whole suffer under this "incipient class apartheid."[4]

In the political arena, there are differing responses to crises in family life. Typically, those on the right lament a "decline in morals" on

---

[1] Thus begins Lisa Sowle Cahill's seminal text, *Family: A Christian Social Perspective* (Minneapolis: Fortress, 2000), 1. For a more extended treatment of this topic, see Don S. Browning, Bonnie J. Miller-McLemore, Pamela D. Couture, K. Brynoff Lyon, and Robert M. Franklin, *From Culture Wars to Common Ground: Religion and the American Family Debate* (Louisville: Westminster John Knox Press, 1997).
[2] Robert Putnam, *Our Kids: The American Dream in Crisis* (New York: Simon & Schuster, 2015), 19, 31.
[3] Putnam, *Our Kids,* 37. Putnam finds that the "sorting of households into distinct neighborhoods by income was significantly higher in 2010 than it was in 1970" (38). This residential segregation translates "into de facto class-based school segregation" since "Schoolchildren from the top half of the income distribution increasingly attend private schools or live in better school districts" and are more likely to "attend a highly selective college" (39). Moreover, Putnam finds evidence of "increasing endogamy" (marrying within one's own social class), which means that "rich Americans and poor Americans are living, learning, and raising children in increasingly separate and unequal worlds, removing stepping-stones to upward mobility" and as result, "members of the upper middle class are less likely to have firsthand knowledge of the lives of poor kids and thus are unable even to recognize the growing opportunity gap" (40-41).
[4] Putnam, *Our Kids,* 39.

the individual level and call for greater personal responsibility.[5] Alternatively, those on the left bemoan the systems and structures that generate unearned privileges for some groups and create unjust barriers for others.[6] In response, conservatives might criticize progressives for endorsing government overreach and entitlements that foster dependence in a so-called "welfare state," whereas progressives would take issue with conservatives for imposing their moral code on others and for being too simplistic in their social analysis.[7] In Christian moral theology, these either/or positions are inadequate, and instead the goal should be to aspire for inclusive human flourishing and right-relationship by promoting human dignity, rights, and the common good in connecting the individual, social, and institutional spheres.

This is the vision Pope Francis shares in his 2016 apostolic exhortation, *Amoris Laetitia*. This document, written in response to the synods on the family in 2014 and 2015, takes heed of the chaos and crises experienced within the institution of marriage and the family unit. Francis writes, "The life of every family is marked by all kinds of crises, yet these are also part of its dramatic beauty" (*Amoris Laetitia*, no. 232). Rather than dwell on these difficulties, Francis aims to inspire families to foster support as "schools of solidarity"[8] and imagine new possibilities as a "factory of hope."[9] The pope calls families to

---

[5] For instance, Seth Dowland traces the focus on family values in the rise of evangelicalism and political conservatism in his book, *Family Values and the Rise of the Christian Right* (Philadelphia: University of Pennsylvania Press, 2015).

[6] See, for example, Richard V. Reeves, *Dream Hoarders: How the American Upper Middle Class is Leaving Everyone Else in the Dust, Why that is a Problem, and What to Do about It* (Washington, DC: Brookings Institution Press, 2017).

[7] These opposing views were on display in the wake of Housing and Urban Development Secretary Ben Carson's comments that poverty is a "state of mind" in May 2017. Carson, the former Republican candidate for President, remarked, "I think poverty to a large extent is also a state of mind. You take somebody that has the right mind-set, you can take everything from them and put them on the street, and I guarantee in a little while they'll be right back up there." He added, "You take somebody with the wrong mind-set, you can give them everything in the world – they'll work their way right back down to the bottom." While those on the right might applaud this emphasis on individual accountability, those on the left would reinforce the necessity of having access to services (like housing, education, employment, and healthcare) to meet basic needs.

[8] Pope Francis used this phrase in an address on December 29, 2014. See also Mary M. Doyle Roche, *Schools of Solidarity: Families and Catholic Social Teaching* (Collegeville: Liturgical Press, 2015).

[9] This phrase comes from an unscripted address at the Festival of Families in Philadelphia, whereas the official version released by the Vatican uses the phrase "workshop of hope." Pope Francis, "Prayer Vigil for the Festival of Families," 26 September 2015, w2.vatican.va/content/francesco/en/speeches/2015/september/documents/papa-francesco_20150926_usa-festa-famiglie.html.

stay committed to each other, cultivate honest and gentle communication, and adopt practices of forgiveness and reconciliation.[10] In a word, Francis exhorts families to practice mercy, which he defines as "opening one's heart to wretchedness."[11] This emphasis on mercy coincided with the Jubilee Year of Mercy, dedicated to teaching and showing that mercy is who God is and what God wants for and from God's people.

Considering the state of familial crisis and Pope Francis's appeal to mercy, solidarity, and hope, this essay explores whether and how the practice of mercy within and between families can help parents and children endure and overcome these challenges in striving for personal and collective flourishing. It proceeds in three steps: first, by identifying and describing some of the root causes of the chaos and crises being experienced by parents, children, and adolescents; second, by analyzing the church's response in *Amoris Laetitia* and Pope Francis's emphasis on mercy; third, by proposing James Keenan's four cardinal virtues—prudence, self-care, fidelity, and justice—as practices of mercy in order to become more attentive and responsive to the needs of families today at the personal, social, and institutional levels.

FAMILIES IN CRISIS

To understand the experience of children today is to view—as Putnam does in *Our Kids*—family life through the lens of unjust inequality in America. Not only does Putnam find that inequality is rising at an "almost unprecedented" rate, but the main factors—class, race, and education—shatter myths of "equal opportunity" and "social mobility" so central to the American Dream.[12] Putnam's book is littered with "scissor charts" illustrating the widening gap between the rich and poor, whites and people of color, college-educated and high-school-educated. For instance, Putnam compares the net worth of college-educated households, which grew by 47% from 1989 to 2013 while the

---

[10] Most of the crises discussed pertain to those experienced by a married couple. See *Amoris Laetitia*, nos. 233-236.

[11] He continues, "Mercy is the divine attitude which embraces, it is God's giving himself to us, accepting us, and bowing to forgive ... we can say that mercy is God's identity card." Pope Francis, *The Name of God is Mercy*, trans. Oonagh Stransky (New York: Random House, 2016), 8-9.

[12] Putnam, *Our Kids*, 36. Putnam explains, "Inequality in the United States increasingly operates through education—a scarce resource in our knowledge-based economy and a measure that is closely correlated with parental socioeconomic status .... Black parents in America remain disproportionately concentrated among the poor and less educated, so black children continue to be handicapped from the start .... Black children live in poorer neighborhoods than white children at that income level, and black children experience less upward mobility and more downward mobility than their white counterparts who started at the same income level" (18-19).

net worth of high-school-educated households dropped by 17%.[13] He concludes by stating that children of well-educated and affluent parents get a "double dip" in benefits whereas children of less educated and poorer parents get a "double whammy" of disadvantage.[14] Putnam's findings are a prelude to the even more recent work of historian Richard Reeves, who argues that not only are upper middle class Americans "leaving everyone else behind," but they are hoarding opportunities that create a "glass floor," a protection "against the risk of downward mobility."[15] As Reeves sees it, "Inequality and immobility thus become self-reinforcing," or as he explains, the problem "is not just class separation, but class perpetuation."[16]

Putnam contends that when it comes to economic opportunity and social mobility, variables of sex and gender, race and ethnicity matter less than the level of educational attainment.[17] Family structure is one such example. The "traditional model" (sometimes referred to as the "nuclear family" that includes parents and children) remains mostly intact for the college-educated, upper third of American society. These families are characterized by two working parents, a mostly egalitarian division of domestic duties, and a smaller chance of experiencing divorce. Putnam contrasts this with the high-school-educated, lower third of the population, depicted by a "new, more kaleidoscopic pattern" of family structure, wherein "childbearing became increasingly disconnected from marriage and sexual partnerships became less durable."[18] For this segment of the country, Putnam adopts the description of "fragile families" (coined by the sociologist Sara McLanahan) to connote instability in marriage, higher rates of divorce, and widespread instances of single parents or step-parents and step-siblings. Putnam finds that educational attainment can be linked to family structure and stability: the ratio of divorced to married couples for college graduates is 14 per 100 couples and double that for high-school-educated Americans.[19] When parents are not able to earn a college degree, their families are more likely to take on a "complex, impermanent structure" that results from multi-partner fertility; compared to college

---

[13] Putnam, *Our Kids*, 36.
[14] Putnam, *Our Kids*, 125.
[15] Reeves, *Dream Hoarders*, 3, 12.
[16] Reeves, *Dream Hoarders*, 10. Reeves's focus is mostly economic, although more attention should be given to the cultural divides between urban and rural Americans. See, for example, Jose A. DelReal and Scott Clement, "Rural Divide," *The Washington Post*, June 17, 2017, www.washingtonpost.com/graphics/2017/national/rural-america/?tid=sm_tw&utm_term=.1d24cb665c51.
[17] Putnam reasons that insofar as college is often linked to good jobs and higher incomes, to describe someone as "college-educated" is to imply someone who is rich whereas someone who is "high-school-educated" would signify someone who is poor (44-45).
[18] Putnam, *Our Kids*, 63.
[19] Putnam, *Our Kids*, 67.

graduates, high-school-educated dads are four times more liable to live apart from their children and 50% less likely to visit them.[20] Overall, half of American children can expect to experience a single-parent family before reaching age 18, and poor children are twice as likely as rich children to have a single parent.[21]

The primary cause for family breakdown seems less a function of a "decline in morals" but more likely determined by socioeconomic status. Putnam asserts, "poverty produces family instability, and family instability in turn produces poverty."[22] Mass incarceration is another pervasive and pernicious factor, especially for families of color. As an example, Putnam finds that more than 50% of black children born in 1990 (whose parents do not have a college education) have had at least one parent incarcerated in their lifetime.[23] When so many children experience poverty and instability, and have parents who are imprisoned or struggle to find employment, they endure high rates of stress.[24] Putnam contends that stress is one of the most influential factors for the financial instability and social immobility of American households, and that insecurity and scarcity compound the effects of stress. Focusing on childhood brain development, Putnam describes how the consistent presence of caring adults enhances cognition and empathy, executive functioning, and non-cognitive skills like grit, self-control, and conscientiousness.[25] When children endure chronic stress and neglect, they fall behind in this development. If children demonstrate these developmental delays (whether cognitive or emotional difficulty), this increases parental stress, which in turn initiates a vicious cycle that creates more stress for children and thus for parents as well.[26]

Although all families experience stress, Putnam emphasizes that "healthy brain development in American children turns out to be closely correlated with parental education, income, and social class" and moreover, that "class-based disparities in cognitive, emotional, and social capabilities emerge at very early ages and remain stable

---

[20] Putnam, *Our Kids*, 68-69.
[21] Putnam, *Our Kids*, 70.
[22] Putnam, *Our Kids*, 74. Putnam adds, "The places in America where single-parent families are most common are the places where upward mobility is sluggish" (*Our Kids*, 79).
[23] Putnam, *Our Kids*, 71.
[24] Pamela Couture underscores the fact that "Childhood and poverty always intersect: children comprise the largest subset of persons who are poor, and poverty shapes the lives of children and their families, chronically and for short 'spells' of poverty." Pamela Couture, *Child Poverty: Love, Justice, and Social Responsibility* (St. Louis: Chalice Press, 2007), 2.
[25] Putnam, *Our Kids*, 110-111.
[26] Putnam summarizes, "Stressed parents are both harsher and less attentive parents" (*Our Kids*, 130).

over the life course."[27] This is significant because the stress a child experiences in the earliest years of life affects who that child becomes as well as his or her ability to access economic opportunities and achieve social mobility. *Our Kids* illuminates an important trend: while all parents experience stress, there is a growing class gap in parental stress caused by scarcity. Single parents and poorer, less educated parents are twice as likely to experience stress due to family income and debt as their married, wealthier, and better educated peers.[28] No household is immune from financial worry,[29] but the way parents handle their stress has a significant impact on child development, especially for mental health.

It is axiomatic that every parent wants what is best for his or her child. However, well-educated and affluent parents are poised to strategize for their kids' present achievement and future success whereas less educated and poorer parents are more inclined to be consumed with basic tasks like keeping them safe, out of trouble, and in school.[30] Though parents may be united by shared aspirations for their children, differences in parental education and socio-economic class account for growing inequalities in a number of areas, including school readiness, attendance, and performance.[31]

Putnam highlights one compelling exception to these rising inequalities: family dinners. Children who ate dinner with their parents at

---

[27] Putnam, *Our Kids*, 115, 117.
[28] Putnam, *Our Kids*, 130-131. In their book *Scarcity*, two behavioral economists explain how cognitive abilities (like problem-solving) are rendered less effective and efficient by scarcity. What is sometimes considered to be a lack of parental ability, concern, commitment, or persistence can result from the parent's mind being overburdened. "Good parenting," they observe, "requires bandwidth. It requires complex decisions and sacrifice. Children need to be motivated to do things they dislike, appointments have to be kept, activities planned, teachers met and their feedback processed, tutoring or extra help provided or procured and then monitored. This is hard for anyone, whatever his resources. It is doubly hard when your bandwidth is reduced." Sendhil Mullainathan and Eldar Shafir, *Scarcity: Why Having Too Little Means So Much* (New York: Times Books, 2013), 156.
[29] For an illuminating overview, see the Board of Governors of the Federal Reserve System's "Report on the Economic Well-Being of U.S. Households in 2016," www.federalreserve.gov/publications/files/2016-report-economic-well-being-us-households-201705.pdf.
[30] College-educated parents exemplify what Putnam calls "concerted cultivation" habits that often result in autonomous, independent, self-directed children with solid self-esteem and strong abilities to make good choices, the result of their parents "promotive" strategies for success. Alternatively, high-school-educated parents tend to focus more on discipline and obedience, conformity to rules, and tend to adopt what Putnam describes as "preventative" strategies (Putnam, *Our Kids*, 121).
[31] For example, the academic achievement gap between children from high and low income families is more than twice the achievement gap between black and white students. On this subject, see Mary E. Walsh and Maria D. Theodorakakis, "The Impact of Economic Inequality on Children's Development and Achievement" *Religions* 8, no. 4 (2017): dx.doi.org/10.3390/rel8040067 (at p. 4).

least five times each week were found to be less likely to drink, smoke, use recreational drugs like marijuana, have premarital sex, fight in school or get suspended; they also earned higher grades and were more likely to report they expected to attend college.[32] Although eating meals together does not solve all problems families face, it does represent an intentional commitment to be present to one another; it is a marker of availability and accompaniment in a time when many households report being busy, stressed, and overwhelmed.[33] Generally, parents are spending more time with their children than was the case fifty years ago, and while this is true for all parents regardless of education and income level, it is still the case that well educated and affluent parents are spending more time on "developmental activities" than their less educated, poorer peers.[34] Not only do children of poor, less educated parents experience more stress in the home, but they receive less parental guidance and support, an apt illustration of the "double dip" versus "double whammy" effect of these yawning class-based inequalities.

CHILDREN IN CRISIS

As cogent and indispensable as Putnam and Reeves's scrutiny of class-based inequality may be, families are in crisis and the "American Dream" is in peril for more than economic reasons. A 2007 UNICEF report ranked the United States second-to-last among 21 OECD countries for overall child wellbeing, family and peer relationships, and behaviors and risks; the U.S. was even worse for children's health and safety.[35] In the late 1990s, the CDC-Kaiser Permanente Adverse Childhood Experiences Study revealed that childhood trauma is not just pervasive, but generates long-lasting effects. A child's ACE Score—determined by experiences of verbal, emotional, physical, or sexual abuse, neglect, parental substance abuse, family instability (caused by separation, divorce, abandonment, or incarceration), or mental illness—indicates a child's exposure to stress. The CDC found that two-thirds of their study participants experienced at least one of these child trauma factors, and more than twenty percent reported

---

[32] Putnam, *Our Kids*, 122. Putnam cites child development specialist Jane Waldfogel, *What Children Need* (Cambridge: Harvard University Press, 2006), 161.

[33] Undoubtedly, there are parents who are simply unable to be home for family dinners because of their work schedule (sometimes because they work more than one job), so this is not to suggest that parents who are not home for family dinner are less dedicated to their children.

[34] Putnam, *Our Kids*, 127. This difference amounts to about 45 minutes per day more for college educated, affluent parents than high school, poor parents – a noticeable departure from the mid-1970s, when there was no significant gap between parents across class lines.

[35] "Child Poverty in Perspective: An Overview of Child Well-Being in Rich Countries," *UNICEF* (2017), www.unicef.org/media/files/ChildPovertyReport.pdf.

three or more such experiences.³⁶ As exposure to trauma increases, so does the likelihood for alcoholism and substance abuse, mental illness, suicide ideation and suicide attempts, financial stress, diminished performance at school and work, risk of intimate partner violence, sexual promiscuity, sexually transmitted infections, and unplanned pregnancies.³⁷ Survivors of childhood trauma often feel stigmatized and ashamed, and only a fraction seek treatment.

Putnam briefly acknowledges childhood trauma in his chapter on parenting. However, he views the importance of the ACE Scale through the lens of the class gap and observes that kids raised by low-income, less educated parents are "two to five times more likely than their less impoverished peers" to experience trauma.³⁸ Putnam attributes these harmful conditions to parental stress, whether caused by the daily routine, their own mental health issues, or their children acting out in response to parental stress (causing a vicious cycle). Putnam frames parental stress mostly in terms of the gap in parental investment in time and money, which correlates to income and education level.³⁹ His chapter on parenting underscores a central theme of the book: the "disadvantages facing poor kids begin early and run deep."⁴⁰ However, Putnam fails to adequately address how children are suffering precisely because their parents are fixated on improving their economic opportunity and social mobility.

Notwithstanding socioeconomic class, children of job-first parents are experiencing greater anxiety, toxic stress, and isolation. This results from parental busyness, sleeplessness, and burnout⁴¹ and exacerbates a broader trend of worsening childhood mental health. Suicide

---

[36] Shanta R. Dube et. al., "Childhood Abuse, Neglect, and Household Dysfunction and the Risk of Illicit Drug Use: The Adverse Childhood Experiences Study," *Pediatrics* 111, no. 3 (2003): 564-572.

[37] Vincent J. Felitti et al., "Relationship of Childhood Abuse and Household Dysfunction to Many of the Leading Causes of Death in Adults," *American Journal of Preventative Medicine* 14, no. 4 (1998): 245-258.

[38] Putnam, *Our Kids*, 114.

[39] Putnam, *Our Kids*, 131-132. In yet another "scissor chart," Putnam shows that parental financial worries are twice as high among high school educated parents as their college educated peers. He briefly notes that single parents are more likely to experience such stress, "even when education and income are held constant."

[40] Putnam, *Our Kids*, 134.

[41] According to Silvia Bellezza and her colleagues, "busyness" has become a more important status symbol than luxury items. See Silvia Bellezza et al., "Research: Why Americans Are So Impressed by Busyness," *Harvard Business Review*, December 15, 2016, hbr.org/2016/12/research-why-americans-are-so-impressed-by-busyness. A 2017 CareerBuilder survey found that 61% of employees feel burned out in their current job, 31% reported feeling high or extremely high levels of stress at work, and 33% of workers said they did not plan to take vacation this year. A 2016 study by Rand Corporation found that the U.S. economy loses $411 billion annually through tired or absent employees. A 2016 Price Waterhouse Cooper survey found only 34%

rates have doubled among American youth; it is now the second-leading cause of death among those aged 10-24.[42] Even as more teens are diagnosed with depression, anxiety, and other forms of mental illness, there has been no corresponding rise in treatment.[43] Children as young as 10 are expressing higher rates of feeling worried, stressed, and overwhelmed: more than two million adolescents report experiencing depression that impairs their ability to function on a daily basis while 6.3 million have been diagnosed with an anxiety disorder.[44] By age 17, 13.6% of boys and 36.1% of girls have been or are diagnosed as depressed.[45] Some describe today's youth as being fragile and entitled, but more work needs to be done to uncover the root causes of the decline in mental health among American children. High academic expectations and stress as well as bullying in school and via text, social media, and the internet all appear to be contributing factors.[46] Parents who place a premium on ambition and achievement—whether their own or their children's—tend to exacerbate insecurity among today's youth. If children need anything, it is the safety and stability generated by parental love and consistency.

Insufficient attention has been paid to the pressure being put on parents and children to perform, achieve, and get ahead. This barely registers as a contributing factor to families in crisis in *Our Kids*; Putnam takes ambition for granted as part of the backdrop for American families. The drive to succeed is not a new phenomenon; in 1970, sociologist Robin Williams identified achievement as a core American

---

of employees feel supported in work-life balance. According to the Deloitte Shift Index, four in five workers are dissatisfied with their jobs.

[42] For years, the CDC has been issuing warnings about the rise in child and teen suicide ideation and attempts. In 2016, the CDC released a report showing that among children age 10-14, the suicide rate doubled from 2007-2014. In that age group, suicide is now more prevalent than car accidents as a cause of death. See the report by Kenneth D. Kochanek et al., "Deaths: Final Data for 2014," *National Vital Statistics Reports* 65, no. 4 (2016): www.cdc.gov/nchs/data/nvsr/nvsr65 /nvsr65_04.pdf.

[43] For example, a study drawn from the National Surveys on Drug Use and Health found a 37% rise in teenage depression from 2005 to 2014, without an increase in mental health treatment. See the report by Ramin Mojtabai et al., "National Trends in the Prevalence and Treatment of Depression in Adolescents and Young Adults" *Pediatrics* 138, no. 6 (2016): e20161878.

[44] Susanna Schrobsdorff, "Teen Depression and Anxiety: Why the Kids Are Not Alrigh,t" *Time*, October 27, 2016, time.com/4547322/american-teens-anxious-depressed-overwhelmed/.

[45] Joshua Breslau et al., "Sex Differences in Recent First-Onset Depression in an Epidemiological Sample of Adolescents," *Translational Psychiatry* 7, no. 5 (2017): e1139.

[46] Lara Korte, "Youth Suicide Rates Are Rising. School and the Internet May Be to Blame," *USA Today*, May 30, 2017, www.usatoday.com/story/news/nation-now/2017/05/30/youth-suicide-rates-rising-school-and-internet-may-blame/356539001/.

value, second only to equal opportunity.[47] It is long past time to more closely examine the effects of the "get ahead" mentality whereby the need to succeed strains the relationship between parents and children, warps how children see themselves and one another, and foments divisive competition between individuals, families, and communities.

When children learn from their parents that ambition or achievement is the greatest good, their identity and self-worth get measured by this standard. In this framework, gratitude and generosity take a back seat to maximizing every resource or opportunity in a social milieu that orbits around scarcity and competition. There is no time for leisure or play; joy and relaxation are not just superfluous, but counterproductive. Curiosity is too time consuming and can lead to making mistakes. Instead of learning from mistakes, children come to believe missteps are unacceptable signs of a weakness or flaw pushing them farther from their goal to succeed. Shortcomings get internalized and children question their fundamental dignity and value. This results in children feeling less secure, connected, and supported. It can also leave children wondering if they are loved, lovable, and capable of loving others.

YOUTH CULTURE OF CONNECTIVITY

As teens prepare for and attend college, they increasingly self-identify with the same word: overwhelmed. Facing pressure to stand out in competitive high schools, meet lofty parental expectations for success, shoulder the financial burden associated with tuition and housing, navigate new freedoms in college life, and endure uncertainty about securing employment after college, college-bound teens are daunted if not exhausted.[48] Many encounter additional unexpected challenges like experiences of racial bias, gender-based discrimination, bullying and hazing, intimate partner violence or sexual assault, and food insecurity and hunger.

Not only are teens struggling in the transition to the independence that corresponds with college life and adulthood[49] but psychologists have detected a diminished ability to connect with their peers. Reports of a rise in narcissism and a drastic decline in empathy—down 40%

---

[47] John J. Macionis, *Sociology* (New Jersey: Pearson Prentice Hall, 2005), 66.
[48] See, for example, Richard Kadison and Theresa Foy DiGeronimo, *College of the Overwhelmed: The Campus Mental Health Crisis and What to Do About It*. (San Francisco: Jossey-Bass, 2004).
[49] Today, even the independence associated with college life and the milestones that come with turning 18 or 21 do not yet equate to "adulthood." Most Americans say one becomes an adult at age 25 and a growing number of psychologists and sociologists point to trends of "prolonged adolescence," "emerging adulthood," or even the neologism, "kidulthood," to describe ages 18-25; critics lament this as the dawn of the "Peter Pan Generation."

according to a study at the University of Michigan[50]— might be the result of children who are trained to think more of themselves and their feats and less about others, especially those in need. Although young people are more connected than ever before—especially through smartphones and social media—they report rising rates of feeling insecure, isolated, and lonely.[51] There appears to be a direct correlation between the amount of time children spend with a screen (phone, tablet, computer, or television) and happiness; according to a 2011 study, 32 percent of teens who use media for 16 or more hours per day reported feeling sad, whereas only 22 percent of teens reported feeling unhappy among those who used media for three hours or less.[52]

Although it never registers in *Our Kids*, it is difficult to overstate the significance of screen time on American families. The average individual spends more than ten and a half hours in front of a screen (an hour more in 2016 than was the case 2015). Aside from sleep, children spend more time consuming digital media than any other activity.[53] The volume, velocity, and ubiquity of digital content and connections can create a hyper-other-directedness wherein self-worth gets measured by how many people one has "friended" or has "following" them, has "liked" their comments or pictures, or responded to their status updates, tweets, Instagram photos, and Snapchat stories. Therapists warn that children are becoming addicted to the "digital drug" of their screens; brain imaging research shows the brain responds to screens as it would cocaine and detects elevated dopamine levels similar to what is experienced during sex.[54]

While technology does not deserve all the blame for these trends in youth culture, its prevalence shapes what has become normative for social interaction. Psychologist Sherry Turkle describes this digital milieu as fashioning a mentality of, "I share, therefore I am" resulting

---

[50] Sarah H. Konrath et al., "Changes in Dispositional Empathy in American College Students Over Time: A Meta-Analysis," *Personality and Social Psychology Review* 15, no. 2 (2011): 180-198.

[51] Sherry Turkle, *Alone Together: Why We Expect More From Technology and Less from Each Other* (New York: Basic Books, 2011), 157.

[52] This study is the result of the ERIAL Project, a collaborative effort between five Illinois universities. See the published findings in *College Libraries and Student Culture: What We Now Know* (Chicago: American Library Association, 2012).

[53] Douglas A. Gentile et al., "Protective Effects of Parental Monitoring of Children's Media Use," *JAMA Pediatrics* 168, no. 5 (2014): 479-484. Researchers found that the more parents can limit their kids' screen time, their children sleep and behave better and improve their performance in school.

[54] See, for example, Nicholas Kardaras, *Glow Kids: How Screen Addiction is Hijacking Our Kids—And How to Break the Trance* (New York: St. Martin's Press, 2016).

in a fragile sense of identity that demands constant validation by others.[55] One consequence of all these digitally-mediated interactions is living in a state of constant distraction or endless busyness. Turkle claims, "We have moved from multitasking to multi-lifing" in our "world of continual partial attention."[56] With smartphones as portals to limitless amounts of content or connections, everything has become subject to interruption. Turkle asserts that this trains users to actually crave connection and interruption.[57] This makes it much more difficult to sustain attention to a particular subject or person. In fact, today's students express fear at the prospect of not using their phones or being busy; they have been trained to be constant consumers, stuck on a hedonic treadmill in pursuit of instant gratification. They are always tethered to their phones, which they cling to as a lifeline for social belonging and status, while their self-esteem and happiness plummet. Students are aware that they are "splitting themselves in two," and yet they feel like they have to continue to follow this script to maintain if not improve their social status.[58]

In effect, digital youth culture encourages the kind of habituation that undermines integrity and authenticity. This increases the conditions that cause fragmentation, both within a person and between persons. At the same time, it also constructs a vision of the self that stands in stark contrast to Charles Taylor's description of a "buffered self" who is able to disengage from one's surroundings, and protect oneself from "distressing or tempting experiences."[59] Instead, it seems more

---

[55] Turkle, *Alone Together*, 302. Turkle describes this as a kind of narcissism that "cannot tolerate the complex demands of other people but tries to relate to them by distorting who they are and splitting off what it needs, what it can use. So, the narcissistic self gets on with others by dealing only with their made-to-measure representations … You can take what you need and move on. And, if not gratified, you can try someone else" (177).

[56] Turkle, *Alone Together*, 160-161.

[57] Turkle, *Alone Together*, 171, 227.

[58] Donna Freitas, *The Happiness Effect: How Social Media is Driving a Generation to Appear Perfect at Any Cost* (Oxford University Press, 2017), 10. Freitas highlights the fact that many students are unnerved by these digital norms, but they are reluctant to give voice to these concerns because they do not want to give others the impression they are vulnerable or struggling. This points to a need to address this topic in our homes, schools, and churches so students feel more supported and less alone. Freitas writes, "While young adults and college students buckling under the pressure to project a false self online may not be as sexy (literally) as teens sexting nude photos to each other, it's a pervasive struggle, and we need to talk about it with them" (11).

[59] Charles Taylor, *A Secular Age* (Cambridge: Harvard University Press, 2007), 38. Taylor asserts that Western civilization has changed from the previous age of the "bounded self" or the "porous self." A "buffered self" can disengage at will; he explains, "My ultimate purposes are those which arise within me, the crucial meanings of things are those defined in my responses to them" that allow the "buffered self" to "avoid distressing or tempting experiences." The "buffered self" is a master of one's own meanings, in that they are not necessarily guided by religious or social bonds. He later adds that the "buffered self" "breeds pusillanimity" (373).

accurate to speak of a "networked self" who is always tethered to others and expects access to content on-demand. This state of constant connectivity can create conditions for belonging and support while also leaving young people feeling like they continuously have to impress or entertain others. Teens spend countless hours carefully curating their digital profiles in an unending task of "impression management."[60] In this cultural context, there is never enough time to perfect one's image or brand, and it subjects young people to steady surveillance from others, setting them up to feel like they can never measure up to the meticulously polished highlight reels that flood their social media newsfeed or timeline. Social media intensify the age-old "compare and despair" dynamic, exposing today's young people to a steady dose of feeling unworthy and fearful of being authentic.

Nonstop surveillance—which comes from always being connected and ready to share— would put anyone on edge; for children and adolescents, this exacerbates a stage of development already marked by uncertainty and vulnerability. Social media foments insecurity because "anything they say or do can easily be taken out of context" by "audiences [that] are invisible" to a particular person.[61] On the one hand, teens feel constantly exposed and privacy seems more unattainable than assured. This leaves them feeling unsafe and craving social conditions that foster a sense of security. Tolerance and nonjudgmentalism are adopted to mitigate social risks like ambiguity and awkwardness. Teens contort themselves to social norms and distort who they are, edit what they believe and value, and even go back to filter out any undesirable digital interactions.[62] On the other hand, teens have unique power to manipulate their social media account and interact with others in order to attract attention, boost their visibility, and elevate their status. They can network personally and professionally, connect with others who share their preferences, and find a sense of community across physical distance. The internet and social media are like mirrors and magnifiers that depict the gauntlet of youth culture today. Teens can express their hurt, celebrate their accomplishments, share their experiences, showcase their relationships, and make friends with people they might not otherwise meet offline. In some

---

[60] danah boyd, *It's Complicated: The Social Lives of Networked Teens* (New Haven: Yale University Press, 2014), 47. Here, boyd cites sociologist Erving Goffman, who uses this term to describe the "social rituals involved in self-presentation" created by individuals in the context of wider groups (which establish norms for what might be considered popular, funny, sexy, etc.).

[61] boyd, *It's Complicated*, 53.

[62] Freitas describes this as a "Facebook Cleanup": removing expressions of negative emotions, mean comments, unpopular or divisive opinions (e.g., about religion or politics), evidence of embarrassing or illicit behavior, posts with few "likes" or "favorites," and anything that makes one look boring, silly, or otherwise unpopular (Freitas, *The Happiness Effect*, 48).

ways, digital technology and social media make youth culture more visible than was the case for previous generations. This presents a unique opportunity to be more attentive and responsive to young people who are struggling.

Online behaviors produce a variety of offline effects. Young people are not always cognizant of the "impact imprint" of the tools and apps they use.[63] One crossover effect of digital youth culture is shaped by the incessant desire for connection and desire for instant gratification learned by the delivery of digital content and connections on-demand. As Sherry Turkle describes, this has created an abundance of "modern Goldilockses."[64] The cultural norms that encourage self-interest and fickle tastes combined with competitive academics and athletics reinforce a "get ahead" mindset that makes it easier to view others with distrust and become more insensitive to others' struggles and needs.

MORALLY ADRIFT

A growing number of young people live by the motto, "I do me, you do you," meant to convey radical tolerance and nonjudgmentalism. Such a philosophy is problematic because it gives the impression that one can isolate individual behavior from social or moral norms and it ignores the impact one's behavior has on others. A male student might think it is harmless to watch pornography or sext, but he fails to consider the broader beliefs, practices, and structures that divorce sex from love and procreation, denigrate and exploit women, promote misogynist norms, and contribute to the market for sex trafficking. Indeed, sexting and pornography are rampant on college campuses, although most students are reluctant to consider the morality of such behavior on the personal, social, and structural levels.[65] This is especially important because of the dehumanizing effects caused by pornography as viewers internalize the objectification of female bodies, subjugation to (white, heterosexual) male pleasure and power, and the physical and verbal abuse contained in the vast majority of pornographic film scenes.[66] A growing number of marriage counselors and divorce attor-

---

[63] The phrase "impact imprint" refers to the manner in which technologies transfer "their essential qualities" to their users. See Nancy K. Baym, *Personal Connections in the Digital Age* (Malden: Polity Press, 2010), 26.

[64] Turkle, *Alone Together*, 15.

[65] See, for example, Karen Peterson-Iyer, "Mobile Porn? Teenage Sexting and Justice for Women," *Journal of the Society of Christian Ethics* 33, no. 2 (2013): 93-110.

[66] Gail Dines argues that most Americans' idea of pornography is "twenty years out of date." Most people might think of images of naked bodies or the act of sex, when in fact, most pornography is aggressive if not violent, and usually depicts women as passive participants—in ecstasy, no less—to the advances of more than one man at a time, who are often verbally and physically abusive (in fact, one study found nearly

neys have expressed concern about the negative effects that pornography has on marriage and family life; according to the American Academy of Matrimonial Lawyers, more than half of divorce cases involve one party having "an obsessive interest in pornographic websites." Sexual exploitation and violence have become normalized due in part to the pervasiveness of pornography.[67] Not only is porn saved to a quarter of all smartphones, but experts estimate that about one-quarter of high school students and one-third of college students have sent a nude or semi-nude picture of themselves. More than 90% of college men and more than 60% of college women reported being exposed to pornography before they turned 18 (more than half of boys and almost a third of girls are exposed to porn before they turn 13). Roughly two-thirds of college men and one-fifth of college women view porn at least once per week, while another 17% of men and 30% of women watch porn one or two times a month. Most college students say viewing porn is acceptable or normal.[68] It should be no surprise that the National Center on Sexual Exploitation calls pornography a "public health crisis."

In the face of all these problems—ranging from mental illness and suicide to sexual exploitation and violence—why isn't there greater moral outrage among our young people? Among the likely explanations, let us consider five possibilities. First, this may be due partly to the high rates of stress, busyness, and connectivity. If young people are living in a constant state of interaction and interruption, it can contribute to what Ervin Goffman describes as "civil inattention."[69] Civil inattention refers to the process when strangers in close proximity show recognition of the other without imposing on them (e.g., an acknowledging glance and then looking away). Although this behavior might be motivated by beneficence (to respect personal boundaries, for instance), it can generate feelings of invisibility and loneliness and reduce social responsibility. Civil inattention fits seamlessly with the "I do me, you do you" mantra, but as the philosopher John Dewey

---

90% of scenes contained at least one aggressive act; the overall average is 12 aggressive acts per scene). See Gail Dines, *Pornland: How Porn Has Hijacked Our Sexuality* (Boston: Beacon Press, 2010), xviii-xxii.

[67] Michael Kimmel describes it this way: "With gross sales of all pornographic media ranging between $10 and $14 billion annually, the porn industry is bigger than the revenues of ABC, NBC, and CBS—combined....More than 260 new pornographic videos are produced every week. Adult bookstores outnumber McDonald's restaurants in the United States by a margin of at least three to one. On the Internet, pornography has increased 1,800 percent, from 14 million web pages in 1998 to 260 million in 2003 and 1.5 *billion* downloads per month in 2005" in *Guyland: The Perilous World Where Boys Become Men* (New York: Harper, 2008), 170.

[68] These statistics are drawn from the 2015 Covenant Eyes Report, available at www.covenanteyes.com/pornstats/. Figures for teen boys are especially concerning: 35% say they have viewed pornographic materials "too many times to count."

[69] Cited by boyd, *It's Complicated*, 58.

warned ninety years ago, "live and let live" just as easily becomes "live and let die"; this is precisely what leads to the "eclipse of the public."[70] In other words, youth culture marked by connectivity can produce young people who are too easily distracted from and not sufficiently invested in the public sphere. Already feeling overburdened and motivated by the social value tied to ambition, there is little incentive to consider issues apart from self-interest.

A second factor is related to the priority given to tolerance and nonjudgmentalism implicit in "I do me, you do you." Michael Kimmel describes this phenomenon as a "culture of silence," which he finds particularly prevalent among young men. Kimmel argues that a "culture of silence"—which requires young men "to suffer without speaking of it and to be silent witnesses to acts of cruelty to others"—is rooted in fear.[71] Fed by a fear of being marginalized, socially shamed, or even becoming a victim of violence, guys learn to keep their mouths closed when they hear offensive remarks, witness other guys get teased or tormented, observe loutish behavior, or learn their teammates gang raped a classmate. Kimmel insists this "culture of silence" is not unique to guys, but it is what gives license to the idea that "boys will be boys" who are not always held accountable for their words and actions.[72] In this social milieu, loyalty trumps all lesser goods like honesty, compassion, or fairness.[73] If students learn to keep quiet about their own pain as well as that of their peers, a generation of young people begin to believe that it is okay to suffer in silence. What is more, to abide by the motto "I do me, you do you," is to cower in fear of appearing intolerant or judgmental, even in the face of harmful beliefs, actions, relationships, and systems that deserve to be denounced and resisted.

A third reason for the lack of moral outrage could be tied more directly to the learned behavior associated with digital technology and social media. Although screens are portals for connection and engagement, they can also be venues for mindless distraction or escapism. It is no small task to overcome the inertia that results from nearly eleven daily hours with a screen. This fosters a "spectator culture" wherein

---

[70] Dewey writes, "Till the Great Society is converted into a Great Community, the Public will remain in eclipse. Communication can alone create a great community. Our Babel is not one of tongues but of the signs and symbols without which shared experience is impossible." See John Dewey, *The Public and its Problems* (New York: Henry Holt and Company, 1927), 142.

[71] Kimmel, *Guyland*, 61.

[72] Kimmel quotes a college student who, speaking from a female perspective, admits, "We know that it's wrong …. But we know that if we go along with it, the cool guys will like us. No big deal. It isn't like they're hitting *us*, is it?" (Kimmel, *Guyland*, 62).

[73] Kimmel contends, "Breaking the silence is treason, worse, perhaps, than the activities themselves" (Kimmel, *Guyland*, 67).

scrolling through endless amounts of content—whether carefully edited Instagram pictures, silly Snapchat stories, adorable kitten videos on YouTube, or impressive sports highlights—encourages a passive form of consumption that trains users to prefer banal entertainment to new and challenging ideas or perspectives.[74] According to the Pew Research Center, 70% of college students play video games and more than half say gaming keeps them from studying "some" or "a lot."[75] Experts are trying to keep up with how the brain responds to all the cognitive and emotional overstimulation that follows so much screen time.[76] A moral analysis of "spectator culture" might take issue less with the inclination for leisure or entertainment than how this shapes whether and how young people respond when exposed to evil or injustice.

"Spectator culture" would seem to produce more passive bystanders than social activists. Evaluating the moral formation that results from these digitally-mediated interactions, it is necessary to acknowledge the potential of the screen to appease, buffer, and disempower. Users can opt out of any contact or content they find undesirable; the rise of "filter bubbles" results from the penchant to participate in "echo chambers" that affirm one's biases and assumptions. This allows people to ignore other perspectives and experiences, or even hide from them. As Elisabeth Vasko argues, Christians have a moral responsibility to confront the reality of "sin as hiding" via "apathy and mindless conformity." This can be detected in the way that the screen can function as a hiding "from God, one another, and ourselves" in a "lack of self-assertion" and segregation by participating "in the ongoing creation of separate and unequal worlds. Privilege creates myopic vision wherein the periphery is hidden from view. It encourages a culture of escapism where time and attention are delivered from the suffering of others to the trivial."[77] Although screens can be thresholds to encounter and share diverse perspectives, embrace vulnerability and experience intimacy, forge new connections and cultivate rapport, these experiences are even more formative when they lead to or flow from offline interactions and experiences. This does not imply a Luddite rejection of technology, but it does invite more intentional study of how these tools are being used, especially to help or hurt.

---

[74] This is Neil Postman's prescient concern in *Amusing Ourselves to Death: Public Discourse in the Age of Show Business* (New York: Penguin Books, 1985).

[75] Maeve Duggan, "Gaming and Gamers," *Pew Research Center*, December 15, 2015, www.pewinternet.org/2015/12/15/gaming-and-gamers/.

[76] Erik Qualman reports the average attention span online is just 7 seconds in *Socialnomics: How Social Media Transforms the Way We Live and Do Business* (Hoboken: John Wiley & Sons, 2013).

[77] Elisabeth Vasko, *Beyond Apathy: A Theology for Bystanders* (Minneapolis: Fortress Press, 2015), 143-144.

A fourth characteristic is informed by Christian Smith's research on the moral formation of "emerging adults" as part of the National Study of Youth and Religion. In light of the data collected since 2001, Smith and his colleagues describe youth culture as awash in "moral therapeutic deism," an individualistic and morally relativistic ethos that prizes personal subjectivity, feeling, and self-fulfillment at the expense of shared moral norms and obligations.[78] At first blush, this view seems innocuous enough: American Christian youth say they believe "God wants people to be good, nice, and fair to each other," and that "the central goal of life is to be happy and to feel good about one's self."[79] However, working out the implications of this morality, it becomes clear that "moral therapeutic deism" defies any normative understanding of the good (or evil) necessary for establishing common agreement and accountability. In "moral therapeutic deism," youth can be self-indulgent without any thought of social (or ecological) responsibility. Community is an afterthought if not an encumbrance.[80] Emerging adults show little interest and do not make much time for civic or political engagement: 69% said they were not at all political, compared to 4% who considered themselves to be actively political.[81] Many survey respondents admitted feeling apathetic, uninformed, distrustful, and disempowered in the political sphere. Though emerging adults affirm the value of volunteering and charitable giving and aspire to incorporate these habits into their later adulthood, many say they do not have the time or resources to be involved in such efforts at the present time. This is problematic for at least two reasons: first, emerging adults fail to recognize that present priorities and practices establish patterns for the future; second, too many emerging adults do not believe they can or should make a difference in the world. In fact,

---

[78] Christian Smith with Melinda Lundquist Denton, *Soul Searching: The Religious and Spiritual Lives of American Teenagers* (Oxford University Press, 2005), 162.

[79] Smith and Denton, *Soul Searching*, 162-163.

[80] As an example, two-thirds of those surveyed say involvement in congregations is unnecessary to be religious (Smith and Denton, *Soul Searching*, 76). More to the point, Smith finds a surprising lack of civic engagement among emerging adults, with very few claiming to be active in their neighborhood or local organizations, or politically aware and invested. Smith argues that digital technology and social media make it easier to create a state of "nearly total submersion of self into fluidly constructed, private networks of technologically managed intimates and associates." See Christian Smith et al., *Lost in Transition: The Dark Side of Emerging Adulthood* (New York: Oxford University Press, 2011), 223.

[81] Smith notes that these surveys were collected in 2008, a year that has typically been described as crucial for empowering youth involvement in politics. On the contrary, the National Study of Youth and Religion data show that most emerging adults feel "disempowered, apathetic, and sometimes even despairing when it comes to the larger social, civic, and political world beyond their own private lives." The 4% who claimed to be "actively political" were almost exclusively male. The remaining 27% reported being only "marginally political," which included such low standards as reading the news to be somewhat informed (Smith et al., *Lost in Transition*, 196, 206-208).

according to Smith's findings, less than five percent of emerging adults are confident they can make a difference.[82] If all God wants is for me to be happy, then I can be content to focus on my own comfort, status, and achievement. There is little room—or need—for social concern or moral outrage in such a worldview.

Part of the reason why today's young people are loath to commit to moral norms is because they have trouble identifying them. Smith and his colleagues find that today's young people are deeply confused and disoriented when it comes to morality. Moral duties are viewed as inessential to character formation or spiritual maturity; they are considered to be "largely avoidable displeasures to be escaped in order to realize a pleasurable life of happiness and positive self-esteem."[83] Six in ten respondents stated that morality is a matter of personal choice or opinion while one in three indicated they did not know what makes anything morally right or wrong.[84] The NSYR data show that two-thirds of emerging adults were unable to consistently, coherently, and articulately respond to questions about moral dilemmas in their lives. Instead, they made sporadic appeals to generic platitudes like "do no harm," the Golden Rule, or Karma, without being able to describe how these relate to established religious and ethical systems. As many as 60% of emerging adults say their morality is situational, with roughly half explaining that they determine what is moral based on whether it might hurt someone.[85] Smith and his colleagues contend that emerging adults demonstrate very little concern for religious obligation or love for God; rather, their moral motivation is social order, efficiency, and prosperity under the safeguard of tolerance. This would seem to generate a moral schizophrenia, lacking both moral truth and moral judgment of better or worse choices. Smith and his colleagues conclude that parents, educators, and religious leaders have done an "awful job when it comes to moral education and formation."[86]

A fifth and final factor is a lack of leadership, especially moral leadership. In light of the previous four factors, it is evident that today's youth culture is wounded by a dearth of social courage.[87] Fear—

---

[82] Smith et al., *Lost in Transition*, 270, n. 5. Smith finds that nearly 70% of emerging adults identify as apathetic, uninformed, distrustful, or disempowered (197-204).

[83] Smith and Denton, *Soul Searching*, 173.

[84] Smith et al., *Lost in Transition*, 21, 36.

[85] These statistics are reported by Christian Smith in *What Is a Person?: Rethinking Humanity, Social Life, and the Moral Good from the Person Up* (University of Chicago Press, 2010), 38-39. Smith reports two-thirds of the emerging adults he studied were incapable of coherent moral discernment (59).

[86] Smith et al., *Lost in Transition*, 59-66 (at p. 60). Incidentally, this is true among Catholic emerging adults, for whom "morality is simply not a pressing issue for many of them" (Smith and Denton, *Soul Searching*, 215).

[87] Michael Kimmel might describe this as a "culture of complicity," a corollary to the "culture of silence" (Kimmel, *Guyland*, 67).

of so many things, whether being marginalized or excluded, losing social status by being considered intolerant, ignorant, offensive, judgmental, boring, or awkward, failing in ambition or achievement, unable to measure up to lofty expectations from parents, teachers, peers, and self—can be paralyzing. In the midst of chaos and crisis, young people need affirmation, support, and hope. They need role models, mentors, and moral exemplars who can provide a template for choosing the kinds of words, actions, relationships, and patterns of belonging that promote personal and collective wellbeing.[88] Young people need leaders who are attentive listeners and have a high capacity for empathy. They desire a vision of life that can offer meaning and purpose, provide comfort and strength, and bring people together in unity across differences. Emerging adults crave freedom and yet are anxious about navigating a daunting array of choices and making mistakes; they need older peers and other adults who can accompany them in reflection and discernment and help them glean wisdom from their experiences. Young people want to feel valued and cared for as much as they want to feel pride in their accomplishments. They would prefer trust and cooperation to judgmentalism and competition. They want a place to feel safe, to find a sense of belonging, and to be empowered to be freely and fully themselves in contributing to the greater good.[89] The experiences of crisis in family life and especially among children and adolescents underscore the necessity of producing more leaders who can imagine new possibilities for the future.

FAITH THAT DOES MERCY

In spite of this lack of leadership, there seems to be at least one person who is garnering attention and respect, both in the United States and across the globe. A 2017 Pew Research survey found that Pope Francis has a 70% approval rating among American adults, while a 2016 WIN/Gallup International poll named the pontiff the "world's most popular leader." Surely much can be said about Francis' message and style, his piety and simple lifestyle, humility and honesty, concern

---

[88] When Kimmel interviews guys who break the "Guy Code" and stand up for themselves or another, he finds two common threads: individual resilience and "they all spoke of at least one adult who made a difference, 'someone who believed in me and stood by me'" (Kimmel, *Guyland*, 271).

[89] For an insightful reflection on leadership, see Simon Sinek, *Leaders Eat Last: Why Some Teams Pull Together and Others Don't* (New York: Penguin, 2017). Sinek asserts that leadership begins with making people feel safe, which he describes as a "Circle of Safety" that abolishes the threat of intimidation, humiliation, rejection, and failure. Instead, the "Circle of Safety" builds empathy and trust and gives people the power to make decisions, thereby making them feel valued and essential to the group (24-26).

for the poor and outcast, and emphasis on accompaniment and inclusion.[90] A central theme of his pontificate has been urging people to cultivate a "culture of encounter," by which he means an openness to share life with others, especially those who are different, vulnerable, or marginalized.

Seven months after his election, Pope Francis called an Extraordinary General Assembly of the Synod of Bishops on the theme "The Pastoral Challenges of the Family in the Context of Evangelization," held in the Vatican in October 2014. The following year, there was an Ordinary General Assembly of the Synod of Bishops to focus on the theme "The Vocation and Mission of the Family in the Church and in the Contemporary World." This preceded an extraordinary Holy Year of Mercy, which was celebrated by the global Catholic church from December 2015 through November 2016. These events demonstrate Francis's commitment to be attentive and responsive to the hopes and fears, needs and desires of the lay faithful. They speak to his aspiration to be a leader who is intent on listening and fostering dialogue and then coordinating a collaborative pastoral response in the spirit of accompaniment.

Pope Francis issued *Amoris Laetitia,* the post-synodal apostolic exhortation, to provide the vision for a pastoral response to the concerns addressed at the synod gatherings in 2014 and 2015. Released in April 2016, *Amoris Laetitia* has generated controversy, in part because Francis has tried to give priority to extending mercy over enforcing rules. Not everyone has welcomed this call to tenderness, forgiveness, and inclusion; in fact, some argue that this has only caused greater uncertainty about how to apply the spirit of *Amoris Laetitia* and remain faithful to church teaching. However, in many ways, *Amoris Laetitia* is a fitting response to what was expressed by the lay faithful when they were asked for feedback in preparation for the 2015 synod. The bishops organized a 46 question survey to help them better understand "the context and challenges of the family" in the contemporary world.[91] Responses to the survey made it abundantly clear that families are struggling (for many of the reasons described in the foregoing

---

[90] When asked, "Who is Jorge Mario Bergoglio?" Pope Francis introduces himself by saying, "I am a sinner. This is the most accurate definition. It is not a figure of speech, a literary genre. I am a sinner." Francis describes his vision of the church as a place of welcome for all: "This church with which we should be thinking is the home of all, not a small chapel that can hold only a small group of selected people. We must not reduce the bosom of the universal church to a nest protecting our mediocrity. And the church is Mother; the church is fruitful. It must be" (Pope Francis interview with Antonio Spadaro, SJ, "A Big Heart Open to God," *America*, September 30, 2013, www.americamagazine.org/pope-interview.)

[91] The fact that the survey contains 46 questions is problematic in and of itself. Many respondents complained that it was too long, used unclear and highfalutin language, and as a result, the response rate was typically evaluated to be "poor" (both in terms

pages) and many Catholics are dissatisfied with the church's pastoral approach to families.[92] A large number find the church to be more focused on following rules than what is best for the people involved in a specific situation. They lament that their home parish is out of touch with their needs and desires and that churches have been reduced to places where sacraments are dispensed. They wish to belong to a vibrant and inclusive faith community that offers support to families navigating all that life brings. They want a church that can imagine new possibilities for building right-relationship with God and one another in light of the "signs of the times."

Amoris Laetitia does not provide a perfect response to families experiencing chaos and crisis, but it does try to take seriously these daunting experiences. The document is also tasked with trying to speak to Catholics across the globe, who are all experiencing marriage and family in a diverse array of socio-cultural, political, and economic contexts. On the whole, *Amoris Laetitia* aspires to live up to Pope Francis' vision of the church as a field hospital; Francis explains, "The thing the church needs most today is the ability to heal wounds and to warm the hearts of the faithful; it needs nearness, proximity. I see the church as a field hospital after battle."[93] *Amoris Laetitia* calls the church to be oriented by mercy and encourages "everyone to be a sign of mercy and closeness wherever family life remains imperfect or lacks peace and joy" (*Amoris Laetitia*, no. 5).

The second chapter of *Amoris Laetitia* is dedicated to highlighting the ways in which families are being scarred in the battlefield of an unjust social order. For example, the document identifies that families are wounded by decreasing support from social structures and institutions (no. 32), rising individualism (no. 33), a lack of commitment (no. 34), loneliness and powerlessness (no. 43), "excessive idealization" of marriage and family (no. 36), a "culture of the ephemeral" (no. 39), and various personal and social sins including sexual exploitation like

---

of the number of completed surveys as well as the quality of the responses). The survey is available as part of the *Lineamenta* on the Vatican website, www.vatican.va/roman_curia/synod/documents/rc_synod_doc_20141209_lineamenta-xiv-assembly_en.html.

[92] Technically, the survey was meant to inform the Synod of Bishops and not designed for the responses to be released to the public. A few U.S. dioceses published summaries of what they collected from the lay faithful. In a research project funded by Xavier University's College of Arts and Sciences and in cooperation with a number of dioceses (including Burlington, Knoxville, Portland, Scranton, St. Petersburg, and Wichita), I was able to review some of what was submitted to the bishops. Overall, the survey responses expressed a good deal of frustration with church teachings and practices, including the exclusionary treatment of LGBTQ individuals, the complex, prolonged, and expensive annulment process, hurt caused by the church's teaching on divorce and remarriage (including whether one can receive Eucharist), and significant disagreement with the prohibition on artificial contraception.

[93] Pope Francis, "A Big Heart Open to God."

pornography, prostitution, and sex trafficking (no. 41), lack of affordable housing and dignified employment (no. 44), sexual abuse of children (no. 45), hardships faced by migrants, refugees, and those living in extreme poverty (no. 46), the isolation of the elderly (no. 48), drug use and domestic violence (no. 51), patriarchy and abuse of women (no. 54). All of these examples are listed without ever using the phrase "social sin." The document lacks a well-developed framework for how families are acted upon, complicit with, and called to resist and reform the beliefs, actions, and policies that contribute to social sin.[94]

Instead, responding to these wounds, Francis appeals to the tender embrace of God (no. 28) and the need to reclaim the vocation of the family, which is to incarnate God's infinite love and tenderness in the world (no. 59). The document proceeds by articulating a soaring vision of family life where love is an experience of the common good (70), the family is the "sanctuary of life" (no. 83), and the church is a "family of families" (no. 87), that is charged with supporting its members, especially those in greatest need (no. 197). Francis writes, The Gospel of the family responds to the deepest expectations of the human person: a response to each one's dignity and fulfillment in reciprocity, communion and fruitfulness. This consists not merely in presenting a set of rules, but in proposing values that are clearly needed today, even in the most secularized of countries" (no. 201). Parishes are called to be more than places where sacraments are dispensed; they are tasked with being on the front lines of caring for families: "The main contribution to the pastoral care of families is offered by the parish, which is the family of families, where small communities, ecclesial movements and associations live in harmony" (no. 202). Francis anticipates this will require a more robust commitment to pastoral outreach and a "more adequate formation" of priests, deacons, women religious, catechists, and parish staff (no. 202).[95]

The remaining passages offer families advice on facing crises (nos. 232-238), reinforce the need for accompaniment (nos. 241-246), emphasize the importance of the ethical formation of children in freedom, virtue, and conscience-formation (nos. 263-267) and portray family

---

[94] This lacuna might be explained by paragraph no. 35: "It is true that there is no sense in simply decrying present-day evils, as if this could change things. Nor it is helpful to try to impose rules by sheer authority. What we need is a more responsible and generous effort to present the reasons and motivations for choosing marriage and the family, and in this way to help men and women better to respond to the grace that God offers them." Later, *Amoris Laetitia* includes an extensive quote from Martin Luther King Jr. on enduring evil and defeating unjust systems with an attitude of love (no. 118).

[95] This is in direct reference to the responses from the lay faithful in the *Lineamenta*. Francis writes, "In the replies given to the worldwide consultation, it became clear that ordained ministers often lack the training needed to deal with the complex problems currently facing families."

life as an educational setting, the first school of values, especially faith, hope, and love (nos. 274-279). In addressing the church as a whole, Pope Francis calls for gradualness in working for change (no. 295), discernment in being attentive and responsive to the presence and power of the Holy Spirit (nos. 296-300), and steadfast in adopting a praxis of mercy (nos. 309-310). Francis also acknowledges the special challenge tied to the "teaching of moral theology" (no. 311), which ought to be shaped by "pastoral discernment" that aspires to "open our hearts to those living on the outermost fringes of society" (no. 312). The document concludes with the claim that "All family life is 'shepherding' in mercy" (no. 322).

Amoris Laetitia breaks new ground for an ecclesial document that tries to speak to and from the lived experience of the lay faithful. It is inspired by Pope Francis' leadership, characterized by "drawing near" to God's people. However, the success of the synod on the family—as well as the next synod, "On Young People, the Faith, and Vocation Discernment," scheduled for October 2018—is more a matter of reception than promulgation. The church needs its bishops and priests, women religious and deacons, pastoral staff and lay leaders to commit to dialogue around the document and creatively imagine effective practices to appropriate it. So far, there have not been many U.S. bishops who have publicly made this an important priority, aside from Bishop Robert McElroy of San Diego.[96] *Amoris Laetitia* will only bring about change if the church generates leadership—especially on the parish level—to engage, discuss, analyze, and apply the wisdom it seeks to share.

The dialogical method of *Amoris Laetitia*, moving between Scripture and Tradition and the various features of the socio-cultural, political, and economic context, puts into practice the "culture of encounter" highlighted so often by Pope Francis. However, there are a number of ways in which *Amoris Laetitia* misses the mark in terms of being attentive and responsive to the needs of families today. For example, as the second line of the document makes clear, "the many signs of crisis in the institution of marriage" are of greater concern than the difficulties experienced between parents and children. In nearly every instance where the document alludes to families in "crisis," the reference is to the relationship between a married couple.[97] There are a few

---

[96] Amy Morris-Young and Dan Morris-Young, "San Diego Diocesan Synod Seeks to Put 'Amoris Laetitia' into Action," *National Catholic Reporter*, October 31, 2016, www.ncronline.org/news/parish/san-diego-diocesan-synod-seeks-put-amoris-laetitia-action.

[97] See, for example, paragraphs nos. 41, 232 and 233, 238, 240, 244 and 300. The only exceptions—aside from a brief overview of main concerns expressed in the *Lineamenta* in paragraphs nos. 50-51—are references to a "demographic crisis" which is the result of families feeling "abandoned due to a lack of interest and attention on the part of institutions" and a rift between family and society and between family and the

times where the document addresses difficulties between parents and children, but this is framed mostly in terms of fallout from divorce, marital strain, or the faith-formation of the child. One promising line reads, "The Church, while appreciating the situations of conflict that are part of marriage, cannot fail to speak out on behalf of those who are most vulnerable: the children who often suffer in silence" (246). But the passage continues, "Despite our seemingly evolved sensibilities and all our refined psychological analyses, I ask myself if we are not becoming numb to the hurt in children's souls ....Do we feel the immense psychological burden borne by children in families where the members mistreat and hurt one another, to the point of breaking the bonds of marital fidelity?" The document is so focused on the hurt caused by divorce and marital strain that it largely fails to address the experiences of chaos and crisis of families that remain intact. It largely ignores the challenges and setbacks children and adolescents face in their own development as persons, not just in their journey of faith. It does not assess how families are affected by and participate in social sin, or how the family can be an agent of grace, not just interpersonally but in building "structures of grace."[98]

Another problematic feature of *Amoris Laetitia* is the way that crisis is discussed. In several cases, the crisis experienced by a couple is described as a test or trial, which for some, could imply that crises are part of God's plan.[99] Describing chaos, crisis, or a challenge in terms of a lesson could suggest that such difficulties—whether personal, relational, or systemic—should be endured rather than denounced and resisted. The experiences of families in crisis described in the preceding pages are not just part of "God's mysterious plan"; they are the result of human finitude and moral failure, caused by personal and social sin. Economic and educational inequality, mass incarceration, food insecurity and hunger, access to clean drinking water, affordable housing, a living wage, mental health and wellbeing, a proper work-

---

school, wherein "the educational alliance between society and the family is in crisis" (*Amoris Laetitia*, nos. 43 and 84).

[98] This term is inspired by Kevin Ahern, who uses it in reference to Catholic NGOs. Given that families are the "building block" of church and society, they should also be considered vital to building "structures of grace" at the local, regional, national, and international levels. See Kevin Ahern, *Structures of Grace: Catholic Organizations Serving the Global Common Good* (Maryknoll: Orbis, 2015).

[99] This is the case in paragraph no. 232, where Francis writes, "Couples should be helped to realize that surmounting a crisis need not weaken their relationship; instead, it can improve, settle and mature the wine of their union ....Each crisis becomes an apprenticeship in growing closer together or learning a little more about what it means to be married. There is no need for couples to resign themselves to an inevitable downward spiral or a tolerable mediocrity. On the contrary, when marriage is seen as a challenge that involves overcoming obstacles, each crisis becomes an opportunity to let the wine of their relationship age and improve .... Each crisis has a lesson to teach us; we need to learn how to listen for it with the ear of the heart."

life balance, protection from abuse, neglect, violence, and war—the list could go on—are all shaped by individual beliefs and actions, social norms, and institutional practices and policies. In some cases, the decisions made at the personal, social, and structural levels promote human dignity and rights, encourage right-relationship, and contribute to the just ordering of society for the common good. However, in cases of moral failure where human dignity and rights are eclipsed by economic greed or political expediency, some are marginalized and excluded from participation or exercising agency; self-interest trumps social and ecological responsibility; and an unjust status quo is not questioned, resisted, or reformed, then Christians have a moral duty to take a stand against such sin and evil. It is inconsistent to expect the lay faithful to possess a clear and coherent moral framework if church documents do not clearly and effectively teach how morality is connected between the personal and social spheres. Moreover, to ignore the moral obligation to stand up to personal and social sin is to fail to live up to the demands of mercy.

WHY MERCY?

Mercy is popularly understood as compassion, kindness, or forgiveness. Pope Francis has exhorted Christians to embrace the practice of mercy in order to initiate a "revolution of tenderness."[100] He introduced the Jubilee Year of Mercy by stating,

> It is the favorable time to heal wounds, a time not to be weary of meeting all those who are waiting to see and to touch with their hands the signs of the closeness of God, a time to offer everyone, everyone, the way of forgiveness and reconciliation. May the Mother of God open our eyes, so that we may comprehend the task to which we have been called; and may she obtain for us the grace to experience this Jubilee of Mercy as faithful and fruitful witnesses of Christ.[101]

Francis is not the first pope to emphasize the centrality of mercy to the Christian life. In a 2008 homily, Pope Benedict XVI stated that mercy is "the central nucleus of the Gospel message; it is the very name of God, the Face with which he revealed himself in the Old Covenant and fully in Jesus Christ, the incarnation of creative and redemptive

---

[100] This is a term Pope Francis has been using with increasing frequency since 2014, including in his TED Talk, "The Only Future Worth Building Includes Everyone," April 2017, www.ted.com/talks/pope_francis_why_the_only_future_worth _building_includes_everyone?language=en.
[101] Pope Francis, *Misericordiae Vultus*, April 11, 2015, w2.vatican.va/content/francesco/en/apost_letters/documents/papa-francesco_bolla_20150411_misericordiae-vultus.html.

Love."[102] While mercy may be *en vogue* because of the attention given to it by Pope Francis, this is actually a much-needed retrieval of a core biblical theme. The Hebrew word for mercy, *hesed*, appears nearly 250 times in Scripture. This repetition is anything but incidental or ancillary; the rich and diverse meaning of *hesed* illustrates the essential character and purpose of God as well as what God desires for and from God's people.

When Scripture describes who God is, *hesed* comes first: God is merciful and gracious, slow to anger, abounding in steadfast love and faithfulness (Exodus 34:6-7). *Hesed* refers to God's steadfast love, a love that is always faithful and never fails, a love marked by loyalty and tenderness, an overabundance that is hardly expressed by the popular shorthand for mercy, "loving-kindness" (Joshua 2:12; 1 Samuel 20:14-17; Isaiah 54:8-10). *Hesed* reflects God's goodness that endures for a "thousand generations" (Exodus 20:6) and unlimited forgiveness of sin (Numbers 14:18-19; Micah 7:19) within a web of relationships as part of God's covenant with God's people (Leviticus 19:2, 17-18; Deuteronomy 15:4, 7; Psalm 13:6). *Hesed* is the very basis for the covenant with Yahweh (Deuteronomy 5:2, 10; Hosea 2:16-21; Isaiah 55:3) and the manifestation of solidarity among God's people, as the demands of solidarity are illustrated by fidelity and obligation (2 Samuel 7:11-16). *Hesed* highlights the gratuitous love of God expressed in mercy that endures forever and embraces all creation (Deuteronomy 7:7-9; Psalm 111:4, 136:1; Daniel 7:9-14). It illustrates God's will to save humanity and restore them to the Promised Land (Psalm 25:6; Jeremiah 42:12), and importantly, *hesed* is not limited to the human family, as God's mercy extends to all creation (Psalm 33:5, 145:9). *Hesed* defines faithfulness (Hosea 6:6; Micah 6:8; see also Matthew 12:7, 23:23) and characterizes those who love God (Ruth 1:8, 2:20, 3:10). The Hebrew Scriptures make clear that *hesed* is inseparable from justice, judgment, piety, compassion, and salvation (Psalm 72:1-4, 82:3, 140:13).

Some biblical scholars have suggested that the word *charis* (grace) in the Christian Scriptures is a closer equivalent to *hesed* than the Greek *eleos*, which is translated as "mercy." Identifying mercy with grace reinforces the idea that insofar as grace is God's self-gift, then God makes Godself known through mercy. *Eleos* appears in the New Testament dozens of times to fortify the witness of the Hebrew Scriptures that mercy describes God's own being (Luke 6:36, 15:11-32; 2 Corinthians 1:3; Ephesians 2:4) and how God treats God's people (Luke 1:58; 1 Peter 2:10). Jesus' teaching and healing ministry is framed in terms of mercy: it is what he teaches (Matthew 5:7) and practices (Mark 5:19). It is the way to love one's neighbor and inherit

---

[102] Pope Benedict XVI, *Regina Caeli*, March 30, 2008, w2.vatican.va/content/benedict-xvi/en/angelus/2008/documents/hf_ben-xvi_reg_20080330.html.

eternal life (Luke 10:25-42), the standard for unlimited forgiveness (Matthew 18:21-35), and what makes faithfulness possible (Romans 12:1-2; 2 Corinthians 4:1). It is the heart of God's desire for God's people (Matthew 9:13, 12:7, 23:23) and linked to wisdom (James 3:17) and the reason for hope (1 Peter 1:3). In the end, mercy triumphs over judgment (James 2:13); put differently, mercy gets the last word.

Francis has refocused Catholic vision through the lens of mercy, which also ignites the imagination for new possibilities for what it means to be human, to belong to each other and to all creation. Mercy becomes the antidote for the chaos and crisis through embracing tenderness and being willing to encounter others in need. Francis's emphasis on mercy frames his call to build a "culture of encounter" so that disciples will "leave the nest which encloses us" and burst the "soap bubbles" of self-concern.[103] He laments the vanity of these isolating soap bubbles, the deceptive fantasy that creates the illusions of innocence and separateness and renders peace impossible because peace is not the absence of conflict, but *shalom*: interpersonal balance and wholeness in the fullness of life, the fruit of right-relationship with God, our neighbors, and all creation. To be a Christian is to be who God is in the world. If "the name of God is mercy," then disciples should follow the example of the Good Samaritan—whose actions are characterized as merciful (Luke 10:37)—by drawing near to those who are in need (instead of moving farther away from the one who was beaten, robbed, and left for dead like the priest and the Levite, who depict the "globalization of indifference"[104]). Mercy inspires the vision and values to connect personal and social responsibility so that family life does not stop at the front door, but passes through this threshold in order to help and heal people in crisis as well as creatively imagine new possibilities for empowering a more integral and inclusive flourishing.

---

[103] Carol Glatz, "In Homily, Pope Compares Vain Christians to Soap Bubbles, Peacocks," *Catholic News Service*, September 25, 2014, www.catholicnews.com/services/englishnews/2014/in-homily-pope-compares-vain-christians-to-soap-bubbles-peacocks.cfm.

[104] In a homily at Lampedusa, Pope Francis compared Jesus' teaching in the story about the Good Samaritan with today's "globalization of indifference." He preached, "We see our brother half dead on the side of the road, and perhaps we say to ourselves: 'poor soul...!' and then go on our way. It's not our responsibility, and with that we feel reassured, assuaged. The culture of comfort, which makes us think only of ourselves, makes us insensitive to the cries of other people, makes us live in soap bubbles which, however lovely, are insubstantial; they offer a fleeting and empty illusion which results in indifference to others; indeed, it even leads to the globalization of indifference. In this globalized world, we have fallen into globalized indifference. We have become used to the suffering of others: it doesn't affect me; it doesn't concern me; it's none of my business!" (Pope Francis, "Homily," July 8, 2013, www.vatican.va/holy_father/francesco/homilies/2013/documents/papa-francesco_20130708_omelia-lampedusa_en.html).

FAMILIES: AMBASSADORS OF MERCY, SCHOOLS OF SOLIDARITY, AND FACTORIES OF HOPE

To say that families are in crisis is to say that families are in need of mercy. This is true within the family unit as much as it is true for how families are affected by social, economic, and political systems and structures. As building blocks of the church and society, families teach, learn, and practice values; the family is a *habitus* of morality.[105] Parents and children can realize their innate dignity and rights, experience freedom, build trust, exercise virtues like compassion and courage, patience and forgiveness, and participate in relationships and practices that promote inclusive right-relationship in and beyond the family. At the same time, when families experience hurt of any kind—deprivation of dignity or rights, neglect or abuse, betrayal or exploitation—these moral failures have the potential to become opportunities for redemption by aspiring for healing, forgiveness, and reconciliation. In the face of so many challenges and such crises, this is a critical time to respond to James Gustafson's classic question, "What is God enabling and requiring us to be and to do as participants in the patterns and processes of interdependence in marriage and family life?"[106] God is enabling and requiring families to embrace their moral agency as people who are "acted upon as much as they act,"[107] in order to be ambassadors of mercy, schools of solidarity, and factories of hope.

Practicing mercy should inspire an emboldened moral imagination that stretches the boundaries of what is possible for the parents, children, relatives, and friends who belong to and build up families. It should motivate a commitment to cultivate tenderness for each person, celebrate the gifts and tasks that correspond to intimate relationships, raise awareness and affirm responsibility for personal and social sin as well as redemption, and promote an ever-more-inclusive vision of all people belonging to a single human family. In this way, mercy can generate the empathy, understanding, and love that connect concern for self and others and fosters solidarity, or unity across difference. Everyone belongs to a family, a common thread that that connects the social fabric, excluding no one. Insofar as mercy means drawing near to others in need, then families can and should practice moral responsibility that balances the demands within and beyond one's family of origin.

---

[105] I use *habitus* in reference to the work of sociologist Pierre Bourdieu, who describes it as a system of embodied attitudes and inclinations that organize the ways that individuals interpret and respond to their social context; *habitus* alludes to the place where agency is practiced and how it reflects and reproduces social norms. See Pierre Bourdieu, *Outline of a Theory of Practice* (Cambridge University Press, 1977), 72-95.

[106] James M. Gustafson, *Ethics from a Theocentric Perspective,* Vol.2 (University of Chicago Press, 1984), 153.

[107] Gustafson, *Ethics from a Theocentric Perspective*, 155.

Heaping more obligations onto the family unit will do little to help families in crisis. However, no household is immune from social responsibility, as each family is called to contribute to the common good.[108] Each individual and family will have to practice the virtue of prudence to discern what God is "enabling and requiring us to be and to do as participants in the patterns and processes of interdependence" that connect family and social life. In an American context, this will mean reimagining family life and reevaluating the quintessential American values of ambition and achievement so that, in a spirit of mercy, we can better address the root causes of chaos and crisis. The virtues of prudence and mercy can also be helpful to avoid being overwhelmed by "compassion fatigue" in the face of so many challenges within and between families today.

Francis's appeal to mercy lacks an ethical framework to address the many demands on individuals, families, and communities. However, it coheres with James Keenan's proposal that prudence, self-care, fidelity, and justice better fit the relational anthropology and contemporary needs of today's Christians than the classical cardinal virtues (prudence, temperance, fortitude, and justice).[109] As Keenan explains, "As persons, we are relational in three ways: generally, specifically, and uniquely. And each of these relational ways of being demands a cardinal virtue. As a relational being in general, we are called to justice. As a relational being specifically, we are called to fidelity. As a relational being uniquely, we are called to self-care."[110] Mercy plays a central role in the tenderness of self-care, the inclusive loyalty of fidelity, and the courage, compassion, and solidarity that characterize justice in the social order. Mercy can inform the virtue of prudence so that individuals, families, and communities can refine their discernment of what is most fitting. As Aquinas points out, the virtue of *epikeia* should be practiced for one's own moral growth and to contribute to the common good in relation to what befits one's ability and needs.[111]

---

[108] Pope John Paul II made this claim in his 1981 apostolic exhortation, *Familiaris Consortio*, asserting that families ought to "work for the building of a more just and human world; for the promotion of just laws favoring the right social order with full respect for the dignity and every legitimate freedom of the individual and the family, on both the national and international level; for collaboration with the school and with the other institutions that complete the education of children, and so forth" (no. 72).

[109] James F. Keenan, "Proposing Cardinal Virtues," *Theological Studies* 56, no. 4 (1995): 709-729.

[110] Keenan, "Proposing Cardinal Virtues," 723.

[111] See Thomas Aquinas, *Summa Contra Gentiles*, 1.3, c. 125 and c. 122. Thomas describes *epikeia* in terms of right reason, which requires freedom to apply the relevant moral norm. This is not to encourage moral dispensation or relativism, but to grow in wisdom.

The virtue of self-care is especially relevant, given the levels of overwhelming stress and anxiety, struggles with substance abuse, sexual exploitation and violence, addiction to digital technology and social media, and diminishing mental health experienced by so many family members. Self-care follows from the "unique responsibility to care for ourselves, affectively, mentally, physically, and spiritually."[112] Embracing this virtue would require carving out the time and space for individuals—regardless of age, status, or ability—to affirm their value in who they are and not just what they do. It implies the discipline to become more attentive and responsive to one's abilities and needs. It seeks balance with an ethic of sacrifice in the spirit of mutuality and interdependence. It subverts the dominant paradigm framed by scarcity and competition by celebrating abundance in gratitude and generosity. Self-care restores and renews to avoid feeling depleted; it builds resilience and deepens the capacity to face and overcome challenges. Self-care aims to preempt the tendency to be overscheduled or overcommitted, always busy or distracted. At its best, self-care disposes a person to the constant presence and power of God in order to more readily recognize the goodness in and around each person, and thereby position each one to more fully receive and offer grace. Self-care is an invitation to grow in love, wisdom, freedom, compassion, and courage.

The virtue of fidelity orders our commitments to those who are nearest; it guides a special care and concern for those who have particular demands on us, "whether by blood, marriage, love, or sacrament."[113] Fidelity grants preference and priority to one's spouse or children, parents or siblings, extended family or closest friends over and against the universal and impartial demands of justice. It is what justifies spending more on tuition for one's own child than what one might donate to charity to support other children in need. Importantly, however, fidelity also demands that family responsibilities come ahead of other demands, especially those that are inessential. Parents who work excessively or who obsess over the next promotion may be falling short of the demands of fidelity. The same could be true of parents who are overcommitted to responsibilities outside the home, even if that includes worthy acts of service to a school, neighborhood, or parish. Like self-care, fidelity aims to prevent too many or overly demanding obligations outside the family unit. This includes a disordered attachment to goods, or a rate of consumption that triggers the need for more work in order to afford a more luxurious lifestyle. Many Americans assume that "luxury" only applies to the top 1%, but it actually refers to excess. In a socio-cultural context that embraces the

---

[112] Keenan, "Proposing Cardinal Virtues," 727.
[113] Keenan, "Proposing Cardinal Virtues," 725.

motto "more is better," luxury is the norm and standard for which people aspire, even if it ought to be regarded as a vice.[114] Fidelity can be useful for interrupting a status quo that overestimates how happy a good or service will make us,[115] and instead give greater priority to being present to family members and finding joy in each other's company.

The virtue of justice is essential for ensuring that family ties do not become idolatrous, such that fidelity to one's kin or intimate relationships overrides his or her moral obligation to pursue what is right, true, good, and just for one's neighbor. As the example of the Good Samaritan teaches, not only is every person to be recognized as one's neighbor, but the command to "Go and do likewise" (Luke 10:37) is an exhortation to *be* a neighbor to others in need.[116] Justice orients people to work for equality; as Keenan explains, "Apart from all specific relations, we belong to humanity and are expected to respond to all its members in general, equally and impartially."[117] While many families adopt practices of charitable giving and other forms of service, these generous gestures are necessary but insufficient for meeting the demands of justice. Justice requires a fundamental re-ordering of society to more equitably distribute privileges and access as well as burdens and obligations. The USCCB asserts, "Basic justice demands the establishment of minimum levels of participation in the life of the human community for all persons."[118] As a principle of justice, the "preferential option for the poor" implies an "obligation to evaluate social and economic activity from the viewpoint of the poor and the powerless" insofar as "Those who are marginalized and whose rights are denied have privileged claims if society is to provide justice for *all*."[119] For American Christians to live up to the demands of justice, families must break free from the "economic structures that are enmeshed in an

---

[114] See, for example, David Cloutier, *The Vice of Luxury: Economic Excess in a Consumer Age* (Washington, DC: Georgetown University Press, 2015). Cloutier dedicates Chapter 2 to demonstrate how luxury degrades individuals, work, and communities.

[115] Happiness studies indicate "that a life devoted to the accumulation of ever-more material goods is not a path to satisfaction, and may be harmful … One author even goes so far as to propose that the data should lead us to 'applying the ancient virtue of thrift'" (Cloutier, *The Vice of Luxury*, 62).

[116] On this passage, Augustine reflects, "all people are to be recognized as neighbors." Augustine, *De Doctrina Christiana* trans. R.P.H. Green (Oxford: Oxford University Press, 1999), 1.30.32. The Samaritan's example "obliterates boundaries that close off compassion or that permit racism or attitudes of superiority," according to Klyne Snodgrass in *Stories with Intent: A Comprehensive Guide to the Parables of Jesus* (Grand Rapids: Eerdmans, 2008), 358.

[117] Keenan, "Proposing Cardinal Virtues," 724.

[118] USCCB, *Economic Justice for All: Pastoral Letter on Catholic Social Teaching and the U.S. Economy* (Washington, DC: USCCB, 1997), no. 77.

[119] USCCB, *Economic Justice for All*, no. 87.

abundance/scarcity dialectic that generates most of the real poverty in the world" as well as

> find ways to enable the kind of genuine empathy that draws people into a spiritual journey that leads one out of the enclave of the American ethos. This spiritual journey requires a community devoted to spiritual poverty and solidarity with the real poor throughout the world. It also requires a shared hope that all forms of genuine solidarity are ultimately joined to a universal and transcendent process of transformation that will prevail.[120]

In this way, a commitment to justice is connected to hope, a disposition oriented to imagining new possibilities for human flourishing in *shalom*. Families are not fated to endure the chaos and crisis being experienced today; transformation and transcendence are possible. To the extent that people embrace their innate dignity and freedom, uphold their rights and responsibilities, and adopt the beliefs, actions, and relationships that promote personal and collective wellbeing, families can live their way into a richer and more just communion of love, in and beyond the household. Cardinal virtues like prudence, self-care, fidelity, and justice provide the framework and vision, but unless and until these become household habits, families will fall short of the goal of becoming ambassadors of mercy, schools of solidarity, and factories of hope.

FAMILIES: A *HABITUS* OF MERCY

Aristotle's enduring insight is that we are what we repeatedly do. No one sits down at the piano for the first time and plays a sonata; that feat can only be accomplished after learning how to read music, play the right keys, and perform songs of increasing complexity. Similarly, families can be a *habitus* of virtue if and only if they make virtue a shared practice by integrating them into their conversations, daily habits, and major decisions. Virtue ethics emphasizes the possibility and practice of moral growth, giving reason to hope that the challenges facing today's children and the problematic features of youth culture can be resisted and reformed. Human nature is not a fixed or static given; to be human is to change and to make the world new. As Rabbi Abraham Heschel contends,

> It is a fatal illusion to assume that to be human is a fact given with human being rather than a goal and an achievement. To the animals, the world is what it is; to man this is a world in the making, and being

---

[120] John J Markey, *Moses in Pharaoh's House: A Liberation Spirituality for North America* (Winona: Anselm Academic, 2014), 138.

human means being on the way, striving, waiting, hoping. Neither authenticity of existence nor the qualities of being human are safe properties. They are to be achieved, cultivated, and protected.[121]

The goal, then, is for families to be households that achieve, cultivate, and protect virtue, aspiring for moral growth, both personally and collectively. To this end, families can be a *habitus* of mercy expressed through prudence, self-care, fidelity, and justice. As Robert Putnam and David Campbell have observed, when it comes to moral formation of religious individuals, belief matters less than belongingness; people are shaped more by their relationships and shared practices than by their beliefs and values.[122] Julie Hanlon Rubio describes how families can live up to the four major tasks outlined in *Familiaris Consortio*—to communicate love; to serve life; promote social order through hospitality, political engagement, and a preferential option for the poor; build up the church as a "domestic church"—through concrete and ordinary practices.[123] Practicing self-care, fidelity, and justice can supplement the valuable disciplines Rubio proposes (which focus on prayer, service, tithing, sharing meals, and sexual fidelity).

It is worth noting that a virtue is a mean between two extremes, one of excess and the other of deficiency. Self-care is the midpoint between the excess of self-indulgence and the deficiency of self-sacrifice that becomes self-annihilation. Practicing the virtue of self-care implies that parent's model making time for rest, relaxation, and rejuvenation. It means living up to the commandment to honor the Sabbath by carving out time from the busyness, the stress, and the gambit of nonstop ambition. Self-care is about restoration; it can be practiced through prayer, worship, and the Sacramental life; through meditation or contemplation; yoga, running, or other forms of exercise; listening to music, reading for pleasure, taking a walk in the neighborhood, or going for a hike and enjoying nature. When children see parents and other adults making time for such practices, they learn the value—and see the effects firsthand—of taking time to be renewed even in the

---

[121] Abraham Heschel, *Who Is Man?* (Palo Alto: Stanford University Press, 1965), 41.

[122] Robert Putnam and David Campbell, *American Grace: How Religion Divides and Unites Us* (New York: Simon & Schuster, 2010), 444, 468-475. Putnam and Campbell insist, "Mobilization or exhortations by clergy seem not to be a major factor" whereas "friends in general have a powerful effect on civic involvement." They continue, "Having close friends at church, discussing religion frequently with your family and friends, and taking part in small groups at church are extremely powerful predictors of the range of generosity, good neighborliness, and civic engagement" (471-472).

[123] Julie Hanlon Rubio, *Family Ethics: Practices for Christians* (Washington, DC: Georgetown University Press, 2010). This book is framed by the convictions that "distinctive disciplines or practices are necessary if families are to resist the culture and live their faith" and that "family practices are directed not only to communion within the family but to solidarity with the poor and social change" (9).

midst of a busy schedule or demanding workload. When these disciplines are shared with children and young people are able to practice self-care, they adopt habits that will build self-worth and expand their capacities to develop and grow. They experience mercy as tenderness for oneself, a self who is always worthy of tenderness. In a social context where scarcity, insecurity, and ambition rule, self-care is a reminder that our goodness is inherent, not earned. In the eyes of Christian faith, self-care is an invitation to bask in and savor God's abundant blessings, be filled with gratitude, and be empowered to be generous.

The practice of self-care means that people take action in becoming attentive and responsive to their physical, emotional, intellectual, spiritual, and social needs. It requires that parents and children become more intentional about how they spend their time. Americans report feeling more exhausted and overwhelmed than ever before, but this may have more to do with wasting time than being overcommitted at work or in the home.[124] It also ensures that people receive professional care, especially in cases of physical and mental illness or experiences of abuse. One in five Americans experience mental illness and nearly 21 million Americans struggle with substance abuse, but only a small fraction seek the treatment they need.[125] More work needs to be done to remove the stigma associated with therapy so that it can be more widely recognized as a meaningful avenue to practice self-care. Children and adolescents—especially following experiences of instability or trauma—should be provided coping skills for managing difficult situations, thoughts, and emotions. In light of the fragile state of mental health and self-esteem in today's youth, it is crucial for parents to speak and model affirming messages.[126]

In the case of digital technology and social media, self-care does not require that people abandon their phones or leave their networks, but it is an invitation to adopt a more chastened use of these tools.

---

[124] See Brigid Schulte, *Overwhelmed: How to Work, Love, and Play When No One Has the Time* (New York: Picador, 2014). Schulte acknowledges that even though time use studies show Americans are not working more and actually have more time for leisure than previous generations, the perception is that Americans are more "crunched for time" than before, and that women are more likely to feel a time crunch than men (14).

[125] For example, only one in ten seek treatment for substance abuse issues, according to the Surgeon General's report issued in November 2016 (Nicole Lyn Pesce, "One in 7 Americans Will Face Addiction, Surgeon General Warns," *New York Daily News*, November 18, 2016, www.nydailynews.com/life-style/health/surgeon-general-warns-1-7-americans-face-addiction-article-1.2877932).

[126] Psychologist Jim Taylor identifies nine messages for parents to communicate to their children, including: unconditional love; growth in competence; home as a safe place; compassion and gratitude; respect and responsibility; and how to process good and bad feelings. See Jim Taylor, *Your Children Are Listening: Nine Messages They Need to Hear from You* (New York: The Experiment, 2011).

There are apps that can be useful for facilitating self-care, like "Happify" and "GPS for the Soul" that assist users with managing stress and anxiety, carving out time for meditation or reflection, navigating the busyness and distraction of digital life, and replacing the superficial with more substantial matters (like a "gratitude journal") to regain perspective and focus. Digital practices of self-care are especially important for children and adolescents so that they can integrate healthy approaches into their use of technology from an early age. To prevent harmful or excessive effects of screen time, it is more effective to begin with a prudent approach to content and connections than to try to correct a dysfunctional habit that has already been formed. It is never too early to begin showing children how to engage their world—online and offline—in a way that is safe, well-informed, and demonstrates responsibility and accountability. Parents should ensure open lines of communication with their children so that kids know their household is a safe space to discuss uncomfortable or uncertain situations. Building trust within the family increases the margins for error and thereby helps parents and children feel safe, creates conditions for everyone to be honest, vulnerable, and less suspicious or defensive, and makes it possible for mutuality in the pursuit and practice of self-care.

As a mean between two extremes, the virtue of fidelity is the harmonious balance between the excess of obsession and the deficiency of ambivalence. Practicing the virtue of fidelity in the family means first of all making sufficient time to accompany one another. In a time when ambition and achievement fuel busyness, the "gift of presence" is invaluable. Just as Putnam highlights the significance of family dinners for predicting child wellbeing (holding constant other factors like class or education),[127] Rubio also emphasizes the way that sharing meals together can combat the growing trend of "loosening family bonds."[128] Fidelity can be shared in other practices that prioritize time together, whether one-on-one or when part or the whole household participates together. This can include sharing a chore like raking leaves, tending to a garden, running errands, or enjoying a more leisurely activity together like playing a game, taking a trip to a park, or going for a bike ride. Families practice fidelity when they make time to attend church together, plan a vacation, or serve others in the community. Fidelity is cultivated when family members make and keep

---

[127] Putnam, *Our Kids*, 122-123.
[128] Rubio, *Family Ethics*, 130. Rubio is quoting Putnam in *Bowling Alone: The Collapse and Revival of American Community* (New York: Simon & Schuster, 2000), 100. Putnam finds that "virtually all forms of family togetherness became less common over the last quarter of the twentieth century."

promises, honor their commitments to one another, and build a household marked by tenderness and affection, respect and acceptance, forgiveness and reconciliation.

Opening one's home in hospitality can cultivate fidelity within the family as well as extend welcome and a place of belonging in a more inclusive manner. Taking time to visit with others—whether friends, extended family, neighbors or strangers—is an important practice to avoid the excess of fidelity. Jesus made clear that fidelity cannot be confined to one's biological family; he subordinated the duties to kin to the tasks of his teaching and healing ministry (Mark 3:31-35). As Lisa Sowle Cahill describes, Jesus's example suggests that "loyalty to one's own group and dedication to the status of that group over all others and at the expense of whoever stands in the way are incompatible with a life of mercy, service, and compassion for the neighbor in need or for the social outcast and the poor."[129] Inclusive hospitality and solidarity are essential for expanding the circle of a family's fidelity. This means combating civil inattention by welcoming those who are outcast or marginalized and working to heal difficult relationships or showing support for those who are struggling and in need. One indictment of familial infidelity is the fact that 40% of homeless youth identify as LGBT, many of whom have been disowned by their families.[130] A hallmark of fidelity is to suffer through difficulty and disagreement together, not just to be loyal when it is comfortable, convenient, or on one's own terms.

Fidelity becomes idolatrous kin-obsession if it fails to incorporate the virtue of solidarity. The Christian vision of family life involves compassion for those who are suffering, experiencing deprivation, and otherwise in need. Mercy demands so much more than tolerance and renders nonjudgmentalism void. Mercy, understood as a practice of loyalty to God and God's people, is measured by drawing near to the outcast and marginalized, the vulnerable and deprived. As Rubio explains, this helps to reveal "not only the privilege of the rich but also the poverty of the rich," and "encourages an awareness of neediness that is fundamental." In other words, families serve others not just to fulfill a social duty, but to grow in their fidelity to brothers and sisters among and beyond their blood relatives.[131] Service is a pathway to

---

[129] Cahill, *Family*, 29.

[130] Laura E. Durso and Gary J. Gates, *Serving Our Youth: Findings from a National Survey of Service Providers Working with Lesbian, Gay, Bisexual, and Transgender Youth who are Homeless or At Risk of Becoming Homeless* (Los Angeles: The Williams Institute, 2012), williamsinstitute.law.ucla.edu/wp-content/uploads/Durso-Gates-LGBT-Homeless-Youth-Survey-July-2012.pdf.

[131] Rubio, *Family Ethics*, 206. Rubio continues, "As families serve together, they may find themselves more able to approach relationships inside the family with humility and a willingness to sacrifice, more ready to risk intimacy ... more willing to welcome sinners like themselves to the table, more joyful about spending less in order to give

transformation, both personal and social. It expands the ability to understand the daunting challenges others face and reduces the inclination to judge them as lazy, unmotivated, or scheming to take advantage. It also exposes the unearned privileges and luxuries that too many Americans take for granted. Service obliterates the passivity of spectator culture or bystander culture that abdicates one's agency and duty. It becomes transformative especially when it moves beyond unidirectional charity and becomes a true encounter marked by free and open dialogue, mutual sharing, and the fostering of friendship. This kind of service resists depersonalization and fragmentation; it builds bridges to forge unity across difference. This is a crucial practice in a time when Americans report being divided by political ideology, class, and race. The rise of lifestyle enclaves indicates that "Americans' social networks are collapsing inward, and now consist of fewer, denser, more homogenous, more familial (and less nonkin) ties."[132] As an example, according to one recent study, 75% of white Americans say they do not have a single black friend and 65% of black Americans indicate their social circle is entirely black.[133] If a family is to become a *habitus* of mercy, this requires that families change their social location, build more inclusive friendships across racial, class, and religious differences, and cultivate fidelity that builds communion in and beyond the household.

Too many Christians think that justice is satisfied by their acts of service or charitable giving from their surplus. Meeting the immediate needs of the poor and even befriending the poor are necessary but insufficient dimensions of the work required to establish a more just, inclusive, and equitable society. The virtue of justice refers to the right-ordering of society and right-relations between people, an equitable distribution of goods and access to opportunity and power, contributions from all members of society based on ability and need, fitting consequences to deter unlawful conduct and make amends for a crime, and reparations to restore what has been denied from those who have been wronged. In short, families must commit to advocacy for structural change as a practice of justice. Each family cannot be committed to every possible injustice, so the virtue of prudence can be helpful in deciding what would be most fitting, according to a family's abilities and needs.

---

more .... Direct service is practice in love, a school of virtue with the potential to transform those who make it an essential part of their lives."

[132] Putnam, *Our Kids*, 211. Putnam continues, pointing out that "American's disengagement and their retreat to relative social isolation ... 'affects members of the lower classes disproportionately, ultimately reinforcing differences between social classes.'"

[133] Daniel Cox, et al., "Race and Americans' Social Networks," *PRRI*, August 28, 2014, www.prri.org/research/analysis-social-network/.

Insofar as justice incorporates the social, economic, and political spheres, it need not be regarded as a partisan issue. Following the 2016 presidential election, 85% of Americans reported the country is more deeply divided than in recent history and nearly six in ten respondents said they were dissatisfied with how democracy is working in the U.S.[134] As Pope Francis urged in his homily at Pentecost, Christians should avoid becoming people who identify with the "right" or the "left" "before being on the side of Jesus," as this results in "diversity without unity" when the goal ought to be unity in diversity, the mark of catholicity.[135] The predominance of tolerance and nonjudgmentalism—which some claim to be like a new "11th Commandment"[136]—might be intimidating for Christians who are anxious about "going public" with their faith or morals, especially amid so much division and political angst. But engaging the world on matters of justice isn't optional for those who follow the example of Jesus Christ, who worked for transformation in the face of personal and social sin. The virtue of mercy requires that Christians dedicate themselves to living in a society that meets the basic needs of each person and provides opportunities for everyone to exercise agency, access resources, and contribute to the community. Christian Smith and Robert Putnam express alarm at the trend of decreasing civic engagement among all citizens, especially among the young[137] and less educated.[138] Our democracy depends on children learning and practicing civic duty. Insofar as mercy is connected to solidarity, Christians are charged with building common ground, participating in dialogue, and leveraging networks for collaboration. This does not mean that it falls on the nonpoor to "fix" or "save" the poor, but to support and stand together to

---

[134] Jennifer Agiesta, "CNN/ORC Poll: A Nation Divided, and Is It Ever," *CNN*, November 27, 2016, www.cnn.com/2016/11/27/politics/cnn-poll-division-donald-trump/.

[135] Pope Francis, "Homily," June 4, 2017, w2.vatican.va/content/ francesco/en/homilies/2017/documents/papa-francesco_20170604_omelia-pentecoste.html.

[136] Alan Wolfe, *One Nation, After All: What Middle-Class Americans Really Think About: God, Country, Family, Racism, Welfare, Immigration, Homosexuality, Work, the Right, the Left, and Each Other* (New York: Penguin Books, 1998), 54. Wolfe suggests that the prevailing middle class morality is characterized by a "quiet faith" and "morality writ small" that "should be modest in its ambitions and quiet in its proclamations" (290).

[137] See note 81 above.

[138] Putnam states that a yawning class gap in political participation can be found across generations, and is especially true for young people: "More than twice as many high-school-educated youth are completely detached from virtually all forms of civic life, compared to college-educated youth" (Putnam, *Our Kids*, 235-236). He adds that this makes citizens more "vulnerable to demagogic mass movements" and cites Pope Francis as a much-needed leader calling for engagement and responsibility (240-241).

strengthen families, so many of which find themselves in chaos and crisis.[139] This is the work of justice.

Families can practice the virtue of justice in a variety of ways. Justice can and should inform what and how families purchase and consume, although we should be mindful of Willis Jenkins's keen observation that Christians should not be so easily convinced that they can "eat their way to justice." Americans have embraced an unsustainable level of consumption of goods and energy; if everyone on the planet consumed at the same rate, we would need at least four earths worth of resources. Taking a more prudential approach to purchasing products and services would garner the attention of corporations, as companies are bent on maintaining and increasing customer loyalty. American families wield tremendous purchasing power, which ought to be leveraged by advocating for just wages, broad access to healthcare, and other benefits like paid leave and childcare.[140] Moreover, justice can be incorporated into habits as an employee or employer, an investor or stockholder as well as into decisions about where a family lives, which schools children attend, the friends they make, and their ability to participate in extracurricular programs.[141] In the face of such widespread division and segregation, practicing the virtue of justice means taking up the cause of racial justice, advocating for criminal justice reform, and ending mass incarceration.[142]

---

[139] Julie Hanlon Rubio, *Hope for Common Ground: Mediating the Personal and Political in a Divided Church* (Washington, DC: Georgetown University Press, 2016), 112. Rubio dedicates Chapter 4 to the way that family life can build up common ground, but it is more focused on promoting marriage, healing families in the case of divorce, and support for job training and just wages than it is on parenting or practices that bring families together in political activism.

[140] Putnam points to childcare as an important way to reverse increasing class inequality. The U.S. ranks 32nd out of 39 countries in the OECD in terms of childcare services and while the best childcare is provided by parents, more work needs to be done to increase paid parental leave, workplace flexibility, and access to childcare (Putnam, *Our Kids*, 249).

[141] A main theme in *Our Kids* is the negative impact of neighborhood segregation on individuals, families, and schools. Putnam highlights the need for more subsidies for affordable housing and "massively more compensatory funding" for schools in poor neighborhoods, as well as greater funding for extracurricular activities, which are a deciding factor in upward mobility, not just for résumé building, but to grow "soft skills and character," forge networks of belonging, and gain access to mentor relationships (Putnam, *Our Kids*, 174-176, 252).

[142] According to a *Washington Post-ABC News* 2016 survey, 63% of whites and 72% of blacks reported race relations are "generally bad," the highest rate since 1992. The U.S. has the highest rate of incarceration, per capita, in the world. 60% of women in state prisons have a child under 18, and children who have at least one parent in jail or prison are more likely to be sexually abused, perform worse in school, and more likely to be imprisoned themselves. A 2011 Russell Sage Foundation Report found that incarceration of a family member is associated with a 64% decline in household assets, affecting 2.6 million children every day.

There is no shortage of injustices that need to be addressed in our country. Gun violence claims 30,000 lives every year and 48 youth are shot every day, resulting in seven fatalities on a daily basis. The CDC reports that the growing opioid epidemic took the lives of 52,000 Americans in 2015, while more families are ravaged by parents who are jailed or killed and more drug-exposed babies are born each year. Food insecurity and hunger affect 49 million Americans, including one in five children who experience hunger each day (for children of color that number slides to one in three). In 2014, the U.S. Department of Agriculture reported that one in seven Americans are enrolled in SNAP and nearly half are children. According to a 2010 CDC report, ten million children are exposed to domestic violence every year. Every minute, 20 Americans are victims of intimate partner violence, affecting 1 in 4 women and 1 in 7 men in their lifetime (women of color experience abuse at rates 35% higher than white women). To practice the virtue of justice would mean advocating for the kinds of laws and funding that can better address these crises, which means overcoming sectarian debates and partisanship on the "right" or "left." The virtue of justice thwarts any temptation to claim that problems facing "those children" are beyond our moral concern. As Putnam would remind us, children in need—wherever they may live and whatever they might face—"are our kids." Practicing the virtue of justice means taking a leadership role in addressing these issues in our households, schools, and neighborhoods instead of waiting for experts, professionals, or politicians to solve these problems for us.

In short, the virtue of justice requires that more American families—especially middle class families—take personal responsibility for right action, advocate for more equitable policies, renounce unearned privileges, and make more sacrifices to reverse the trend of "opportunity hoarding" that has come at the expense of less educated and low income Americans.[143] Too often middle-class power is marshaled to protect the status quo, with too many families focusing more on merit than mercy.

Families will need to be supported in coming to terms with the ways they benefit at the expense of lower-class families, while at the same time managing their own challenges and crises. The church is in a unique position to serve and support families, especially at the parish level. This kind of pastoral ministry is an ideal way to live up to Pope Francis's vision of the church as a field hospital. In a time when four

---

[143] In *Dream Hoarders*, Richard Reeves outlines a number of concrete practices, ranging from initiating home visits to help with parenting (especially in cases of unplanned or unwanted pregnancies in low income households), recruit better teachers for the poorest school districts, generate more public funding to help finance college education (and end legacy admissions to top schools), expand fair housing legislation and limit exclusionary zoning, and open up job training and internship opportunities as a pathway to better employment (123-152).

in ten Americans say that churches contribute little or nothing to solving important social issues, this is a crucial opportunity for the church to effect change, especially for families in need.[144] If the church is to be more than a place where sacraments are dispensed, it must open its doors in a merciful embrace of all. Even more, it must leave its brick-and-mortar edifice and meet families where they are, accompanying them in sharing life together. If, as Putnam has argued, moral formation is more a matter of belongingness than belief, then the church must be a community that practices virtue and promotes trust. Trust is essential for overcoming fear, establishing a sense of safety, and fostering the conditions that prime the pump for moral courage. Trust should not be a luxury reserved for those who live in gated communities or are digitally connected to close-knit lifestyle enclaves; it is a gift and task meant for all.[145]

Insofar as mercy is the core of who God is and what God wants for and from God's people, then mercy—understood as steadfast love and faithfulness, abundant generosity, tenderness, forgiveness, and inclusive solidarity—must be the primary practice of Christian life. This is true for the local and global church as well as the domestic church. Adopting the virtues of prudence, self-care, fidelity, and justice can initiate personal and collective transformation. Families are in crisis, but if they become a *habitus* of mercy, schools of solidarity, and factories of hope, they will live their way into new possibilities for human flourishing and right-relationship at the personal, social, and institutional levels. M

---

[144] Michael Lipka, "Are Churches Key to Solving Social Problems? Fewer Americans Now Think So," *Pew Research Center*, July 18, 2016, www.pewresearch.org/fact-tank/2016/07/18/are-churches-key-to-solving-social-problems-fewer-americans-now-think-so/. In 2001, only 21% of Americans thought churches, synagogues, and other houses of worship contributed "not much" or "nothing" to solving social problems.

[145] Trust is a key ingredient to building social capital, and Putnam finds that it has been dwindling in the present social context. This is true for young people of all backgrounds and especially for low income children, where only one in seven kids agree that generally "people can be trusted" (compared to one in four rich kids). In one sobering vignette, Putnam recounts a child from a low income neighborhood who reflects, "Love gets you hurt, trust gets you killed" (Robert Putnam, *Our Kids*, 220-221).

Transgender Bodies, Catholic Schools, and a Queer Natural Law Theology of Exploration

Craig A. Ford, Jr.

THIS ESSAY IS DEDICATED TO A GIRL NAMED Leelah. During the 2014-2015 Christmas season, she walked onto a highway in order to end her life. In her wake, she left a note:

After a summer of having almost no friends plus the weight of having to think about college, save money for moving out, keep my grades up, go to church each week and feel like shit because everyone there is against everything I live for, I have decided I've had enough. I'm never going to transition successfully, even when I move out. I'm never going to be happy with the way I look or sound. I'm never going to have enough friends to satisfy me. I'm never going to have enough love to satisfy me. I'm never going to find a man who loves me. I'm never going to be happy. Either I live the rest of my life as a lonely man who wishes he were a woman or I live my life as a lonelier woman who hates herself. There's no winning. There's no way out. I'm sad enough already, I don't need my life to get any worse. People say "it gets better" but that isn't true in my case. It gets worse. Each day I get worse.[1]

Leelah—it will be obvious by now—was transgender. She was also imprisoned by a despair, by an anger, by a hopelessness that was the result of a lethal cocktail of loneliness, of treatment that arguably constituted parental abuse, and of an operative theology that is, I will show, as tendentious as it is deadly. In her note, Leelah goes on to describe how, upon revealing her trans* identity to her parents, she was forced to see therapists who told her that she was "selfish and wrong and that [she] should look to God for help." Two years later, when she was sixteen, her parents took away her laptop and phone and forbid her from interacting with anyone on social media. This was in response to Leelah's coming out to her friends at school. A year later,

---

[1] Leelah's suicide note is transcribed in full in Joseph Patrick McCormick, "Trans Teen Publishes Heartbreaking Suicide Note: 'This Life Isn't Worth Living,'" *Pink News*, December 30, 2014, www.pinknews.co.uk/2014/12/30/trans-teen-publishes-heartbreaking-suicide-note-this-life-isnt-worth-living/.

when her phone privileges were returned, her friends abandoned her. "That's the gist of it," she writes, "that's why I feel like killing myself." Leelah walked onto the highway when she was seventeen.

Of the three ingredients in the cocktail that took Leelah's life, this essay mounts a challenge only to its theological component. But however its contribution is judged, this essay is manifestly insufficient to address the time of crisis in which this essay meets you, the reader. This crisis cannot be doubted or denied. Take, for example, Samantha Hill, another transwoman who was sexually assaulted eight different times in five different federal prisons. Her reason for going to jail? Robbing banks in order to get the money she would need in order to move forward in the process of her transition. Her reasoning: if she gets the money, she can afford to continue the process; if she gets caught, she goes to prison, where they are legally obligated to treat her at no additional cost.[2] She is joined by the other 30% of transgender persons who report physical or sexual assault by prison facility staff or fellow inmates, a rate five to six times higher than the U.S. incarcerated population in total.[3] Or consider the fact that, in 2015, 50% of transgender persons experienced rejection by their families.[4] Or that 70% of all trans* respondents to a survey reported being harassed, assaulted, or denied access when attempting to use a public restroom.[5] Or that transgender persons are 3.7 times more likely to experience police violence compared to cisgender survivors and victims; are seven times more likely to experience physical violence when interacting with the police compared to cisgender survivors and victims; are, if the person is a transgender person of color, six times more likely to experience physical violence from the police compared to white cisgender survivors and victims; and are, if the person is a transwoman, nearly twice (1.8x) as likely to experience sexual violence when compared with other survivors.[6]

Theology must own up to its part in this crisis. After all, it is not insignificant that Leelah was still a teenager when she committed suicide. In fact, it is on the stages of America's primary and secondary

---

[2] German Lopez, "Prison is Horrifying. For Transgender People, it's Hell," *Vox,* April 11, 2016, www.vox.com/2016/4/11/11355702/prison-transgender.
[3] Sandy E. James, Jody L. Herman, Susan Rankin, Mara Keisling, Lisa Mottet, and Ma'ayan Anafi, *The Report of the 2015 U.S. Transgender Survey* (Washington DC: National Center for Transgender Equality, 2016), www.transequality.org/ sites/default/files/docs/usts/USTS%20Full%20Report%20-%20FINAL%201.6.17.pdf, 191.
[4] James, Herman, Rankin, Keisling, Mottet, and Anafi, *The Report of the 2015 U.S. Transgender Survey*, 65.
[5] Jack Drescher, "Five Myths on Being Transgender," *Washington Post,* May 13, 2016, www.washingtonpost.com/opinions/five-myths-about-transgender-issues/2016 /05/13/eca17dbc-177e-11e6-9e16-2e5a123aac62_story.html.
[6] These last set of statistics are all drawn from the National Coalition of Anti-Violence Projects, "Hate Violence against Transgender Communities." *Anti-Violence Project,* avp.org/wp-content/uploads/2017/04/ncavp_transhvfactsheet.pdf.

schools—particularly America's *Catholic* primary and secondary schools—where the effects of anti-queer theology most profoundly reverberate, intimidating queer youth. Erected as a shield by school administrators and bishops alike, Catholic theology stands in as the ultimate justification for a variety of positions taken that either deny accommodations to transgender students or eliminate the bodies of transgender persons from Catholic spaces altogether. Take, for example, the case of Damian Garcia. In 2013, he was a senior at Saint Pius High School in Albuquerque, New Mexico. Despite having legally changed his name, and despite the fact that students, family, and teachers referred to him as Damian, the administration ruled that he would not be able to graduate in the gown designated for boys. In defense of its actions, the school cited the remarkably specific policy stipulating that students at graduation must dress in gender-specific attire according to the gender filed on the student's birth certificate. Damian ended up not participating in his own graduation.[7] May 2014 saw the case of another Catholic High School, this time a Sacred Heart Cathedral Prep in San Francisco, which chose to remove Jessica Urbina's yearbook photo because she would be depicted wearing a tuxedo rather than a dress. The school initially upheld its decision, citing archdiocesan policy, but then reversed itself on grounds that "it was clear that the school had not adequately communicated to Jessica or her parents the decision made several months ago regarding senior portraits."[8] As another example, for roughly a month in March 2016, the Mount St. Charles Catholic High School in Woonsocket, Rhode Island, planned to adopt a formal policy for its 2016-2017 handbook in which transgender students would not be able to enroll or continue to enroll in classes. The proposed policy was worded, "Mount St. Charles Academy is unable to make accommodations for transgender students. Therefore, MSC does not accept transgender students nor is MSC able

---

[7] Sunnivie Brydum, "Transgender High School Senior Skips Graduation Over School's Transphobic Policy," *Advocate*, May 23, 2013, www.advocate.com/politics/transgender/2013/05/23/transgender-high-school-senior-skips-graduation-over-schools. See also Glennisha Morgan, "Damian Garcia, Transgender Student, Must Wear Girl's Graduation Attire, School Rules," *HuffPost*, May 17, 2013, www.huffingtonpost.com/2013/05/17/damain-garcia-transgender-graduation-n_3287936.html.

[8] Francis DeBernardo, "What's So Doctrinal about Gender Normative Clothing?" *Bondings 2.0 Blog*, May 20, 2014, www.newwaysministryblog.wordpress.com/2014/05/20/whats-so-doctrinal-about-gender-normative-clothing). The original text of the letter was posted to the school's website but, at the time of writing, has been taken down.

to continue to enroll students who identify as transgender."⁹ Explaining its actions, school administrators wrote on March 4, 2016, that

> The policy that currently appears in the Mount Saint Charles Student Handbook is not intended to be discriminatory toward transgendered students nor is Mount Saint Charles Academy's intent or desire to exclude transgender students. The policy was put in place for the simple reason that Mount Saint Charles feels that its facilities do not presently provide the school with the ability to accommodate transgender students.[10]

By the end of the month due to public outrage, the school had decided not to implement the policy. It is unclear what changed about the school's facilities.

Then there are the firings. In 2008, Jan Buterman was fired from his job in St. Albert School District in Canada after completing his transition. The school maintained that he was fired for "not embodying Catholic values." A day after filing a complaint with the human rights commission, the school offered Buterman $78,000 to settle in exchange for Buterman's dropping his complaint.[11] Before her firing in 2011 from Saint Francis Preparatory School in Queens, Marla Krolikowski heard that she was "worse than gay," in response to her acknowledging that she was transgender. She was later fired on grounds of insubordination. Krowlikowski sued. Justice Duane A. Hart, who heard the case, thought it was intriguing that the dismissal, which occurred after 32 years of teaching, coincided with Krolikowski's revealing her gender identity. Apparently not interested in pursuing the intrigue any further, the school agreed to settle outside of court on undisclosed terms.[12]

It is interesting to examine how magisterial theology is functioning in this economy of policy-wielding, retractions, and settlements. Most striking on any analysis will be how few theological arguments are

---

[9] Quoted in Linda Borg, "Mount St. Charles Academy Rescinds Policy Against Transgender Students," *Providence Journal*, March 10, 2016, www.providencejournal.com/news/20160310/mount-st-charles-academy-rescinds-policy-against-transgender-students.

[10] "Statement Regarding Transgender Students at MSC," Mount Saint Charles Academy, March 4, 2016, www.mountsaintcharles.org/podium/ default.aspx?t=204&nid =839021.

[11] Janice Johnston, "Alberta Transgender Teacher Fired in 2008 Loses Case in Appeal Court," *CBC News Edmonton*, June 23, 2017, www.cbc.ca/news/canada/ edmonton/trans-gender-teacher-fired-jan-buterman-1.4176026. The appeal concerned the question of whether Buterman had agreed to settle. Buterman's argument in this instance was not successful.

[12] Sam Roberts, "Marla Krolikowski, Transgender Teacher Fired for Insubordination, Dies at 62," *New York Times*, September 27, 2015, www.nytimes.com/2015 /09/28/nyregion/marla-krolikowski-transgender-teacher-fired-for-insubordination-dies-at-62.html?mcubz=0&_r=0.

being invoked in the process. Either theological argument is assumed to have already been advanced—as in the cases when school administrators cite policies which are, presumably, the practical applications of theological claims—or substantive theological argument is avowed to be forthcoming—as in the cases where a school cites Catholic "values" as the reason why one of its teachers was fired, without subsequently specifying principles from which an argument based in those values could be given. The truth is that, with respect to gender, Catholic theology is profoundly unsettled. As an illustration, let's take one more example. This is the 2016 case of Gabriel Stein-Bodenheimer, the chair of the English department of Mercy High School in San Francisco, who also happens to be Jewish. As a stark counterexample to the trend described in relation to transgender teachers at Catholic secondary institutions, the Sisters of Mercy did not terminate Stein-Bodenheimer when he publicly identified as transgender. Instead, in a letter written to the families at the school, Sr. Laura Reicks, president of the West Midwest Community of the Sisters of Mercy, wrote, "We believe the Sisters of Mercy's statement of Catholic identity for our secondary schools underscores the importance of quality relationships for everyone associated with the school. And, we strive to witness to mercy when we honor the dignity of each person in a welcoming culture that pursues integrity of word and deed."[13] Perhaps equally surprisingly, in a statement released on the following day, San Francisco Archbishop Salvatore Cordileone expressed gratitude for how the Sisters engaged the question, and furthermore, said that the school's decision fell within "the legitimate range of prudential judgment."[14] Stein-Bodehimer was allowed to keep his job.

What exactly is going on here theologically? Of note first is to examine how the trope of "Catholic values" is circulating here. In 2008, when Jan Buterman was fired after acknowledging his transgender identity, the school cited its "Catholic values" as the reason why Buterman's employment was terminated. Conversely, in 2016, the Sisters of Mercy cited a principle of Catholic social teaching—namely, the dignity of the human person—as the reason undergirding their decision to retain Stein-Bodenheimer as chair of Mercy High School's English department. If one grants that both "values" are valid expressions of the relevant aspect of the Catholic tradition, then how does one explain the completely divergent outcomes with respect to

---

[13] Letter to Parents of Mercy High School, May 11, 2016, www.scribd.com/doc/312408489/Letter-to-parents-of-San-Francisco-s-Mercy-High-School-students-released-May-11.

[14] Dan Morris-Young, "Catholic School Won't Fire Transgender Teacher," *National Catholic Reporter*, May 12, 2016, www.ncronline.org/blogs/ncr-today/catholic-school-wont-fire-transgender-teacher.

the teaching careers of these two transmen? It is here where Cordileone's "legitimate range of prudential judgment" commentary comes in to make the point—precisely by clarifying nothing. To say, as he did, that the choice to retain Stein-Bodenheimer was an exercise of prudential judgment within, presumably, a legitimate range of such judgment is *just as* compatible with the view that retaining Stein-Bodenheimer was the right thing to do *as it is* compatible with the view that retaining Stein-Bodenheimer was the lesser of two evils (which, all other things being equal, would have dictated that retaining Stein-Bodenheimer would have been the wrong thing to do). Precisely the question that is left suspended above this legitimate range of judgments is the question to which everyone wants an answer: is it wrong to fire transgender employees at Catholic institutions? It is a question that can be asked in a more general way, one that brings both the plight of transgender students and transgender teachers into relief: is it right to accommodate an individual's chosen gender identity in a Catholic educational environment, even if that chosen identity is not the same as the one written on that individual's birth certificate?

As both Cordileone's comments and the competing realizations of Catholic values suggest, we do not know exactly what it is going on theologically. But I do think that we can make some headway towards an answer, and—more than this—towards an answer that says *yes*, it is right that a Catholic educational environment accommodate an individual's chosen gender identity (whatever that happens to be), and that says *yes*, it is possible to give an answer within the natural law idiom of Catholic thought. What is required to get there first, though, is an account of what elements in Catholic theology are being deployed in the debate around gender, including a formulation of a magisterial argument. Next, I give an analysis of the theological conversation surrounding gender theory, noting the particular challenges that exist with respect to a trans*friendly theology in the Catholic tradition. Last, I give the beginnings of a theological account that I believe meets these challenges.

A Genealogy of Magisterial Teaching with Respect to Transgender Persons

At present, there is no official Catholic document that engages transgender persons directly as its principal subject. The result is that a determination about what exactly counts as "official church teaching" on the matter is complex, since any answer will essentially involve a collation of teachings, comments, and resources put out by the magisterium—more or less in passing—while focusing on other matters. Nevertheless, it is possible to bring some order into this collation. We just have to work backwards, beginning with Pope Francis, whose comments related to transgender persons are among the most popularly circulating when other Catholics—namely the bishops—talk about transgender persons.

Outside of addresses given to specific audiences, Francis's formal comments relating to transgender persons have been given in his 2015 Encyclical *Laudato Si'* and his 2016 Apostolic Exhortation *Amoris Laetitia*. One can locate the heart of Francis's teaching where he describes the intellectual space known as the "ideology of gender." Such ideology, he explains,

> "Denies the difference and reciprocity in nature of a man and a woman and envisages a society without sexual differences, thereby eliminating the anthropological basis of the family. This ideology leads to educational programs and legislative enactments that promote a personal identity and emotional intimacy radically separated from the biological difference between male and female. Consequently, human identity becomes the choice of the individual, one which can also change over time." It is a source of concern that some ideologies of this sort, which seek to respond to what are at times understandable aspirations, manage to assert themselves as absolute and unquestionable, even dictating how children should be raised. It needs to be emphasized that "biological sex and the socio-cultural role of sex (gender) can be distinguished but not separated."... It is one thing to be understanding of human weakness and the complexities of life, and another to accept ideologies that attempt to sunder what are inseparable aspects of reality. Let us not fall into the sin of trying to replace the Creator. We are creatures, and not omnipotent. Creation is prior to us and must be received as a gift. At the same time, we are called to protect our humanity, and this means, in the first place, accepting it and respecting it as it was created (*Amoris Laetitia*, no. 56).[15]

In this paragraph, Francis is both drawing together a variety of threads within the tradition of Catholic teaching on gender and sexuality while also deploying them anew. The first thing to note here is the complete absence of the word 'transgender'—indeed, the absence of *any* specific sexual or gender identity—from this discussion. The reason why is because what Francis has set his sights upon is much more expansive: Francis is not interested in talking about *persons*; he's interested in talking about *beliefs* that those persons may have. Crucially, these are the people who believe, as he says, that "human identity becomes the choice of the individual, one which can also change over time." Consequently, Francis has transcended a discussion based in identities: if you've adopted this new "gender ideology," as it were,

---

[15] Both internal quotes are places where Francis is quoting the *Relatio Finalis* of the bishops from the 2015 Synod on the Family.

then Francis is speaking to you. Identifying as transgender or cisgender; homosexual or heterosexual; or conservative or progressive does not matter in the least. The problem, to use other words, is an infectious idea, and Francis gathers all opposition to current magisterial teaching with respect to sex and gender and gives it the name of 'ideology.' To do this, he creates a dichotomy between those who believe the truth, which is coextensive with the magisterium's position, and those who do not so believe the truth, who choose instead to give in to 'ideology.'

Defining one's audience essentially in this negative way does indeed have its rhetorical advantages. If it does nothing else, it allows Francis and the bishops to name the terms of the debate. For example, this is not the first time that the bishops have named opposition to their teaching related to sex and gender as ideology—and, by continuing to use this language, Francis gives to his current teaching a theological provenance within other magisterial teaching. We've seen this dichotomy before, for example, in the 1986 letter *On the Pastoral Care of Homosexual Persons*;[16] in the 2003 letter *Considerations Regarding Proposals to Give Legal Recognition to Unions Between Homosexual Persons*;[17] and again—this time more directly related to gender— in the 2004 *On the Collaboration of Men and Women in the Church and the World.*[18] However, exemplary on any discussion of ideology is the

---

[16] "Nevertheless, increasing numbers of people today, even within the Church, are bringing enormous pressure to bear on the Church to accept the homosexual condition as though it were not disordered and to condone homosexual activity....These latter groups are guided by a vision opposed to the truth about the human person....*They reflect, even if not entirely consciously, a materialistic ideology which denies the transcendent nature of the human person as well as the supernatural vocation of every individual*"(Congregation for the Doctrine of the Faith, *On the Pastoral Care of Homosexual Persons*, no. 8, emphasis mine).

[17] "The Church's teaching on marriage and on the complementarity of the sexes reiterates a truth that is evident to right reason and recognized as such by all the major cultures of the world. Marriage is not just any relationship between human beings. It was established by the Creator with its own nature, essential properties and purpose. *No ideology can erase from the human spirit the certainty that marriage exists solely between a man and a woman, who by mutual personal gift, proper and exclusive to themselves, tend toward the communion of their persons*" (Congregation for the Doctrine of the Faith, *Considerations Regarding Proposals to Give Legal Recognition to Unions Between Homosexual Persons*, no. 2, emphasis mine).

[18] "Recent years have seen new approaches to women's issues. A first tendency is to emphasize strongly conditions of subordination in order to give rise to antagonism: women, in order to be themselves, must make themselves the adversaries of men.... In order to avoid the domination of one sex or the other, their differences tend to be denied, viewed as mere effects of historical and cultural conditioning. In this perspective, physical difference, termed *sex*, is minimized, while the purely cultural element, termed *gender,* is emphasized to the maximum and held to be primary. The obscuring of the difference or duality of the sexes has enormous consequences on a variety of levels. *This theory of the human person, intended to promote prospects for equality of*

2000 letter issued by the Pontifical Council of the Family, in which the word 'ideology' or 'ideological' occurs seven times in reference to opposition to the magisterium's position.[19]

The biggest liability to such an approach, however, is that in defining a class of people by what they *don't* believe, Francis and the bishops run the risk of misrepresenting what it is that people who disagree with magisterial teaching *actually do believe*, precisely because they never give a substantive account of it. In other words, the problem that plagues Francis and the bishops when they write in this way is the problem of creating intellectual strawmen and generating a field of intellectual distortions that do nothing to clear up the terms of what is actually being debated. There's also the rather embarrassing problem of poor uses of logic, resulting in the construction of invalid arguments and the production of inflammatory, unsubstantiated assertions.

Consider again the document put forward by the Pontifical Council for the Family. The authors promise us a "serenely impartial perspective free from any arbitrary or demagogical positions (no. 9)." But then they proceed to write, "The ideology of 'gender' found a favorable environment in the individualistic anthropology of radical neo-liberalism." Appended to this massive charge is a footnote advising the reader that "Marxism" and "structuralism" are to blame. Yet neither term is defined, and such a diagnosis becomes unintelligible to the extent that, for example, Marxists (who generally divide the world into those who have access to the means of production and those who don't) would be surprised to hear that they were "individualists." These same Marxists would even be more surprised to find that they were parties to "radical neo-liberalism," which, on its face, would seem to be more at home within certain libertarian forms of capitalism, like that put forward by Milton Friedman in his classic *Capitalism and Freedom*. Moreover, in the same footnote we are given putative examples of those who constructed this "ideology of gender"—Wilhelm Reich, a psychoanalyst; Herbert Marcuse, a philosopher; Margaret Sanger, the birth control advocate and infamous founder of Planned Parenthood; and Simone de Beauvoir, French feminist—all of whom died before 1980, with the exception of Beauvoir, who died in 1986.

---

women through liberation from biological determinism, has in reality inspired ideologies which, for example, call into question the family, in its natural two-parent structure of mother and father, and make homosexuality and heterosexuality virtually equivalent, in a new model of polymorphous sexuality" (Congregation for the Doctrine of the Faith, *On the Collaboration of Men and Women in the Church and the World*, no. 2, emphasis mine).

[19] "In the process that could be described as the gradual and cultural human de-structuring of the institution of marriage, the spread of a certain ideology of 'gender' should not be underestimated. *According to this ideology, being a man or a woman is not determined fundamentally by sex but by culture*" (Pontifical Council for the Family, *Family, Marriage and "De Facto" Unions*, no. 8, emphasis mine).

This list, to say nothing about the argument that is missing that would draw these rather disparate personages together, nearly completely ignores all scholarship from the 1980's and 1990's, the two decades in which queer theory—the field of study that looked at gender and sexuality critically—began to take off. Thus, we have an example of an inflammatory, unsubstantiated assertion. Who exactly are these individualist, radical neo-liberals, and are any of them alive to defend themselves?

We can return to Francis for examples of intellectual distortions that ground invalid arguments and the construction of strawmen. Consider this passage, also from *Amoris Laetitia*:

> Beyond the understandable difficulties which individuals may experience, the young need to be helped to accept their own body as it was created, for "thinking that we enjoy absolute power over our own bodies turns, often subtly, into thinking that we enjoy absolute power over creation....An appreciation of our body as male or female is also necessary for our own self-awareness in an encounter with others different from ourselves. In this way we can joyfully accept the specific gifts of another man or woman, the work of God the Creator, and find mutual enrichment." Only by losing the fear of being different, can we be freed of self-centeredness and self-absorption. (*Amoris Laetitia*, no. 285)[20]

Questions concerning logic can be generated throughout this passage. What are these "understandable difficulties," and what is the relationship between the young people who experience them and the apparent diagnosis that they are having trouble accepting their bodies as they were created? We do not know; this is merely asserted. And what would qualify this lack of acceptance as the condition of enjoying "absolute power over our bodies"? What's the difference between 'power' and 'absolute power' here? We don't find out. However, as the paragraph continues, we are informed of something new altogether: that these "understandable difficulties" apparently detract from a "self-awareness in an encounter with others different from ourselves." It is hard to envision exactly what this means. What encounters are made difficult—informal ones with friends at the grocery store, traffic stops with the police, sexual encounters, romantic encounters, or what? And what function does "self-awareness" have in this? Doesn't one have to be self-aware in order to have the "understandable difficulties" in the first place, which seem to be a problem with one's own body? We can't say for sure. Yet, evidently, these understandable difficulties inhibit the acceptance of the "specific gifts of another man or woman," understood also to be the "work of God the

---

[20] The internal quotes are where Francis is quoting his encyclical *Laudato Si'*.

Creator," while also making these young people susceptible to "self-centeredness" and "self-absorption." So, on the one hand, these young people with these "understandable difficulties" may not have the requisite sense of self-awareness in order to encounter those different from themselves; yet, on the other, if these difficulties aren't addressed, these young people run the risk of self-centeredness and self-absorption, which, if it suggests nothing else, would seem to presume some sort of (morally problematic) self-awareness. What exactly all this means is anyone's guess: logic is unable to preserve truth among statements, because everywhere throughout the paragraph one finds the introduction of new terms that are not properly related one to the other. We have, then, an invalid argument. To see the strawman that results from this, one need only review Francis's introduction to the 'ideology of gender' that we saw earlier in *Amoris Laetitia* 56. It has an argumentative resemblance to the passage we've just investigated:

> It is one thing to be understanding of human weakness and the complexities of life, and another to accept ideologies that attempt to sunder what are inseparable aspects of reality. Let us not fall into the sin of trying to replace the Creator. We are creatures, and not omnipotent. Creation is prior to us and must be received as a gift. At the same time, we are called to protect our humanity, and this means, in the first place, accepting it and respecting it as it was created.

The assertion is that those who defend the 'ideology of gender' believe—or, rather, *ultimately* believe—that they don't accept or respect creation as God created it. Yet is this actually what these people believe? Most relevantly, can this be held as a credible representation of what *Christians* who disagree with the magisterium believe—Christians who ostensibly accept, as an article of faith, God as the creator?

The answer is, 'Of course not.' But before we can see clearly why this is the case, we need to construct a magisterial position that approaches validity. We have clues about what the problem is—opposition to the magisterium's positions related to sex and gender—and about what the argument has to prove—namely, that an ideology of gender, however defined, ends up denying the magisterium's theology related to sex and gender. We can take for granted that the magisterium's theology related to sex and gender is transparent to its theology of marriage, such that an attack on one is an attack on the other.[21] This

---

[21] As evidenced, for example, by Francis's comment in his address to priests, religious, seminarians and pastoral workers during his journey to Georgia and Azerbaijan (October 1, 2016): "You, Irena, mentioned a great enemy to marriage today: the theory of gender. Today there is a world war to destroy marriage." See the USCCB document "'Gender Theory'/'Gender ideology'—Select Teaching Resources," updated February 1, 2017, www.usccb.org/issues-and-action/marriage-and-family/marriage/

is an important connection to make because, technically, the magisterium has only a theology of marriage; there is no separable theology of sex and gender. Fundamental to such a theology of marriage is the essential complementarity of the genders, a term which actually denotes two things at once. First, that as a metaphysical feature of all human persons *qua* created beings, every person is *always* either a man and a woman who is furthermore constituted *essentially* as male or female, respectively. Such a position, also known in the theological literature as biological or gender essentialism, grounds the magisterium's hesitation to put too much theoretical cleavage between sex and gender without postulating some sort of psychological or cultural pathology. "In a correct and harmonious process of integration," they write, "sexual and [gender] identity are complementary [i.e., not at variance] because persons live in society according to the cultural aspects corresponding to their sex. The category of generic sexual identity ('gender') is therefore of a psycho-social and culture nature."[22] Second, in addition to being essentially gendered, the two genders are understood to be complementary, which is to say that, when considered together, they produce a unified reality, forming a whole that neither of them could form alone. This feature entered Catholic sexual teaching as a concept during the pontificate of John Paul II, especially as he developed it in his collections of homilies that became known as the *Theology of the Body*. "Masculinity and femininity express *the twofold aspect of man's somatic constitution*....This meaning, one can say, consists in *reciprocal enrichment*."[23] Refracting this theological perspective into the natural law tradition, this gender essentialism paired with gender complementarity is understood to be a *natural complementarity* between the genders.

In *Familiaris Consortio*, John Paul II provides a significant illustration of the relationship between this natural complementarity and the existence of marriage. Marriage, understood as "conjugal communion,"

> Sinks its roots in the natural complementarity that exists between man and woman, and is nurtured through the personal willingness of the spouses to share their entire life-project, what they have and what they are: for this reason such communion is the fruit and the sign of a profoundly human need. But in the Lord Christ God takes up this human need, confirms it, purifies it and elevates it, leading it to perfection

---

promotion-and-defense-of-marriage/upload/Gender-Ideology-Select-Teaching-Resources.pdf.
[22] Pontifical Council for the Family, *Family, Marriage, and "De Facto" Unions*, no. 8.
[23] See John Paul II, *Man and Woman He Created Them: A Theology of the Body*, trans. Michael Waldstein (Boston: Pauline Books and Media, 2006), esp. Addresses 8, 9, 12-15; quote at Address 9, no. 5.

through the sacrament of matrimony: the Holy Spirit who is poured out in the sacramental celebration offers Christian couples the gift of a new communion of love that is the living and real image of that unique unity which makes of the Church the indivisible Mystical Body of the Lord Jesus. (*Familiaris Consortio*, no. 19)

Marriage, in its sacramental form, strengthens this natural complementarity found between a man and a woman, providing them with a stable context for realizing certain goods—goods which go all the way back to Augustine: *fides* or faithfulness between the spouses; *proles*, or children; and *sacramentum*, or the indissolubility of the relationship based in Christ's relationship with the Church.[24] It is through this argument that sees marriage as realizing the asserted physical, affective, and spiritual complementarity between the genders that the magisterium, through John Paul II, believes that marriage *by definition* occurs only between a man and a woman such that any attempts to expand marriage to include same-sex partners would, per this definition, involve changing the definition of marriage. Love, therefore, is not enough to make a family, as many political campaigns for marriage equality insisted. It is merely a part, perhaps necessary but not sufficient: "Marriage, in fact, the foundation of the family, is not a 'way of living sexuality as a couple'....Nor is it simply the expression of a sentimental love between two persons: this characteristic is usually present in every loving friendship. Marriage is more than that: it is a union between a man and a woman, precisely as such, and in the totality of their male and female essence."[25]

The connection between natural complementarity, its realization in marriage, and the state is that the magisterium argues that the state has an interest in the preservation of marriage as a societal institution. At the base of this connection is the assertion that the goods in marriage have a public dimension, and that, insofar as these goods have a public dimension, the state has an interest in preserving marriage. The clearest connection comes through examining the good of children. For fairly intuitive reasons, the state has an interest in making sure that there are adults in the society who, most importantly, are able to work and carry on various civil and private occupations. This gives the state an interest in making sure that children are able to make it to this adult phase. From here, the magisterium makes a variety of assertions based in superlatives. The *best* way for the state to make sure that children make it to adulthood in order to serve society is for the state to support

---

[24] Augustine, "On the Good of Marriage," in *Treatises on Marriage and Other Subjects*, trans., Charles T. Wilcox (Washington DC: Catholic University of America Press, 1955), 3-51, at 24.32.
[25] Pontifical Council for the Family, *Family, Marriage, and 'De Facto' Unions*, no. 22.

children in the context of the *family*. The *best* way for the state to support children in the context of the *family* is to support the stability of the *parents of the child*; and the *best* way to support the parents of the child is to support the *stability of an individual marriage*, which, as we have seen, requires the exclusion, by definition, of any arrangement which does not involve solely one man and one woman. Since it makes no sense to support one marriage so defined to the exclusion of others, the state therefore has an interest in *supporting the stability of all marriages*. At this point one can observe an interesting symmetry in the magisterium's argument. In the same way that marriage "sinks its roots" in the asserted natural complementarity of the partners, so does the state "sink" its roots into the three goods of marriage, by incentivizing married couples to have children through, for example, favorable taxation schemes to make raising children less financially burdensome; by promoting the fidelity of the spouses through laws prohibiting adultery; and by promoting the indissolubility of marriage, albeit indirectly, through the discouragement of divorce through the enactment of programs that will keep families from separating. Such a cascade allows us to see what reasoning lies behind otherwise less-than-intuitive claims: like, for example, the claim that legalizing same-sex marriage discriminates against "true" marriage because "[same-sex couples] do not take on the essential obligations to society that are proper to marriage"—ostensibly the "obligation" to sexually reproduce children.[26] Or that children in households headed by same-sex couples may suffer a harm so great that they should not be allowed to be adopted by same-sex couples for the sole reason that the caretakers would be in a same-sex relationship.[27] This cascade also allows us to see why the magisterium has also identified divorce—or, perhaps to be more exact, the so-called *normalization* of divorce—as a threat to the family equal to, if not worse than, the threat posed by same-sex

---

[26] Pontifical Council for the Family, *Family, Marriage, and 'De Facto' Unions*, no. 16.

[27] "The bond between two men or two women cannot constitute a real family and much less can the right be attributed to that union to adopt children without a family," John Paul II's *Angelus* from February 20, 1994, quoted in *Family Marriage, and 'De Facto' Unions*, no. 23. Several years ago, this question was politicized with particular fervor by social scientists, with sociologist Mark Regnerus concluding a study finding that children in households headed by same-sex couples adjusted suboptimally as adults later in life (Mark Regnerus, "How different are the adult children of parents who have same-sex relationships? Findings from the New Family Structures Study," *Social Science Research* 41, no. 4 [July 2012]: 752-770). The study was later widely discredited, drawing a condemnation from the American Sociological Association (American Sociological Association, "ASA Files *Amicus* Brief with Supreme Court in Support of Marriage Equality," March 15, 2015, www.asanet.org/press-center/press-releases/asa-files-amicus-brief-supreme-court-support-marriage-equality).

marriage.²⁸ But most importantly, if not also least intuitively, one can see why the magisterium vehemently recruits the state to oppose legal protections for transgender persons and for same-sex couples: if the state doesn't defend natural complementarity, then, apocalyptically speaking, the entire edifice of marriage will come crumbling down. It is, in other words, a contemporary example of a 'slippery slope' argument.

So runs the argument that draws a connection between the natural complementarity of the man and the woman and the state's mandate to protect marriage. We are also at the point where we can state what the 'ideology of gender' is. Precisely stated, the 'ideology of gender' is the belief or set of beliefs with the conclusion that denies the natural complementarity of the genders as the magisterium defines it. Interestingly, such a denial can deny one, the other, or both components that build up the idea of the natural complementarity of the genders. If one seeks to build room for transgender persons, then one must deny that one is embodied *essentially* either as man or a woman. If one wants to argue for the morality of same-sex sex acts and/or the morality of same-sex unions, then one must deny the *complementarity* of the genders.²⁹

We can reach the conclusion of our reconstruction of this magisterial argument by delineating what threats are posed by denying gender essentialism and gender complementarity, in turn. If it is the case that the magisterium is right, then denying gender essentialism questions the creative wisdom manifested in God's *creating* one as a man or as a woman—something like the sin of ingratitude or spitefulness. This concern is large enough to cast shadows on *all* ways in which transgender persons live out their lives: from changing personal pro-

---

²⁸ Cf. *Charter of the Rights of the Family*, Preamble B. Divorce is also invoked as a "grave offense" to the natural law, which applies to Christians and to non-Christians: "Divorce is a grave offense against the natural law. It claims to break the contract, to which the spouses freely consented, to live with each other till death. Divorce does injury to the covenant of salvation, of which sacramental marriage is the sign" (*Catechism*, no. 2384). Also, "Divorce is immoral also because it introduces disorder into the family and into society" (*Catechism*, no. 2385). Crucially, same-sex marriages are viewed as contrary to the natural law because the Vatican views them as essentially institutionalizations of same-sex sex acts, which are also viewed as contrary to the natural law; see Pontifical Council for the Family, *Family, Marriage and 'De Facto' Unions*, no. 23, n. 41, as well as Congregation for the Doctrine of the Faith, *Considerations Regarding Proposals to Give Legal Recognition to Unions Between Homosexual Persons*, esp. nos. 6-9.

²⁹ Another interesting parallel emerges between magisterial treatments of transgender persons and persons living with same-sex attraction: both are understood to manifest psychological pathology. In the case of the "homosexual" the individual suffers from an "objective disorder" with respect to sexual object, while the trans*person suffers from "gender dysphoria."

nouns, to undergoing hormone treatment, to undergoing sex reassignment surgery. It is at this point that we can make sense of Francis's judgment in *Amoris Laetitia* 56 that the 'ideology of gender' tempts one into assuming the role of the Creator, even as we can see how such a concern is rhetorically overcharged. This set of arguments also bears a family resemblance to arguments going back to Paul VI through Benedict XVI that manifest the concern that technology—though, in our case, technology that intervenes in gender assignment—attempts to master nature in ways that do not accord with authentic human development.[30]

A threat that manifests to gender complementarity if the magisterium is correct is a disregard for the theological significance of human biology, particularly as it applies to human sexual relationships. As we can recall, John Paul II's *Theology of the Body*, through his interpretation of Genesis, maintains that the biological affinity between the penis and the vagina in human sexual reproduction serves as a concrete indication of the metaphysical complementarity between the genders. But, if this construal of metaphysical complementarity is false, then so goes the natural law theological foundation for any argument against same-sex sex acts (and, by extension, same-sex relationships). A final threat has been raised by Francis in particular. Figuring challenges both to gender essentialism and gender complementarity as Western developments in a world sensitized to the global history of colonialism, Francis has identified the incursion of the 'ideology of gender' as a form of ideological neocolonialism of the world by intellectual elites in the West. Thus, any denial of gender essentialism or gender complementarity, rather than seen as marks of societal progress, are understood rather to be signs of societal regress, harking back to, or, alternatively, extending, the domination of the Global South by the Global North.

> In Europe, America, Latin America, Africa, and in some countries in Asia, there are genuine forms of ideological colonialization taking place. And one of these—I will call it clearly by its name—is [the ideology of] 'gender'. Today children—children!—are taught in school that everyone can choose his or her sex. Why are they teaching this? Because the books are provided by persons and institutions that give you money.[31]

---

[30] See, for example, Paul VI, *Populorum Progressio*, no. 34; John Paul II, *Sollicitudo Rei Socialis,* nos. 27-40; and Benedict XVI, *Caritas in Veritate*, nos. 68-77.

[31] Francis, "Address to the Polish Bishops during Apostolic Journey to Poland," July 27, 2016, as quoted in USCCB, "'Gender Theory'/Gender Ideology.'"

THEOLOGICAL ENGAGEMENTS WITH NATURAL COMPLEMENTARITY

This argument is full of vulnerabilities, but we will concentrate our efforts at the base, on the magisterium's assertion concerning the natural complementarity of the genders. Forcing a reconsideration of this concept will thus weaken the cascade in which the state "sinks into" the goods of marriage—goods that, in turn, "sink into" the natural complementarity of man and woman. First, one can question the theological coherence of the concept of natural complementarity, especially as it is put forward by John Paul II. Upon examination, the term 'natural complementarity' seems to represent an ontologization of the perceived genital compatibility of the penis and vagina for reproduction (also called biologism)—an interpretation that becomes all the more plausible to the extent that John Paul II runs into difficulties explaining the integrity of each individual creation as complete in itself when people choose not to marry or when people choose to live a celibate life. To the extent that one *need not*, in order to live a fulfilled life, find one's gendered complement, one is forced to ask how necessary the concept is at the ontological level in the first place, even if one concedes that there seems to be a certain biological affinity in human sexual reproduction.[32] In other words, to use the formulation put forward by revisionist theologians Todd Salzman and Michael Lawler, the problem is how to explain how men and women are complete in themselves while also being simultaneously incomplete as a couple.[33]

---

[32] This is to say that, if sexual reproduction is to happen, this process seems to require the fertilization of an egg by a sperm.

[33] From what I can tell, John Paul II's solution involves giving an account of vocation that realizes complementarity in a way that is realized differently for each person but is nevertheless viewed as theologically equivalent. So, just as the married couple symbolizes the relationship between Christ and the Church, so does the celibate's vow of chastity to God symbolize that same reality through "continence for the kingdom of heaven" (*Theology of the Body*, Address 78, no. 4). For this to work, this solution requires a certain ontologization of gender between Christ (figured as masculine) and the believer (figured as feminine), which is a move John Paul II seems to have taken from von Balthasar. As many have pointed out, this is not without its problems (for one example, see Linn Marie Tonstad, "Sexual Difference and Trinitarian Death: Cross, Kenosis, and Hierarchy in the *Theo-Drama*," *Modern Theology* 26, no. 4 [2010]: 603-631). But even if one puts this aside, such a relationship between Christ and the Church seems accessible to all Christians (if not to all humanity), married or not. So, in the case of married persons, they seem to be realizing *both* this form of complementarity between Christ and the Church *and* the complementarity of man and woman. Precisely what we don't have here is an account of their *equivalency*. Outside of the mere stipulation that they are equivalent, either we have an account of how married persons are realizing *at a greater level* the relationship symbolized by Christ and the Church; *or* we have an account of how the celibate vocation is *a greater realization* of the relationship between Christ and the Church than is the married vocation; *or* we have an account of how the complementarity of man and woman is and the life of the celibate are, at best, derivative from *a more primary ontological complementary* relationship between Christ and the Church (creator and creation?) insofar

For their part, Salzman and Lawler replace the concept of natural complementarity as the magisterium understands it with the concept of 'holistic complementarity', a term that recognizes "biological complementarity" insofar as this seems to be required in cases of human sexual reproduction. Crucially, however, Salzman and Lawler do not see this form of complementarity as prohibitive of same-sex relationships in view of the fact that, in their finding the *apposite* partner for mutual vulnerability and spiritual growth, partners in same-sex relationships fulfill the purpose of marriage theologically considered.[34] This view is isomorphic with other accounts given by theologians who have questioned natural complementarity on grounds that the goods of marriage can be instantiated differently across opposite-sex as well as same-sex couples without any theologically relevant disparities.[35] A third reason to question the account of natural complementarity comes from the observation that many theologians, especially women theologians, have noted concerning how such arguments extend the ideological trajectory that sustains the gendered oppression of women in contemporary society through the maintenance of gender roles.[36]

---

as creation is prior to marriage. To the extent that John Paul II figures the celibate life eschatologically as an anticipation of eternal life, in which persons are no longer given in marriage, I believe that the logic of John Paul II's position leads him to this second solution, despite his own desire to hold that married and celibate vocations are equal in view of the fact that they both challenge individuals to love within their vocations (as he says in *Theology of the Body*, Address 78, no. 3). To say that we are supposed to love in all of our vocations does not address the problem at hand. Choosing the third option is the only option that makes the two vocations equivalent, but, in doing so, he cannot maintain that the natural complementarity between the genders is *ontologically primary*. Salzman and Lawler engage John Paul II's notion of complementarity in their *The Sexual Person: Toward a Renewed Catholic Anthropology* (Washington DC: Georgetown University Press, 2008), 84-91.

[34] See also Patricia Beattie Jung, "God Sets the Lonely in Families," *More than a Monologue; Vol. 2: Inquiry, Thought, Expression*, ed. J. Patrick Hornbeck and Michael A. Norko (New York: Fordham University Press, 2014), 115-133.

[35] This is the consensus view of nearly all revisionist moral theologians. For examples of writings, see Margaret Farley's *Just Love: A Framework for Christian Sexual Ethics* (New York: Continuum, 2006); Stephen J. Pope, "The Magisterium's Arguments Against Same-Sex Marriage: An Ethical Analysis and Critique," *Theological Studies* 65, no. 3 (2004): 530-565; Lisa Cahill, "Same-Sex Marriage and Catholicism: Dialogue, Learning, and Change," in *More than a Monologue: Sexual Diversity and the Catholic Church; Inquiry, Thought, and Expression*, ed. J. Patrick Hornbeck and Michael Norko (New York: Fordham University Press, 2014), 141-155; Salzman and Lawler's *The Sexual Person*, ch. 7; and Jean Porter, "The Natural Law and Innovative Forms of Marriage: A Reconsideration," *Journal of the Society of Christian Ethics* 30, no. 2 (2010), 79-97.

[36] See, for example, Lisa Sowle Cahill's classic *Sex, Gender, and Christian Ethics* (New York: Cambridge University Press, 1996), esp. 1-120, and Margaret A. Farley, "New Patterns of Relationship: Beginnings of a Moral Revolution," in *Changing the Questions: Explorations in Christian Ethics*, ed. Jamie L. Manson (Maryknoll: Orbis, 2015), 1-23. In the not too distant past, this view has been challenged by the "New Feminism," but this view largely seems to be a restatement of John Paul II's view to

These interventions, however, interrogate and reform only natural complementarity *understood as gender complementarity.* It does not offer any sustained critique of *gender essentialism.* In fact, one can remain a gender essentialist while still wanting to dismantle gender complementarity: how this is done is simply to view biological sex as the unalterable bedrock, releasing gender as the socially constructed concept.[37] In other words, gender—one's identity as a man or as a woman— is created by culture, but sex—one's identity as either male or female—is "natural," the foundation on top of which gender is built. As Susannah Cornwall shows, this is more or less the state of the current discussion across Christian denominations.[38] Indeed, Catholicism is not excluded from this paradigm either, especially when one considers recent comments from Francis related to gender. "It is true," Francis writes, "that we cannot separate the masculine and feminine from God's work of creation, which is prior to all our decisions and experiences, and where biological elements exist which are impossible to ignore. But it is also true that masculinity and femininity are not rigid categories" (*Amoris Laetitia,* no. 286).[39]

Without dismantling this gender essentialism in our theology, which simply moves the rigidity of the category of gender back one step into sexual identity, there can be little hope of depathologizing the existence of all trans*persons, since it is precisely the question of the fixity of sexual identity that is at stake, particularly for transgender persons who wish to transition. As it stands, there are theologians who are attempting such a depathologization. Some have taken approaches that attempt to minimize the shock that transgender persons may pose to Christian communities. For example, Luke Timothy Johnson has proposed to view gender identity as among the *adiaphora*—that is, among those non-essential things that should not be an obstacle to Christian unity.[40] And James Childs, for his part, takes the cautious

---

which theologians like Lisa Cahill and Margaret Farley are responding. For an example of the 'New Feminism,' see Michelle M. Schumacher, ed., *Women in Christ: Toward a New Feminism* (Grand Rapids: Eerdmans, 2004).

[37] This, for example, is my reading of Cristina Traina's *Feminist Ethics and Natural Law: The End of the Anathemas* (Washington DC: Georgetown University Press, 1999). See below at n.54.

[38] Susannah Cornwall, "'State of Mind' versus 'Concrete Set of Facts,'" *Theology and Sexuality* 15, no. 1 (2009): 7-28.

[39] For another similar view, see Austen Ivereigh, "Transgender Debates Require Distinction Between Theory and People," *Crux,* October 23, 2016, cruxnow.com/analysis/2016/10/23/transgender-debates-require-distinction-theory-people/.

[40] Luke Timothy Johnson, "The Church and Transgender Identity: Some Cautions, Some Possibilities," *Commonweal,* February 27, 2017, www.commonwealmagazine.org/church-transgender-identity.

road of practicing divine acceptance in the midst of uncertainty.[41] Others, like Virginia Mollenkott—working in the relatively new field of what we would call queer theology—have attempted to build more liberative theologies that focus on confronting Christian communities in their oppression of transgender persons while encouraging Christian communities to use trans*identity—in which sex and gender identities are fluid—as a horizon for an adequate theological anthropology.[42] To similar effect, Elizabeth Stuart argues that, in view of the primacy of Christian baptismal identity, all other identities, including sex and gender, are placed under "eschatological erasure."[43] And as a final example, Mary Elise Lowe highlights how the circumstances that transgender persons face in the larger world allow them to bring particular gifts to all Christians regardless of gender identity.[44]

TOWARDS A QUEER NATURAL LAW THEOLOGY OF EXPLORATION

But these interventions have all been made by non-Catholics. To address such a topic within the idiom of the natural law—since that is the framework through which Catholic teachings on sex and gender are generated—will be the challenge for theologians who wish to speak to the Catholic tradition. This requires the emergence of a theology that is *queer* enough to be able to challenge both gender essentialism and gender complementarity while also using the building blocks of the natural law tradition in order to do so. The Catholic theological discussion has not gotten quite so far. In fact, when one excludes the work that revisionists have done to dismantle gender complementarity (which, once again, includes an interrogation of the rigidity of societal gender roles), one is left with very little to offer against gender essentialism for the benefit of queer people other than the theological imperative "to show hospitality to" and/or "to listen to" the "stranger," even though queer persons have actually been in

---

[41] James M. Childs, "Transsexualism: Some Theological and Ethical Perspectives," *Dialog: A Journal of Theology* 48, no. 1 (2009): 30-41.

[42] Virgina R. Mollenkott, *Omnigender: A Trans-Religious Approach* (Cleveland: Pilgrim Press, 2001).

[43] Elizabeth Stuart, "Sacramental Flesh," in *Queer Theology: Rethinking the Western Body*, ed. Gerald O'Loughlin (Malden: Blackwell Publishing, 2007), 65-75. For other interesting theological work in trans*liberation and eschatology, see Michael Nasuner, "Toward Community Beyond Gender Binaries: Gregory of Nyssa's Transgendering as Part of his Transformative Eschatology," *Theology and Sexuality* 16, no. 1 (2002): 55-65. For work at the intersection of trans*liberation and Christology, see Tricia Sheffeld, "Performing Jesus: A Queer Counternarrative of Embodied Transgression," *Theology and Sexuality* 14, no. 3 (2008): 233-258.

[44] Mary Elise Lowe, "From the Same Spirit: Receiving the Theological Gifts of Transgender Christians," *Dialog: A Journal of Theology* 56, no. 1 (2017): 28-37.

Catholic congregations for centuries.[45] There are two problems with this thinking: one, it continues to draw a wedge between queer Christians and whoever "we" or "us" are in a particular scenario, a posture that only continues to position the queer Christian as the stranger and the one on the outside; and two—and this one is more devastating—the logic of "hospitality," "welcome," and "listening" can be turned on their heads against queer Christians. This was famously done, for example, in 2013, when Cardinal Archbishop Timothy Dolan of New York proclaimed that, while all are welcome in the Roman Catholic Church, "that doesn't necessarily mean we love and respect their actions." Indeed, he continues, "Truth may require that we tell the person we love that such actions are not consonant with what God has revealed."[46] The result: even after welcoming, we are right back where we started at the beginning in this theological argument.

So, then, let's start with our queer natural law argument. In Catholic theological ethics, natural law arguments are normative explorations into *human nature*. For those who are familiar with queer theory, however, this may seem to be exactly the nonstarter, insofar as 'human nature,' like all concepts—scientific or philosophical—is the product of social construction. As such, 'human nature' can become the putatively neutral storehouse for all sorts of prejudices. Indeed, we can see how it *has* been so deployed. Not so long ago there were discussions about whether black persons were sufficiently human to be bearers of equal constitutional rights in the United States, and there was "science" that was held out to provide evidence to support that black people, as a race, were less intelligent than their white counterparts. The same story can be told with respect to sexuality, since we can see—in the present case—that the magisterium maintains that "human nature" excludes sexually queer identities as more or less pathological. This was also the consensus position of many professional psychologists and other social scientists until late in the twentieth century. But it is one thing to know that all of our concepts our socially constructed; another thing to know that our concepts are often deployed by the powerful in order to oppress or structure society in a way that normalizes white supremacy, patriarchy, and heterosexuality (among others); and it's a third thing altogether to believe that knowing the two above items justifies a form of antirealism about truth—that is, that it justifies the belief that truth does not exist because everything asserted as true is the product of social construction, or—what amounts to the

---

[45] Essays of this form are ubiquitous, with one of the most recent entries coming from James Martin, S.J. Note how the title frames the text: *Building a Bridge: How the Catholic Church and the LGBT Community Can Enter into a Relationship of Respect, Compassion, and Sensitivity* (New York: HarperCollins, 2017).

[46] Timothy Cardinal Dolan, "All are Welcome!" *cardinaldolan.org*, April 25, 2013, cardinaldolan.org/index.php/all-are-welcome/.

same conclusion practically—that truth might exist but we have no access to it and no way to verify it.[47] Though a complete argument for such a position lies beyond the scope of this paper, I would maintain instead what Jean Porter has outlined as a speculative realist position, which maintains that we attain genuine, though imperfect, knowledge about the world which we subsequently express through our concepts—concepts that, in turn, adequately correspond to what we're talking about.[48] Or, to use language involving social construction: even though all of our concepts are socially constructed, this by itself is enough to prove only that every concept is imperfect. We may have seen defective accounts of that in which human nature consists, in other words, but this alone is not enough to deny that there is such a thing as human nature.

But why retain the concept of human nature at all? Because, whenever we ask the question—'What sort of beings are we? What are we like?'—we are asking a question about human nature. It is indeed answered in a variety of modes—the human being considered biologically, sociologically, anthropologically, etc.—but we are always asking the question, and asking the question is practically inescapable. The Catholic natural law tradition, especially as developed during the medieval period by theologians like Thomas Aquinas, begins by asking this very question.[49] Thomas's answer, following Aristotle, is that we are the types of beings who go about the world learning the truth—admittedly partial and imperfect—by exploring the world, experiencing it through our senses, representing that world and the things in it to ourselves by abstraction through concepts, and sharing those concepts with others through instruction, through the law, and through customs (ST I q. 84-85; I-II q. 90-97). We cannot and do not learn in any other way.

To say that the Catholic natural law tradition not only investigates human nature but investigates human nature *theologically* is to assert two additional claims: first, that this exploration through the world is related to our knowledge of God, who can truly be known, even if ultimately imperfectly (ST I q. 86, a. 2); and that God's action in the world is, in part, for the sake of our flourishing, otherwise known as

---

[47] This form of antirealism is self-refuting: if it is impossible to determine if a proposition is true, then, if this statement is asserted as true, then there is no way to determine whether it is true.

[48] Jean Porter, *Nature as Reason: A Thomistic Theory of the Natural Law* (Grand Rapids: Eerdmans, 2005), 57-68. Importantly, by saying that our concepts "adequately correspond" to what we're talking about, we are asserting nothing more than a metaphysically realist position: when you and I are talking about *x,* it is the case that *x* really exists as something external to our minds that we can talk *about.*

[49] For an interesting argument along Thomistic lines while also engaging Judith Butler, see, Eugene F. Rogers, Jr., "Bodies Demand Language: Thomas Aquinas," in *Queer Theology*, 176-187.

our salvation, which we have impeded through our own individual actions (individual sins), through our corporate actions (social sin), and through the installation of structures that make individual and social sins practically inescapable (structures of sin).[50] Crucially, this theological natural law framework as constructed by the medieval theologians did not see faith and reason as oppositional. Indeed it saw them as two sources, revelatory of a singular truth about reality, that were subject to dialectical interaction in an elaboration of the natural law.[51] This natural law is nothing more, but crucially nothing less, than our innate capacity as creatures connected to God to know right and wrong as well as to know the very general principles by which such determinations can be made (ST I-II q. 91, a.2).[52]

In our present day, we must persist in such an integrative approach to faith and reason when investigating the natural law in relation to the lives of queer persons. Following the method of the medieval natural lawyers, we must look at what knowledge we gain about human nature through our investigation of how human beings actually exist. In our day, the most respected form of such investigation goes by the name of 'science.' As Susannah Cornwall's research has shown, biologists—particularly through the study of intersex persons—have determined that it is no longer possible to maintain that human sex manifests as a simple binary of male and female.[53] This fiction nevertheless persists because, as queer theorists—among the most notably celebrated, Judith Butler—have shown us, even our experience of the material body *as sexed prior to our encountering it* is itself the result of a temporal process of negotiation through which we have organized reality to fit a certain conception of it.[54] Our present moment invites

---

[50] Thomas relates the action of God to individual sins at ST III q. 1, a. 3, ad. 1, and he relates Christ's work to remedying original sin at III q. 1, a. 4. Among others, Karl Rahner, appropriating Thomas, has argued that original sin operates at a social level. See his *Foundations of Christian Faith: An Introduction to the Idea of Christianity*, trans. William V. Dych (New York: Crossroad, 1995), 106-115. For a plausible theological analysis of structures of sin see Daniel K. Finn, "What is a Sinful Social Structure?" *Theological Studies* 77, no. 1 (2016): 136-164.

[51] See Jean Porter, *Natural and Divine Law: Reclaiming the Tradition for Christian Ethics* (Grand Rapids: Eerdmans, 1999), 121-185.

[52] See also Porter, *Nature as Reason*, 327-342. These principles are indeed very general, and require often complex and difficult operations of practical reasoning in order to determine moral norms—principles which become even more intricately difficult to apply in a given case. See ST I-II q. 94, as well as Porter, *Nature as Reason*, 231-324.

[53] Susannah Cornwall, *Sex and Uncertainty in the Body of Christ: Intersex Conditions and Christian Theology* (Oakville: Equinox, 2010).

[54] See Judith Butler's essay, "Bodies that Matter," in *Bodies that Matter: On the Discursive Limits of Sex* (New York: Routledge, 1993), 3-27. Butler's analysis here is one in which power dissimulates behind what we represent as ontology. Crucially, this is *not* necessarily a denial of the body's materiality that is prior to our encountering it. It is, instead, the observation that there is no encounter with the materiality of

us to reconsider that conception and modify it accordingly. So if gender essentialism (in which sex is prior to cultural signification) is false, then the magisterium's notion of gender essentialism is undermined by the very sort of investigation that is required for a natural law methodology. If we don't appear in the world "in nature" only as male and female, then to claim an ontological binarism along such lines is too simplistic a philosophical analysis for the actual world that God created.

The main crux of magisterial arguments in favor of modified gender essentialism is not scientific, however; it is scriptural, and is generally limited to a citation of Genesis 1 and 2. The bible verse generally quoted, however—"Male and female He created them (Gen. 1:27)"—is completely unable to bear the weight of an argument in favor of gender essentialism because the verse does not make an argument about *what it means* to be embodied before God, which is in part what scientific investigation into human biology seeks to explain.[55] Also, such interpretation does not invite any nuance or any awareness of historical criticism, which is standard procedure in biblical interpretation. This is true even according to the magisterium's own standards in *Dei Verbum*, the Catholic Church's dogmatic constitution on divine revelation.

> However, since God speaks in Sacred Scripture through men in human fashion, the interpreter of Sacred Scripture, in order to see clearly what God wanted to communicate to us, should carefully investigate what meaning the sacred writers really intended, and what God wanted to manifest by means of their words.... For truth is set forth and expressed differently in texts which are variously historical, prophetic, poetic, or of other forms of discourse. The interpreter must investigate what meaning the sacred writer intended to express and actually expressed in particular circumstances by using contemporary literary forms in accordance with the situation of his own time and culture. (*Dei Verbum*, no. 12)

---

the body that is not always already conceptualized. There is, in other words, always a body there, but there is no unmediated access to it. Contrary to how Cristina Traina reads Butler, there is actually no "loss of the body" that leads to a new version of the "mind-body dualism" problem, even as Butler's reading forces us to acknowledge that there is no body that automatically supplies the "concrete criterion of womanhood," that Traina would like (*Feminist Ethics and Natural Law*, 3-4). Stated much more clearly, Butler writes, "If the bodily traits 'indicate' sex, then sex is not quite the same as the means by which it is indicated. Sex is made understandable through the signs that indicate how it should be read or understood. These bodily indicators are the cultural means by which the sexed body is read. They are themselves bodily, and they operate as signs, so there is no easy way to distinguish between what is 'materially' true and what is 'culturally' true about a sexed body" (in "Undiagnosing Gender," in *Undoing Gender* [New York: Routledge, 2004], 75-101, at 87).

[55] Cornwall, "'State of Mind' versus 'Concrete Set of Facts,'" 18-19, esp. 18, n5.

The next paragraph in that same document names an important qualification that is sure to be invoked by anyone who would want to defend the magisterium's position on gender essentialism, however.

> But, since Holy Scripture must be read and interpreted in the sacred spirit in which it was written, no less serious attention must be given to the content and unity of the whole of Scripture if the meaning of the sacred texts is to be correctly worked out. The living tradition of the whole Church must be taken into account along with the harmony which exists between elements of the faith. (*Dei Verbum*, no. 12)

Truly, it cannot be doubted that through the development of the Catholic tradition to the present day, gender essentialism has been operative, both explicitly and implicitly. Equally, one cannot doubt that in the magisterium's contemporary sexual teaching, there is a sort of "harmony" that can be discerned. This can be seen through our construction of the magisterial argument, and such a harmony was that which John Paul II was trying to articulate in his *Theology of the Body*. So, even if Scripture by itself isn't probative with respect to the magisterium's position, might it still be the case that, taking a "wider-view" of the Tradition, one might be able to defend modified gender essentialism, perhaps chiding contemporary biologists into acknowledging that, by and large, human beings do in fact come as male and female, and that contemporary scientific research is simply giving disproportionate attention to genetic and psychological outliers, like intersex persons, transgender persons, and nonheterosexuals? Is the magisterium's formulation of the natural law concerning sex and gender still the best interpretation?

We must answer this question once again in the negative, because a better natural law account—one that takes into account the development of all persons regardless of sexual and gender identity—can be given. Earlier, we established that human beings are the sort of creatures who seek truth through exploration of the world around them, knowing that this exploration, in a theological key, will bring them closer to knowledge of God. This is no less true with respect to phenomena in the external world than it is for individuals who seek the truth about themselves as they attempt to answer the question *Who am I?* Sex and gender identity are among the elements of one's self that one must explore not only introspectively in the sacred space of one's conscience, but also in community—perhaps with one's family, with one's close circle of friends, and even with one's Christian community. Indeed, alongside other elements of one's self that must be investigated along similar axes of conscience and community, living into one's sex and gender identity is part of the larger journey towards fulfillment in one's relationship with one's self, with others, with the world, and with God. Or, as Thomas called it, this is part of a larger journey towards *eudaimonia*, or happiness—which Thomas will identify as a life lived by the virtuous person (ST I-II q. 4, a. 6).

This argument requires some way of connecting one's journey to one's sex and gender identity to the happy life lived by the virtuous person. Clearly, it would be false to assert that people who have found their sex and gender identity are, for that reason, virtuous. (Surely, we can imagine someone who has discovered their sex and gender identity and yet turns out, for other reasons, to be quite vicious.) So, the path will be indirect, but certainly not insignificant. For even though finding one's sex and gender identity might not directly lead one to a life of virtue, it does go a significant distance towards establishing one's *well-being*, which, as Jean Porter explains, is "the normative ideal of flourishing proper to any...kind of creature, and as such, it will include all the components of a humanly desirable life, including life itself, health, security, and participation in a network of family and social relations."[56] And even though well-being may not be sufficient for the virtuous life (indeed, for some people, it may not even be required, since, strictly speaking, one need not have health in order to be virtuous), well-being nevertheless "provides the paradigmatic instance of a virtuous life—paradigmatic, because this reflects the form that the life of virtue will actually take for most people, and paradigmatic in the more basic sense that the exigencies of human well-being will inform the criteria for the ideals of the virtues."[57] To the extent that finding one's sex and gender identity contributes to one's healthy development, to that extent does such a journey contribute positively to one's own well-being. This contribution, in turn, provides us with normatively significant insight, generally speaking, into the possibility of achieving a truly fulfilled—that is to say, virtuous—life. Here contemporary scientific investigations into human sexuality prove useful to the extent that professional societies of medical and psychological professions point out that both heterosexual and homosexual sexual orientations are healthy. But, if one assumes that one's development as cis-gender constitutes a healthy development (something which no one denies), can one say the same for transgender persons? At this point, we simply need to ask them. Here's Terry:

> After a few months on the hormones I started noticing remarkable changes, especially in my bipolar disorder. Before the hormones, I was taking the maximum of six medications but was still not very stable. After the hormones, I was able to drop to three. I am now more stable than I have ever been before.[58]

---

[56] Porter, *Nature as Reason*, 142-143.
[57] Porter, *Nature as Reason*, 174.
[58] Terry Dresser, "Terry's Journey," in *Transgendering Faith: Identity, Sexuality, and Spirituality*, ed. Leanne McCall Tigert and Maren C. Tirabassi (Cleveland: Pilgrim Press, 2004), 40-42, at 41.

And here is Jacob:

> My love for God grows everyday! Without God I would not be the man I am today. God has truly been beside me, guiding me through this journey. God has provided everything that I have needed in my life, and more. I am still searching for a church that will accept the whole me and not judge me because I am transgender. I have so much to give and desire to use it to glorify God, who has touched my life in such a profound way. I would not have been able to make it through all the changes in my life if I had not had Jesus to look to for help and guidance. Every step of the way he has shown himself faithful![59]

Space allows us only to provide two testimonials, but we have a lot here already. We have a natural law account that integrates sex and gender identity development—regardless of how one eventually identifies—into the virtuous life by understanding such development as a component of one's well-being. To get here, we employed the natural law methodology that is analogously operative in our explorations into phenomena in the natural world. It is a better natural law argument than the one put forward by the magisterium because it is an account that is truly *integrative* with the scientific insight of the day, rather than resistant to it. This feature alone strengthens its value as a natural law argument to the extent that one does not have to posit an opposition between what one identifies as a revelation and one what identifies as a deliverance of reason. But it is also a better natural law argument than the one put forward by the magisterium because one does not have to put excessive interpretative weight on passages out of Genesis 1 and 2 that are not able to sustain an argument in favor of gender essentialism. In its place, a natural law argument like the one outlined here could find more vibrant places to look in scripture to achieve the "harmony" between Scripture and Tradition. Instead of Genesis as the scriptural site for understanding one's gender journey, one could take the various motifs offered by examining the life of discipleship, where one follows Jesus in order to discover one's true identity.[60] And last, one can even see how living into one sex and gender identity can be integrated into the Church's virtue tradition insofar as such a journey can be understood as a journey to the virtue of chastity. If one turns in the *Catechism* to the section on the sixth commandment—that is, the one against adultery where all the sexual sins are generally gathered (*Catechism* 2331-2359)—one finds that the heart of the section is not its condemnations, but is, in fact, its exhortation to the development of chastity. At 2337, chastity is defined as "the successful integration

---

[59] Jacob Nash, "My Life Story," in *Transgendering Faith,* 67-70, at 70.
[60] See also Justin Tanis, *Trans-gendered: Theology, Ministry, and Communities of Faith* (Cleveland: Pilgrim Press, 2003), 55-84.

of sexuality within the person and thus the inner unity of man in his bodily and spiritual being." When one is able to drop a gender essentialist lens in one's interpretation of sex and gender identity, one can see how one's exploration of sex and gender can in fact allow one to become more chaste—to encounter the world as a sexual being who is unified, integrated, and who exhibits praiseworthy well-being.

In addition to giving a natural law argument, I also believe that I am giving a genuinely *queer* argument as well. The impulse of this argument is to continue the counterhegemonic tradition of queer thought by pointing a beam of hospitality towards that which is unknown, towards that which is potentially strange and unsettling. Indeed, on the account offered here, one does not need to posit a preexisting natural identity that one was "born with"—as came into vogue with, for example, lesbian and gay rights—in order to legitimately manifest an identity. Instead, this account emphasizes the *journey towards an identity*, without predetermining which identities count, including those identities that are fully chosen without any recourse to a "born this way" rationale.[61] In this way, this account can speak—and I hope *helpfully* speak—to all experiences: to the experiences of transgender persons, asexual persons, genderqueer persons, and questioning persons, not only to the experiences of lesbians, gays, and heterosexuals who have had access to "born this way" justifications for their public visibility.[62] Indeed, if any identity is presumed, it is only

---

[61] As witnessed, for example, in the case of Siân Taylder, "Shot from Both Sides: Theology and the Woman Who Isn't Quite What She Seems," in *Trans/Formations*, ed. Marcella Althaus-Reid and Lisa Isherwood (London: SCM Press, 2009), 70-91.

[62] Indeed, it is, in part, because he relies on this paradigm that David Cloutier's discussion of transgender identity is misguided (in "The Church and Transgender Identity"[see note 40 above]). Essentially extending the magisterium's argument, Cloutier writes, "By contrast, the widespread stability of sex/gender congruence [by which he means 'cisgender'] is far more robustly supported by scientific evidence than is the claim of a fundamental transgender identity." By positing a "transgender identity," he makes the legitimacy of transgender lives depend on whether they can mimic the "born this way" discourse that lesbians and gays have been able to successfully mobilize politically. Rather than question the paradigm, he weaponizes it against transgender persons, by representing them as the latest in a line of "gnostic dualists" who say that "identity is matter of free expression of an internal sense…regardless of his or her embodiment." See above at n. 54 for a response to this unreflective use of 'embodiment.' On the dangers on relying on "born this way" discourse in order to justify identity, see Eve Kosofky Sedgwick, "How to Bring Your Kids Up Gay," in *Fear of a Queer Planet: Queer Politics and Social Theory*, ed. Michael Warner (Minneapolis: University of Minnesota Press, 1993), 69-81. Also, Butler, "Undiagnosing Gender," in *Undoing Gender*, 75-101. On the need for hospitality towards transgender persons as they discover who they are becoming, see Susannah Cornwall, "Apophasis and Ambiguity: The 'Unknowingness' of Transgender," in *Trans/Formations,* 13-40. There are, of course, legitimate ethical worries: what of people who *become* an identity that is problematic—perhaps an identity as a pedophile? That, perhaps mercifully,

that of a seeker. The rest I leave to our personal experiences of conscience, of community, and of the various ways in which we investigate the phenomenon of human life, scientifically, philosophically, or otherwise: What sort of beings are we? What are we like?

And what better place to undertake such an investigation along the lines outlined here of a queer natural law theology of exploration than in our schools—the precise places where we are developing and growing into the identities into which God is allowing us, indeed *moving us*, to become? If the argument given here is convincing, then we have the theological grounds for creating polices that provide spaces for transgender students to explore who they are—from everything from providing the proper facilities for them as they explore, to offering classes that provide accurate sex and gender education. The prudence of administrators in Catholic schools will, of course, be required in a political climate like the one described at the beginning of this essay. Moreover, this framework also provides a theological argument for why the Sisters of Mercy acted justly in refusing to fire one of their transgender instructors: indeed, in view of Stein-Bodenheimer's human dignity as a seeker, it would have been positively immoral to fire him simply because he reached a point of being willing to share the results of that journey with others. This framework also provides a theological argument for moving beyond a revisionist theological conversation that has largely been centered on correcting gender complementarity to the neglect of gender essentialism. By critiquing gender essentialism, we are being more truly responsive to our natural law methodology, and in so doing, we make our moral theology more open, more non-exclusive. And lastly, by offering a constructive argument after showing the pitfalls of the magisterial position, this queer natural law framework may be one that helps save the life of a transgender teenager considering suicide because of the message she hears from ministers and from other church officials—even if it was too late in coming for Leelah. M

---

is a conversation for another day. But the answer involves an account—which I believe is possible to give—of the relationship between queerness and community that, by necessity, brings into being a conversation about norms.

Hooking Up, Contraceptive Scripts, and Catholic Social Teaching

Kari-Shane Davis Zimmerman and Jason King

IN HER 2010 ARTICLE, KARI-SHANE DAVIS Zimmerman wrote, "Given the current 'unhooked' dating practices of today's young men and women, it becomes ever more pressing that moral theologians address the issue of sex and contraception outside of the marital relationship."[1] Seven years later as we near the fiftieth anniversary of *Humanae Vitae*, we believe more work on this issue remains. Therefore, in this paper, we would like to take up this task of discussing "the issue of sex and contraception outside of the marital relationship" by attending to two tasks. First, we seek to address contraception use in American college hookup culture. As our research suggests, a complicated portrait exists, and there are new issues moral theologians ought to be attending to inside the classroom and within the field of sexual ethics. Second, we offer a way forward that can be used in classrooms and other settings that has served us well as we seek to expand both the ways in which twentysomethings approach the issue of contraception specifically and sexual activity more broadly speaking, as well as how they develop and engage their own moral compass when faced with complex decision-making.

We have chosen the context of college hookup culture for this discussion as it suggests two key aspects about contraceptive use outside of marital relationship.[2] First, how college students use contraception

---

[1] Kari-Shane Davis Zimmerman, "Hooking Up: Sex, Theology and Today's 'Unhooked' Dating Practices," *Horizons* 37, no. 1 (2010): 72-91, 90.
[2] Admittedly, this discussion brackets questions of contraceptive use as a prophylaxis. We have done so in the belief that it helps us better identify the social dynamics operative in hookup culture. Based on works like Emily Reimer-Barry's *Catholic Theology of Marriage in the Era of HIV and AIDS: Marriage for Life* (Lexington: Lexington Books, 2015), especially chapter 6, and Mary Jo Iozzio, Elsie Miranda, Mary Doyle Roche, *Calling for Justice Throughout the World: Catholic Women Theologians on the HIV/AIDS Pandemic* (New York: Continuum, 2008) however, we imagine that the positions of vulnerability and privilege shaping students' decisions about the use of contraception would similarly shape the use of contraception as prophylaxis. While supporting this claim would require additional research and a different essay, it would reinforce our argument that a Catholic Social Justice framework is needed to adequately analyze contraceptive use.

reveals some important social forces at play when students make decisions about hooking up. In particular, we argue students' decisions about contraception use are tied to positions of power and privilege or weakness and marginalization within hookup culture. Second, as a result, college hookup culture calls forth a Catholic Social Justice framework for dealing with contraceptive use outside of marriage. Specifically, and in response to the issues of power, the context calls forth the Catholic Social Teaching values of dignity and solidarity.

This essay proceeds in the following way. First, we look at the current context of hooking up and the role contraception plays in this. Research suggests a dynamic not so much about personal choice but rather about power and marginalization. Second, we discuss how this context raises such kinds of problems as objectification and conformity and thus calls forth the need for a discussion on dignity and solidarity. Third, we indicate how these issues can be addressed in the classroom. Particularly, by leading with a discussion of Natural Family Planning, we believe one can open up conversation about the operative social forces at play and so enter into a broader dialogue that is not so much about the specific use of contraception or Natural Family Planning but rather about how one can make responsible decisions in the light of certain power dynamics at play within hookup culture that can affect anyone.

HOOKUP CULTURES AND CONTRACEPTIVE USE

Before we begin, let us mention two things that are needed to understand contraceptive use within hookup culture. First, as Jason King recently argues, there is not one or "a" hookup culture operating on college campuses, but rather there are four hookup cultures.[3] Each of these cultures establishes the meaning of hooking up, and we argue that each sets the context for contraceptive use. Second is the idea of a script. Technically, a script is "a cognitive schematic structure—a mental road map—containing the basic actions (and their temporal and causal relations) that comprise a complex action."[4] More simply put, scripts are mental structures that people rely upon to know how to see, judge, and act. They provide possible courses of actions that are acceptable for particular contexts.[5] Thus, scripts are not pure abstractions but rather social guides. They indicate what is typical and expected, what is acceptable and possible, and what is objectionable

---

[3] Jason King, *Faith with Benefits* (Oxford University Press, 2017), 5-17.
[4] "Script, Definition 2," in Gary R. Vandenbos, ed., *APA Dictionary of Psychology*, (Washington, DC: American Psychological Association, 2007), p. 820.
[5] See *The Complete Dictionary of Sexology* (New York, NY: Continuum, 1995), s. v. "Script": "a repertoire of acts and statuses that are recognize by a social group, together with the rules, expectations and sanctions governing these acts and statuses."

and discouraged. They are less moral guides and more social expectations about how to function in a particular setting. The more people understand the social context, the more people know what scripts to employ and what ones to avoid. To understand contraceptive use in hookup culture, one needs to understand how different contraceptive scripts are operative in different hookup cultures. To that task we now turn.

The first kind of hookup culture operating is referred to by King as *"stereotypical"* hookup culture. It is what most students and researchers assume to be the norm on all college campuses for all students. Students in this category hookup without expectations of anything afterwards, and they do so frequently. However, far from being the statistical norm, it is actually the culture of a select few, around 25% of students.[6] Typically, these young men and women are white and wealthy[7] and, if available, belong to fraternities and sororities.[8] In other words, they tend to be the most privileged students on a campus.

Within *stereotypical* hookup culture, men lean towards not using contraception because they tend to employ a "no contraception" script. Their positions of power, from gender, race, and class, usually mean they need not be concerned about contraception. In "Sexual Esteem in Emerging Adulthood," Megan Maas and Eva Lefkowitz explain, "Through the lens of hegemonic masculinity, men are more privileged sexually and therefore can insist on experiencing pleasure and passion over responsibility."[9] Moreover, their position of power gives them confidence, an attribute associated with "never using contraception during recent penetrative sex."[10]

Yet, the same does not hold true for most of the white women who are a part of *stereotypical* hookup culture. Their contraceptive script differs. Even though they too may have racial and socio-economic privilege, they lack gender privilege. Thus, women in this group tend to use something like the pill or IUD and thus plan their contraception

---

[6] See Caroline Heldman and Lisa Wade "Hook-Up Culture: Setting a New Research Agenda," *Sexuality Research and Social Policy* 7, no. 4 (2010): 323-333, 324, and Megan Manthos, Jesse Owen, and Frank Fincham, "A New Perspective on Hooking Up Among College Students," *Journal of Social and Personal Relationships* 31, no. 6 (2014): 815-829, 824.

[7] Jesse J. Owen, Galena K. Rhoades, Scott M. Stanley, and Frank D. Fincham, "'Hooking Up' Among College Students: Demographic and Pyschosocial Correlates," *Archives of Sexual Behavior* 39, no. 3 (2010): 653-663.

[8] Mark Regnerus and Jeremy Uecker, *Premarital Sex in America: How Young Americans Meet, Mate, and Think about Marrying* (New York: Oxford University Press, 2011), 104.

[9] Megan Maas and Eva Lefkowitz, "Sexual Esteem in Emerging Adulthood: Associations with Sexual Behavior, Contraception Use, and Romantic Relationships," *Journal of Sex Research* 52, no.7 (2015): 795-806, 802.

[10] Maas and Lefkowitz, "Sexual Esteem in Emerging Adulthood," 802.

use ahead of time.[11] According to Maas and Lefkowitz, this should not come as a surprise given that since the invention of hormonal birth control in the late 1960s "the responsibility for contraception has predominantly been delegated to women."[12] In her 2008 book *Unhooked*, Laura Sessions Stepp notes that, since the 1960s women have been told to succeed and have done so, they often have to do so by playing just like men "play."[13] In *stereotypical* hookup culture, this means hooking up without expectations of a relationship. However, it also means that they need to attend to contraception to do so.

In contrast to the above, most students do not embrace *stereotypical* hookup culture but rather a second culture, a *relationship* hookup culture. These students make up a large majority of students on college campuses. While many in this cohort know that hooking up is not supposed to include any subsequent relationship expectations, they indirectly work against this assumption by using hooking up as a way into a relationship. In their 2012 essay "Sexual Hookup Culture", Justin Garcia and his fellow authors found that not only did most people hope for a relationship—65% of women and 45% of men—many people even talked about it—51% of women and 42% of men.[14] Regarding positions of power and privilege, students operating within *relationship* hookup culture tend to be in the middle. They are not the highly privileged; therefore they do not control the social norms of hookup culture. However, they rarely experience social marginalization because of race, sexual orientation, or religiosity. Thus, while many feel like they need to participate in hookup culture in order to establish a personal relationship, they also feel like they can subtly alter its terms.

Men and women in *relationship* hookup culture tend not to plan for contraception use in advance. They have a habit of employing a "spontaneous contraception" script. While those in long-term relationships usually employ reliable and long-term contraception methods, those who are in *relationship* hookup culture are hooking up as a way into relationships but are not yet in a relationship. They are not looking

---

[11] Karen Ingersoll, Sherry Dyche Ceperich, Mary Nettlemen, and Betty Anne Johnson, "Risk Drinking and Contraception Effectiveness Among College Women," *Psychology and Health* 23, no. 8 (2008): 965-981, 976-977; Jinhyung Lee, Abbey Berenson, Pooja Patel, "Characteristics of Females Who use Contraception at Coitarche: An Analysis of the National Survey of Family Growth 2006-2010 Database," *Journal of Women's Health* 24, no. 12 (2015): 972-977, 973; Maas and Lefkowitz, "Sexual Esteem in Emerging Adulthood," 802; Caroline Free, Jane Ogden, and Ray Lee, "Young Women's Contraception Use as a Contextual and Dynamic Behavior: A Qualitative Study," *Psychology and Health* 20, no. 5 (2005): 673-690, 687-688.
[12] Maas and Lefkowitz, "Sexual Esteem in Emerging Adulthood," 802.
[13] Laura Sessions Stepp, *Unhooked: How Young Women Pursue Sex, Delay Love and Lose at Both* (New York: Riverhead Books, 2007), 36.
[14] Justin Garcia, Chris Reiber, Sean Massey, and Ann Merriwether, "Sexual Hookup Culture: A Review," *Review of General Psychology* 16, no. 2 (2012): 161-176, 167-168.

for an anonymous hookup but a way into something more, something that could lead to a relationship. Within this context, they are *not* typically looking for intercourse and thus do not plan for it. When they do hookup however, the sexual activity is often impulsive, so they employ one of three spontaneous contraceptive scripts. First is the use of the condom. However, as some students' sexual activity progresses toward penetrative sex, they often hesitate to stop and discuss contraception for fear of "ruining the 'mood.'"[15] Thus, a second option sometimes chosen by men and women in this large middle is actually the use of no contraception. Third and finally, in order to avoid pregnancy altogether, some will employ an alternative form of contraception: oral or anal sex.[16] This last option has been growing in prominence as men and women "evaluate oral sex as having fewer social, emotional, and health risks, judge oral sex to be more acceptable in dating and non-dating relationships; and consider oral sex less threatening to their values and beliefs than penetrative sex."[17]

A third hookup culture is an *anti-hookup culture*. While it might seem strange to name *not* hooking up as a hookup culture, it is a culture that exists in opposition to *stereotypical* hookup culture. Although not the majority of students, these men and women are a substantive minority, approximately 20% on any given campus.[18] These students tend not to hookup and so find themselves on the fringes of campus life, socially vulnerable and marginalized. These students tend to be racial minorities, those of the lower economic class,[19] members of the LGBTQ community,[20] and those who are highly religiously committed.[21]

The students who find themselves in this context do not hookup and therefore do not resort to using contraception. They utilize a "no contraception" script. The reasons for this vary however. Racial minorities tend not to participate in hooking up because they feel like

---

[15] Sally Brown and Kate Guthrie, "Why Don't Teenagers use Contraception? A Qualitative Interview Study," *The European Journal of Contraception and Reproductive Health Care* 15 (2010): 197-204, 197.
[16] See Heldman and Lisa Wade "Hook-Up Culture," 324-235. See also Maas and Lefkowitz, "Sexual Esteem in Emerging Adulthood," 802: Young men and women "evaluate oral sex as having fewer social, emotional, and health risks, judge oral sex to be more acceptable in dating and non-dating relationships; and consider oral sex less threatening to their values and beliefs than penetrative sex."
[17] Maas and Lefkowitz, "Sexual Esteem in Emerging Adulthood," 796-797.
[18] King, *Faith with Benefits*, 8-11.
[19] Brian Sweeney, "Party Animals or Responsible Men: Social Class, Race, and Masculinity on Campus," *International Journal of Qualitative Studies in Education* 27, no. 6 (2014): 804-821.
[20] Wade and Heldman, "Hooking Up and Opting Out," 130.
[21] Tina Penhollow, Michael Young, George Denny, "Impact of Personal and Organizational Religiosity on College Student Sexual Behavior," *American Journal of Health Studies* 27, no. 1 (2012): 13-22.

they are jeopardizing their college opportunity, viewing it as "a time for assuming adult responsibilities and leaving childish things behind."[22] Similarly, members of the LGBTQ community often do not participate in campus hookup culture because, being unsure if they or their homosexual activity would be welcomed where hooking up occurs, they worry about physical safety.[23] For those in the lower economic classes, cost becomes a factor in not using more reliable forms of contraception like the pill, so they typically do not hookup so they can avoid the risk.[24]

Religiously committed students' contraceptive use is a bit harder to pin down. For the most part, these students do not hookup and oppose hooking up in principle. In *Faith with Benefits*, King's research confirms this, claiming Catholic students who strongly believe that "contraception is wrong" tend to hookup less.[25] To maintain this opposition, these religious students usually form and stay within a network of students with similar beliefs. When they enter into a long-term relationship however, some become sexually active. At this stage, they most often employ hormonal contraception not only to prevent pregnancy but also to hide their sexual activity and preserve their status as a member of their religious group.[26] One can see then that even within this group of marginalized students there is evidence of fear of marginalization.[27]

Lastly, the fourth type of culture is a *coercive hookup culture*. Coercive hookup culture takes stereotypical hookup culture and attempts to legitimize the use of force in sexual activity. This is done in various ways. Some utilize gender stereotypes and cultural norms to legitimize coercion, others tap into beliefs about masculinity and rape, and still others rationalize their actions by blaming alcohol.[28] Whether through

---

[22] Sweeney, "Party Animals or Responsible Men," 817.
[23] Wade and Heldman, "Hooking Up and Opting Out," 130.
[24] Larissa Huber and Jennifer Ersek, "Contraceptive Use Among Sexually Active University Students," *Journal of Women's Health* 18, no. 7 (2009): 1063-1070.
[25] King, *Faith with Benefits*, 53-59.
[26] See Nicholas Hill, Mxolisi Siwatu, and Alexander Robinson, "'My Religion Picked My Birth Control': The Influence of Religion on Contraceptive Use," *Journal of Religious Health* 53 (2014): 825-833. See also Annie Wright, Jennifer Duffy, Sarah Kershner, Shannon Flynn, and Andrea Lamont, "New Opportunities in Teen Pregnancy Prevention: Identifying Individual and Environmental Differences Between Youth Who Abstain, Use Contraception, and Use No Contraception," *Journal of Community Psychology* 43, no. 8 (2015): 931-953, 949-950.
[27] Nicholas Bowman and Jenny Small, "Do College Students Who Identify with a Privileged Religion Experience Greater Spiritual Development? Exploring Individual and Institutional Dynamics," *Research in Higher Education* 51 (2010): 595-614.
[28] See Matthew Hogben, Donn Byrne, Merle E. Hamburger, and Julie Osland, "Legitimized Aggression and Sexual Coercion: Individual Differences in Cultural Spillover," *Aggressive Behavior* 27 (2001): 26-43; Laina Y. Bay-Cheng and Rebecca K. Eliseo-Arras, "The Making of Unwanted Sex: Gendered and Neoliberal Norms in College Women's Unwanted Sexual Experiences," *Journal of Sex Research* 45, no. 4

one of these means or some other, perpetrators' legitimation of the violence enables the rampant sexual assault on college campuses, a coercive hookup culture. According to the Center for Disease Control, 20% of women in college experience completed or attempted rape, and 85% percent of these assailants are known, usually boyfriends, ex-boyfriends, or classmates.[29] Those who are assaulted do not have a choice over the situation and so often cannot employ contraception.[30] Albeit for slightly different reasons, this culture has a "no contraceptive" script like the anti-hookup culture.

THE NEED FOR HUMAN DIGNITY AND SOLIDARITY

The abovementioned survey of hookup cultures and contraceptive scripts within them indicates that viewing contraception simply in a narrow framework of pregnancy prevention cannot adequately account for the multiplicity of meanings attached to contraceptive use. In her original article, Davis Zimmerman applies the concept of a "contraceptive mentality" to help explain these power dynamics within hookup culture. First, she argues the contraceptive mentality that emerges within hookup culture is a view of one's hookup partner as "an object of sexual gratification; the body is merely something to be consumed (devoured almost) and then immediately discarded (or spit out again)."[31] In other words, persons become objectified in a hookup, viewed not as human beings but rather things to be used and manipulated for one's own sexual gratification. The contraceptive scripts within hookup culture suggest one reason why this kind of manipulation can happen. Persons with power and privilege can more easily disregard the impact of their sexual activity upon others, and, as a result, they can disregard their contraception use. Therefore, white, wealthy men tend not to use contraception, and those coercing others not only do not use contraception but also prevent others from choosing it by their very actions. Far from concerns about openness to life,

---

(2008): 386-397; Sarah R. Edwards and David L. Vogel, "Young Men's Likelihood Ratings to Be Sexually Aggressive as a Function of Norms and Perceived Sexual Interest," *Psychology of Men and Masculinity* 16, no. 1 (2015): 88-96.

[29] Center for Disease Control, "Understanding Sexual Violence (2014 Fact Sheet)," https://www.cdc.gov/violenceprevention/pdf/sv-factsheet.pdf.

[30] See Eve Walternaurer, Helene Doleyres, Robert Bednarczyk, and Louise-Anne McNutt, "Emergency Contraception Considerations and use Among College Women," *Journal of Women's Health* 22, no. 2 (2013): 141-146. Women who find themselves vulnerable, even in cases where there is no threat or assault, will often not employ contraception as they assume "contingency and indeterminacy as central to the reproductive experience"; see Don Seeman, Iman Roushdy-Hammady, Annie Hardison-Moody, Winnifred Thompson, Laura Gaydos, Carol Rowland Hogue, "Blessing Unintended Pregnancy: Religion and the Discourse of Women's Agency in Public Health," *Medical Anthropology Theory* 3, no. 1 (2016): 29-54.

[31] Davis Zimmerman, "Hooking Up," 89.

this non-contraceptive use is hostile to life—one turns the other into an object of sexual gratification, regardless of the effects on the other.

Second, Davis Zimmerman contends the contraceptive mentality "contributes to the development of an abbreviated anthropology" that pressures all to conform to the "physically indifferent and psychologically unattached" mentality of those in privileged positions.[32] In other words, those who dominate the culture not only objectify others, but they also have a social influence that pressures others to conform or, at least, comply with their mentality (at least in outward appearance). Others must approach the world as the privileged do. Thus, it is not just that certain individuals are "indifferent" and "unattached" but that the whole culture assumes this "abbreviated anthropology" as the norm for everyone.

This type of pressure to comply with the "abbreviated anthropology" can be seen in two different ways people experience marginalization *within* hookup culture. First, white, wealthy women participating in stereotypical hookup culture experience a kind of marginalization. As explained above, these women tend to choose planned forms of contraception both to participate in hookup culture and to protect themselves from white, privileged men who fail to concern themselves with contraception. Similarly, those who hookup in pursuit of a relationship can experience marginalization. They feel the pressure to conform to the expectations of hookup culture; therefore, they resort to using spontaneous means of contraception, condoms or oral and anal sex, as a way to protect themselves within the system. The exceptions prove the rule. Those who are sexually coerced would chose means to protect themselves but have had this choice hindered or revoked, while those who hookup and unexpectedly move to sexual intercourse will not use contraception in order to preserve the "mood" and thus comply with the dominant norms of stereotypical hookup culture.

A second group of students can be marginalized by being *pushed out* of the system all together for not complying with the "abbreviated anthropology." These students tend to be the highly religious, racial minorities, members of the LGBTQ community, and the economically disadvantaged. While they tend to employ a "no contraception" script, the choice has little to do with preventing conception. Being outside of the system, they take measures to protect themselves, but they are done for their own safety and security. Thus, they tend not to participate in hookup culture, and not using contraception is more the result of not participating. Here too, the exception proves the rule. Highly religious students will employ contraception to preserve their status amongst their peers, choosing to hide their sexual activity in order to conform to the expectations of their group. If one wants to preserve the openness to life that has guided traditional church discourse on

---

[32] Davis Zimmerman, "Hooking Up," 89.

contraception, then we need an approach that also can address the objectification of others and the pressure to conform to an abbreviated anthropology. We argue at least two additional principles must be added: human dignity and solidarity.

First, the notion of human dignity needs to be included in the conversation about contraception in order to respond to the problem of objectification found in hookup culture. The tradition of Catholic Social Teaching argues every human being has an inherent dignity. They are of "equal value" and have a relationship with God, being made in God's image and having a "capacity for God" (*Compendium of the Social Doctrine of the Church*, no. 109-110). This notion of dignity speaks out against the mistreatment of those who are marginalized within hookup culture. The privileged feel free to disregard the effects of their actions upon others, and this lack of concern turns the marginalized into "objects of sexual gratification." Human dignity enables the evaluation of contraceptive use by examining how it can contribute to the instrumentalizing of others, especially the marginalized who are more susceptible to being harmed in hookup culture.[33]

Second, the notion of solidarity is also needed in discussions of contraception to help mitigate the pressure to conform to the "abbreviated anthropology" of hookup culture. Solidarity more broadly speaking refers to that "bond of interdependence between individuals and people," the truth that "we are all really responsible for all," and the "willingness to give oneself for the good of one's neighbor, beyond any individual or particular interest" (*Compendium of the Social Doctrine of the Church*, nos. 192-194). In short, solidarity is about a system of relationships that does not leave people out of community life. Put differently, solidarity implies attending to the reasons for exclusion and working to undo them. Without this category of social analysis, moral theology's discussion of contraceptive use will fail to attend to who is excluded and why, remaining unable to speak about the pressure to fit into hookup culture that guides the choice to use contraception and the social exclusion that renders using contraception pointless.

Together, dignity and solidarity not only address the situation of the vulnerable within hookup culture, but they also have the power to transform the actions taken by the privileged. For example, these concepts can help wealthy, white men understand how hookup culture damages them. As Donna Freitas argues in *The End of Sex*, men face an "emotional glass ceiling." She writes, "We ask that they repress their feelings surrounding their own vulnerabilities and need for love, respect, and relationship so intensely that we've convinced them that to express feeling is to have somehow failed as men; that to express

---

[33] This point echoes Margret Farley's principle of "Do No Unjust Harm" in *Just Love: A Framework for Christian Sexual Ethics* (New York: Continuum, 2006), 216-218.

such feeling not only makes them look bad in front of other men, but in front of women, too."[34] White men grow up hearing, visualizing, and thus internalizing these cultural assumptions that at the heart of their masculinity lies sexual performance and an absence of emotion.[35] They adopt a self-inflicted objectification that neither values their dignity beyond their sexual activity nor allows for solidarity by disparaging emotions. It strips men down to their mere physical existence. If those with power and privilege grasp this self-inflicted damage along with the damage done to the more vulnerable, they can contribute to and thereby hasten the demise of this troubling culture.

Moral theologians stand in a unique position to help both the marginalized and the privileged. Hookup culture's objectification of the body stands in stark contrast to the view of the body put forth by Scripture where the body is a temple to be nourished and cared for and by tradition that values the body through its teaching on the incarnation and resurrection. Moral theologians not only have these resources at their disposal but also the principles of human dignity and solidarity found in Catholic social teaching. To help students appropriate these principles though, they need some way to dislodge the norms of hookup culture. Without this element of moral analysis, the use or non-use of contraception will be inadequately analyzed, failing to account for the ways in which using contraception can protect one's vulnerability and non-use can result from coercion and violence.

TEACHING NATURAL FAMILY PLANNING

One way to get at the values of human dignity and solidarity into the thought processes of college students is by discussing Natural Family Planning (NFP) in the classroom. While NFP is consistent with the teaching of the Catholic church and, as a result, safe and easy to teach on a Catholic campus, this is not why we recommend it. We are advancing it as a pedagogical technique that can open up conversations about the social dynamics at play within hookup culture. This is because NFP presents a different perspective on human sexual relationships because it is so far removed from the typical assumptions about contraception and so very foreign to hookup culture's view of the human person and human body. Thus, teaching NFP challenges the idea that contraception and hooking up are just "the way things are" and so generates a critical examination of this assumption. It does this in three important ways.

---

[34] Donna Freitas, *The End of Sex: How Hookup Culture is Leaving a Generation Unhappy, Sexually Unfulfilled and Confused About Intimacy* (New York: Basic Books, 2013), 115.

[35] Freitas, *The End of Sex*, 100. For a similar view, see Michael Kimmel, *Guyland: The Perilous World Where Boys Become Men* (New York: HarperCollins Publishers, 2008).

First, NFP begins with a discussion of correct biological knowledge as to when and how the sexual act can produce new human life. For some, it will serve as a refresher course from middle school health classes. For others, it will be the first time they have participated in a discussion regarding "female signs of fertility."[36] In either case, it assumes that, if one is going to engage in any sexual act, both persons must be "biologically knowledgeable" of a woman's stage of fertility and infertility. This starting point presumes an equality and respect between men and women as it requires an "information balance." Men, and not just women, have to understand human sexual biology in general and of women in particular. Put differently, teaching NFP builds a foundation of human dignity and solidarity between the sexes because it makes students more knowledgeable about human beings and their biological processes, especially women who are so frequently marginalized in hookup culture.

Second, teaching NFP and its implicit challenge to the assumed norm of hooking up and contraception creates space for students from the margins to participate and speak. They no longer need to feel fearful or isolated because they hold a differing or a minority position, as a differing and minority position already has been put forward in NFP. Thus, the silent minorities can be encouraged to use their voices. The highly religious can more easily speak up in favor of the practice because it has been introduced as basic "biological information" and a legitimate alternative. Women in the classroom can confront the assumption (implicit or explicit) that they are responsible for contraception and men are not, thus tackling the issues of power and privilege. The traditional connection of sex and procreation can be discussed as this is presumed in NFP, and this connection can also be challenged as not using contraception can be a way that people exercise their privilege over others. As NFP has opened the door to challenging norms, those of the LGBTQ community can raise questions about the applicability of NFP to their experiences, as both outsiders and, in some instances, less concerned about pregnancy. In each of these cases, students are encouraged to speak up for their views because the normativity of hookup culture has been destabilized. The result is openings to discuss alternative perspectives, especially those on the margins of hookup culture.

---

[36] For the lack of sexual knowledge in college students see Erin Moore and William Smith, "What college student do not know: where are the gaps in sexual healthy knowledge?" *Journal of American College Health* 60, no. 6 (2012): 436-442, 436 and Jean Claude Martin and Jennifer Y. Mak, "College Students' Sexual Knowledge and Attitudes," *Kentucky Association of Health, Physical Education, Recreation and Dance* 51, no. 1 (2013): 16-25, 17-18.

Finally, leading with NFP enables further conversation about solidarity and what it truly means to pursue a healthy personal relationship. As we have indicated all along, one significant problem with hookup culture is the assumption that everyone must be like or comply with the preferences of the wealthy, white male. It is the pervasiveness of the "abbreviated anthropology" model or in students' minds the idea that "everyone is doing it." This dominance shuts down conversation and makes students fearful and confused about how to talk about and pursue healthy personal relationships.[37] NFP fosters conversations about sexual activity and so fosters communication about relationships. As Julie Hanlon Rubio notes in her "Beyond the Liberal/Conservative Divide on Contraception," NFP can foster a relationship that is not ordered hierarchically, with one receiving and one giving, but one of reciprocity and respect.[38] Based on the testimonies of practitioners, Rubio noted that NFP has the potential for "an increased capacity for total self-giving, growth in mutuality, better communication, higher levels of intimacy, increased sexual pleasure and spiritual growth."[39] The point here is not that this inevitably occurs or to advocate for NFP as an entry way into these kinds of relationships. Rather, noting this testimony and the experience of those practicing NFP reveals to students a different kind of relationship between persons who are (or planning to be) sexually active than that found in hookup culture. Instead of shame, mistrust, fear, lack of vulnerability and authenticity, or the white, wealthy male focus on sexual performance and being unfeeling, NFP proposes a relationship of communication, biological awareness, mutuality, and consideration of the consequences of choices. NFP seeks to consider the whole person and the relationship, the opposite of the "abbreviated anthropology" at the heart of hookup culture. By introducing this aspect that NFP implies, students can then begin to think more clearly and critically about their connections with people in general and their personal relationships in particular, regardless of their actual acceptance of NFP.

CONCLUSION

In this paper, we have attempted to complicate the portrait of hookup culture because research suggests there is not one hookup culture but several hookup cultures operating on any given college campus. Moreover, within those hookup cultures, contraception use var-

---

[37] Olga Khazan, "Why College Students Need a Class in Dating," *The Atlantic*, June 2, 2014, www.theatlantic.com/education/archive/2014/07/why-todays-college-students-need-a-class-on-dating/373823/.
[38] Julie Hanlon Rubio, "Beyond the Liberal/Conservative Divide on Contraception," *Horizons* 32, no. 2 (2005): 270-294.
[39] Rubio, "Beyond the Liberal/Conservative Divide on Contraception," 277.

ies, and what is evident is that power and privilege, as well as marginalization and feelings of vulnerability, shape students' actions. Because such a complicated portrait exists, we contend more work remains in helping students think critically about their and others' possible sexual activity outside of the marriage context. We therefore propose adding the principles of human dignity and solidarity to the discussion to have a more adequate analysis of the use and non-use of contraception within American college hookup culture. These principles help illuminate the dynamics of power and privilege, as well as weakness and vulnerability, which often guide the contraceptive choices young men and women make within hookup culture. Lastly, we contend that teaching NFP can, by challenging the presumed norms of hookup culture and contraception, reinforce the importance of dignity and solidarity for students and their relationships. Doing so, we hope, provides a way for students to make wise decisions about sexual activity and the use of contraception in the context of college hookup culture. **M**

Youth, Leisure, and Discernment in an Overscheduled Age

Timothy P. Muldoon
Suzanne M. Muldoon

THE 2018 SYNOD OF BISHOPS, ON THE theme of youth and vocational discernment, has offered an "opportune time," a *kairos*, for reflection on the question of how the predominating culture of the United States influences children and adolescents in their process of discernment. This essay uses that *kairos* to raise a particular question about a prerequisite for discernment, namely the leisure time that allows for young imaginations to unfold in freedom. It begins with a question: how ought parents and other caregivers of children respond to the time pressures that affect childhood? It presupposes that discernment is a process that unfolds in freedom; involves the use of imagination; and leads, over time, to life decisions that coalesce in a vocational journey. Hence the question about overscheduling children is fundamentally a question about how U.S. culture affords youth the freedom to develop the practices that are constitutive of a discerning life.

Our analysis begins with international and national agencies who have raised concerns about young people's access to leisure, particularly unscheduled free play, in our age. It points to the particular benefits of free play in comparison to goods that arise from scheduled leisure time, especially youth sports, and asks questions about the decline of free play in the United States. This analysis offers a window into a predominant social imaginary governed by economic questions and their impact on youth, and so we turn to the philosopher Charles Taylor and his exploration of the development of modern social imaginaries as a hermeneutic for understanding this decline. We then turn in the latter part of the essay to consideration of larger questions for Christian discernment, relying on a theological exploration of leisure.

YOUTH AND THE RIGHT TO LEISURE

In recent decades, national and international agencies have highlighted leisure as a fundamental right of youth. Article 31 of the United Nations' Convention on the Rights of the Child (1990), for example, calls on states to protect the rights of children to leisure time:

> 1. States Parties recognize the right of the child to rest and leisure, to engage in play and recreational activities appropriate to the age of the child and to participate freely in cultural life and the arts.
>
> 2. States Parties shall respect and promote the right of the child to participate fully in cultural and artistic life and shall encourage the provision of appropriate and equal opportunities for cultural, artistic, recreational and leisure activity.[1]

Similarly, the UN's World Programme of Action for Youth on Leisure-Time Activities articulated its position (1995) this way:

> The importance of leisure-time activities in the psychological, cognitive and physical development of young people is recognized in all societies. Leisure-time activities include games, sports, cultural events, entertainment and community service.[2]

Already by the 1990s, it was becoming apparent to international child advocates that several dynamics impinged on children's access to leisure. Over the next decade, a particular focus of attention at the international level was on digital technology. In 2005, the UN Department of Economic and Social Affairs (UNDESA) World Youth Report raised particular concern for what they called "information and communication technology" or ICT— this, of course, in the still-early days of the Internet and before the use of smartphones. From the mid-nineties to 2005, they write, there was a shift in perception about leisure time activities. They noted the rise of a "global media-driven youth culture," which changed patterns of socialization and had an impact on youth leisure time activities.

> In the traditional view, leisure time is simply seen as "free time", but there has been a growing awareness of the vital contribution discretionary time can make to a young person's social inclusion, access to opportunities and overall development.[3]

They raised concerns about cuts in government spending on leisure programs for youth, highlighting the goods that such programs can cultivate in young people: physical health, development of a positive self-concept, teamwork, and greater commitment to volunteerism, to name a few. They also expressed concern that ICT is making leisure

---

[1] United Nations Office of the High Commissioner, "Convention on the Rights of the Child," http://www.ohchr.org/EN/ProfessionalInterest/Pages/CRC.aspx.
[2] United Nations Division for Social Policy and Development, "Leisure-time Activities," https://www.un.org/development/desa/youth/leisure-time-activities-wpay.html.
[3] United Nations Department of Economic and Social Affairs, "Part II: Youth and Civil Society: The Emergence of a Media-Driven Youth Culture," *World Youth Report 2005*, http://www.un.org/esa/socdev/unyin/documents/wyr05part2.pdf.

time more sedentary and more individualized, thereby compromising some of its benefits. A particular target of their study is the emergence of youth-focused marketing since the Second World War, and the emergence of a youth culture as a result of new forms of communication and consumption.

One area of research which underscored this kind of change was the work done in Fiji by Anne Becker and her colleagues. Their 2002 study was a wake-up call about the extent to which television could contribute to disordered eating among a "media-naive" population—namely, those to whom television was a new medium.[4] The study, along with a follow up 2011 study, offered some clues as to the extent of the influence of media exposure on disordered eating and, by extension, the power of media to shape adolescent social networking.[5] Becker began surveying adolescent girls almost immediately after TV was introduced on the island, seeking to understand the way that contributed to the reshaping of attitudes toward body image. What her research showed was that the new medium had a marked effect on adolescent girls, with hours dedicated to television consumption that negatively affected body image and socialization.

The Becker studies, along with many others, have lent credence to the concerns raised by UNDESA about the cultural reshaping of leisure time for youth. More recently, the World Assembly of Youth, the international coordinating body of national youth councils and organizations, has underscored the importance of policymaking and social support for youth leisure, in order to push back against the decrease of physical activity they see as a consequence of youth media culture. They write:

> In every culture, there are hours in the day when young people are not formally required to be in school or engaged in household or paid work.... These hours, these activities, and often even these programs are considered discretionary. They are viewed as optional nice but not necessary, or even particularly important. These are the hours, the activities and the programs whose absence or disappearance would not be noticed by policy makers but would be very much felt by young people.[6]

---

[4] Anne E. Becker et al., "Eating Behaviours and Attitudes Following Prolonged Exposure to Television among Ethnic Fijian Adolescent Girls," *British Journal of Psychiatry* 180, no. 6 (2002): 509-14.

[5] Anne E. Becker, Kristen E. Fay, Jessica Agnew-Blais, A. Nisha Khan, Ruth H. Striegel-Moore, and Stephen E. Gilman, "Social Network Media Exposure and Adolescent Eating Pathology in Fiji," *British Journal of Psychiatry* 198, no. 1 (2011): 43-50.

[6] World Assembly of Youth, "Youth and Leisure Time Activities," http://www.way.org.my/youth-issues/youth-and-leisure-time-activities.

They point to the manifold benefits that come from a right approach to leisure—that is, an approach that enhances family bonds and promotes cognitive, identity, and social/emotional development in children. They urge governments to fund leisure activities for children as part of an overall commitment to social well-being. They further call on private sector companies and citizens to support youth leisure.

In the United States, the American Academy of Pediatrics has also, in recent years, raised particular concerns about children's leisure time. In particular, it has highlighted the decrease in time allotted to children to engage in free play, citing the UN's recognition of play as a right of every child.[7] Their report highlights various factors that have reduced play: "a hurried lifestyle, changes in family structure, and increased attention to academics and enrichment activities at the expense of recess or free child-centered play."[8] They cite a number of studies that highlight the benefits of play: development of imagination, dexterity, and physical, cognitive and emotional strength; healthy brain development; and many more. They call particular attention to free play, in contrast to play which is controlled by adults:

> Ideally, much of play involves adults, but when play is controlled by adults, children acquiesce to adult rules and concerns and lose some of the benefits play offers them, particularly in developing creativity, leadership, and group skills.[9]

They point to surveys of elementary school principals from 1989 to 1999 which showed a significant decline in the number of schools which had a recess period. They further point to the decline of free time for children that came as a result of the 2001 No Child Left Behind Act, which emphasized reading and mathematics. The loss of free play time, they argue, could have long-term repercussions, due to the fact that children's cognitive abilities are enhanced by a clear change in physical activity. They even speculate that the loss of free play may exacerbate the difference in academic performance between boys and girls, since a sedentary environment may impact boys' learning styles more significantly.

The shift away from free play in the academic environment has also come during a period when parents feel pressure to find structured activities for their children from a very young age, the AAP report argues. Parents devote significant financial resources to securing opportunities for children. While many such opportunities are shown to be beneficial, they are a source of disparity between middle class and

---

[7] Kenneth R. Ginsburg, "The Importance of Play in Promoting Healthy Child Development and Maintaining Strong Parent-Child Bonds," *Pediatrics* 119, no. 1 (2007): 182-191.

[8] Ginsburg, "The Importance of Play," 182.

[9] Ginsburg, "The Importance of Play," 183.

lower-class families. They raise the question of when scheduling becomes overscheduling. "It is left to parents to judge appropriate levels of involvement, but many parents seem to feel as though they are running on a treadmill to keep up yet dare not slow their pace for fear their children will fall behind."[10] Some children show benefits of parental scheduling, but the report points to other research which suggests a connection between overscheduling and child and adolescent depression. There is not yet a direct causal link, but the authors suggest that it important to consider the possibility. They conclude that "the protection of both play and high-quality family time are negatively affected by the current trends toward highly scheduling children."[11]

Taken together, these studies over the past nearly thirty years point to widespread concerns among experts in youth culture about the decline in what might be called "healthy" leisure time. Whereas the American Academy of Pediatrics suggests that active play is so central to childhood that it ought to be part of its definition, today in wealthier communities it is being replaced by highly scheduled time, while poorer children increasingly lack access to active play altogether.[12] The question of the proper balance between structured time and free play for youth is, therefore, an important question for discernment among many stakeholders, including |parents and families, educators, and policymakers.

THE MODERN SOCIAL IMAGINARY AND LOSS OF FREE PLAY

Charles Taylor identifies elements of mass culture that shape interactions between people—elements which are antecedent to people's choices and which provide the contours within which social interactions take place. His use of the term "social imaginary" is a reference to the ways that these elements impact people's ability to imagine what kind of life is even possible in light of their perceptions about the way a society functions. He describes the social imaginary as a "vision of moral order" that made possible the development of Western society and suggests that political ties are an application or extension of this moral order.

The social imaginary provides a prescription for the way that people stand in relation to reality.[13] It conditions what people see and how they respond. It helps people to identify "features of the world, or divine action, or human life which make certain norms both right and...realizable."[14] Taylor's analysis focuses on the change in social

---

[10] Ginsburg, "The Importance of Play," 184.
[11] Ginsburg, "The Importance of Play," 184.
[12] Regina M. Milteer and Kenneth R. Ginsburg, "Maintaining Strong Parent-Child Bond: Focus on Children in Poverty," *Pediatrics* 129, no. 1 (2012): e205.
[13] Charles Taylor, *A Secular Age* (Cambridge: Harvard University Press, 2007), 162.
[14] Taylor, *A Secular Age*, 162-163.

imaginary from the sixteenth to the twenty-first century, highlighting the emergence of three key factors: the modern economy; the public sphere; and the practices of democratic self-rule.[15] These modern elements of the social imaginary, he writes, have significantly impacted the way people relate to one another, and have implications for both politics and religious belief.

Taylor suggests that the modern social imaginary departs from hierarchical classical models influenced by Plato. In those older models, "The mutual service which the classes render to each other when they stand in the right relation includes bringing them to the condition of their highest virtue." The hierarchical model was predicated on a reverence for the organism of a society; individual desires were sublimated for the sake of the organism. Taylor suggests that, today, this model persists to some degree at the level of family, such as when a sibling forgoes education for the sake of maintaining the family property. Indeed, in contexts where there is the threat of indigence, Taylor writes, "The rules of family and community seemed the only guarantee of survival. Modern modes of individualism seemed a luxury, a dangerous indulgence."[16] We have seen this attitude among some marginalized populations in the United States today: it may be that only one child will seek higher education in order to eventually support the family, while others enter the workforce to manage immediate needs. In such cases, commitment to unrestricted freedom of the individual cannot be a theoretical, much less real, commitment because it is simply not imaginable that each child can do whatever he or she wants if the family is to survive.

In contrast, Taylor describes that the modern order is directed toward the ordinary goals of life, liberty, and the sustenance of self and family. This organization serves individuals and families "instrumentally," not in view of virtue but rather in view of basic goods necessary for existence.[17] More specifically, he writes, individuals serve each other through economic exchange—a view that developed in large part through the application of the theories of Locke and Grotius. Locke, in particular, emphasized the necessity of discipline and self-improvement as cornerstones of a divine natural order, meaning that economic activity becomes the model for human behavior in a society. In the modern social imaginary, the freely acting individual is an economic agent, and his or her economic agency is vital for the engine of the public order. Such an imaginary has implications for the way parents understand their role in child rearing, of course. In the modern social imaginary, the primary focus is not on the organism of the family but on the developing freedom and social capital of the youth. To

---

[15] Taylor, *A Secular Age*, 176.
[16] Taylor, *A Secular Age*, 168.
[17] Taylor, *A Secular Age*, 165-166.

be sure, there are strong overlaps in these different imaginaries—both involve the cultivation of virtues, and both can involve recognition of the importance of family life. Yet, in the modern imaginary, there is a stronger emphasis on forming a youth for individual economic agency.

Of course, it would be erroneous to draw too strong a line to suggest that the social construction of childhood in the modern world is a movement away from leisure toward economic agency. To be sure, there is a history of childhood economic agency that stretches back centuries. In the early nineteenth century, for example, child labor was essential for the economy of poor families. Children were important agents in the microeconomies of family farms; their labor contributed to the well-being of the family as a whole. A youth was as much an economic actor as an adult, albeit a not-fully-developed one. During the period of mass immigration to the United States from the mid-nineteenth century to the early twentieth century, children were essential for the assimilation process faced by immigrant families. They acted as translators and guides, because their abilities to adapt outpaced those of their parents or grandparents.

Only later, perhaps in part because of the changing understanding of labor that emerged in the wake of the industrial revolution, could children be seen as needing some measure of exemption from economic activity. Steven Mintz writes that the idea that childhood could be a time of life sheltered from economic imperatives "represented an effort to contain the precocities and uncertainties that had characterized the process of growing up in the nineteenth century."[18] Indeed, by the 1930s, we see evidence of a new dimension of the social imaginary with the passage of child labor laws. These laws, together with the shift away from work to schooling during the twentieth century, created a space for childhood as a social construct distinct from adulthood.

It is possible, therefore, to speak of the growth of youth culture in the United States and elsewhere as the result of both labor policy and the rise of educational systems. Those factors, together with the growth of suburban life after World War II, carved out a social place for childhood that has dramatically shaped the contemporary social imaginary. Yet what the organizations above have highlighted is a growing concern that the space created for childhood is, in effect, condensing and that the key characteristic of childhood—free play—is being compromised in favor of either structured activity ordered toward economic benefit or unstructured, unhealthy pursuits that are sedentary or otherwise harmful.

---

[18] Steven Mintz, *Huck's Raft: A History of American Childhood* (Cambridge: Belknap Harvard, 2004), 87.

Our thesis, then, is that in the modern social imaginary, we see many adults treating children's leisure time in an instrumental way that results in a diminished value of free play. Aristotle viewed leisure as an active condition oriented toward virtue, an end toward which other forms of activity are rightly oriented.[19] In the modern social imaginary, however, free play becomes wasted time—time that might otherwise be oriented instrumentally toward ends that serve economic interests. To be sure, this state of affairs is for many families not so much an object of clear choice as it is an economic necessity. The instrumentalization of children's time is often predicated on work schedules and the need for child care.

In this context, free play is not free. Parents are responsible for finding ways that their children can engage in useful activity that does not offer an extra burden on already-diminished time. To use one preeminent example, what has emerged in recent decades is an outsized role for youth sports, which has developed into a multi-billion dollar industry. To be sure, there are a number of benefits: organized sports offer opportunities for physical activity, countering a significant trend toward obesity in youth.[20] They can encourage the virtues of fair play and cooperation. They can offer children new opportunities for fun activity that they might not otherwise engage in. Still, youth sports can be caught up in economic imperatives that are not in the best interest of children.

The U.S. youth-sports economy, which includes everything from travel to private coaching to apps that organize leagues and games streamed online, is now a $15.3 billion market, having grown 55% since 2010.[21] Yet even with this level of investment, more children are getting shut out of organized sports. Some 41% of children from households earning $100,000 or more have participated in team sports, according to the Sports & Fitness Industry Association, but in households with income of $25,000 or less, participation is 19%. Fewer children have access to sports of any kind—organized or pick-up—compared to a decade ago.[22]

---

[19] Aristotle, *Politics*, 10.7.

[20] According to the Centers for Disease Control and Prevention, "The percentage of children with obesity in the United States has more than tripled since the 1970s. Today, about one in five school-aged children (ages 6–19) has obesity" (Childhood Obesity Facts, https://www.cdc.gov/healthyschools/obesity/facts.htm).

[21] Sean Gregory, "How Kids Sports Became a $15 Billion Industry," *Time*, August 24, 2017, http://time.com/4913687/how-kids-sports-became-15-billion-industry/.

[22] According to the Aspen Institute, "Fewer than half of children ages 6 to 11 meet the U.S. Surgeon General's recommendation for engaging in at least 60 minutes of moderate physical activity most days of the week. One way to address that deficit is through sport activity, especially team sports, as children often enjoy playing in groups. But fewer of them are doing so now than just a few years ago. The federal government does not track sports participation rates among preteens, but according to the Sports & Fitness Industry Association (SFIA), which does, 40 percent of kids

Kids themselves report that they choose to participate in sports because they have fun, not because they like winning or hope to earn external benefits.[23] When sports are an exercise in authentic leisure, rather than another form of following adult directions, they enjoy the experience. Many adults, though, tend to focus on external goods—the benefits that may emerge in a more-or-less utilitarian calculus. The fundamental issue, it appears to us, is that discernment about youth sports and leisure more broadly tends to operate within the context of a modern social imaginary that prizes cost/benefit analysis over a thick understanding of leisure, and especially of free play. We believe that a recovery of a more Aristotelian model will ultimately yield greater good both for families and communities as a whole.

DISCERNING YOUTH LEISURE

For Aristotle, leisure is an end in itself and not an instrumental good ordered toward something greater. "[N]ature herself, as has been often said, requires that we should be able, not only to work well, but to use leisure [*schole*] well; for, as I must repeat once again, the first principle of all action is leisure" (*Politics* 8.3). Leisure is almost synonymous with freedom; it is that which the free person works towards. Unlike the slave for whom there is no leisure (1334a20), the free person can order work toward leisure, a state which allows for contemplation and resting in the existential good of life itself.

For children, leisure and free play are almost synonymous. Free play is the activity towards which children spontaneously order themselves without adult supervision; it is, to recall the words of the American Academy of Pediatricians, practically the definition of childhood. Just as Aristotle held that work was necessary for leisure, we are arguing that adult-supervised activities—from school to organized sports and other activities—must serve free play as a good in itself.

In Christian theology, as in Aristotle's philosophy, leisure is ordered toward contemplation. Leisure is the active condition of being whole and purposeful as a creature of God, without need for any further *telos*. In the *Divine Comedy*, Dante offers an image that is the

---

played team sports on a regular basis in 2013, down from 44.5 percent in 2008. Further, only 52.2 percent took part in those activities even once during the year, down from 58.6 percent." SFIA data provided to the Aspen Institute, based on 2013 statistics. Aspen Institute, "Sport for All, Play for Life," January 27, 2015, https://assets.aspeninstitute.org/content/uploads/2015/01/Aspen-Institute-Project-Play-Report.pdf.
[23] Michael A. Messner and Michela Musto, "Where Are the Kids?," *Sociology of Sport Journal*, 31, no. 1 (2014): 102-122. The Aspen Institute paper cites Messner and Musto's study: "Most of what we know involves kids already in the game, and it suggests extrinsic rewards and 'winning' mean far less to them than to adults. In a 2014 George Washington University study, 9 of 10 kids said 'fun' is the main reason they participate. When asked to define fun, they offered up 81 reasons—and ranked 'winning' at No. 48. Young girls gave it the lowest ratings."

opposite of leisure. It is an image of those souls in Purgatory who have lived selfishly proud lives and who, as a consequence of their always thinking about themselves, must carry around crushingly heavy boulders—the consequence of what they have worked to build for themselves over the course of their lives. For Dante, there is a temptation to treat work as an extension of selfish pride—pointless in itself, save for the way that it can inflate a person's ego. In contrast, he offers images of people who have learned the proper relationship between themselves and God and who, as a consequence, are not tempted to make an idol of their work. There is Mary, the mother of Jesus, and King David, who dances even in the presence of servants out of an exuberant joy at the presence of the Lord. These figures, Dante suggests, are capable of joy because they know themselves to be at the service of God.[24]

What these images suggest for parents and other adults is that they must not superimpose disordered adult understandings of utility onto children's experiences of leisure. Too often we ourselves have seen families who turn children's activities into a gauntlet of resumé-building activities, diminishing simple goods like family dinners, game nights, or even simply time at home together. The organizational responses we outline earlier in this essay suggest to us that such stories are not merely anecdotal but point to an increasingly corrosive social imaginary.

Josef Pieper argues that culture depends on leisure, and that leisure is not possible unless it is related to worship.[25] Following his logic, we suggest that worship is constitutive of a social imaginary: it is that toward which a life is ordered, either consciously or unconsciously. It is not a stretch to point towards the objects of worship in the modern social imaginary: primarily wealth and social capital. It is no surprise that without a transcendent object of worship, the consequence of obtaining the objects of worship is depression.[26] Further, lacking a transcendent object of worship, leisure becomes entertainment, for there is no sense of growth toward a transcendent end.

In contrast, in the context of worship, leisure becomes possible as that which nourishes the soul toward growth and a deepening of life ordered toward happiness. Pieper says it well:

---

[24] Dante, *Purgatorio*, Canto 10.
[25] Josef Pieper, *Leisure the Basis of Culture*, trans. Alexander Dru (New York: Pantheon Books, 1952, 1964).
[26] See, for example, Alice G. Walton, "Why the Super-Successful Get Depressed," *Forbes*, January 26, 2015, https://www.forbes.com/sites/alicegwalton/2015/01/26/why-the-super-successful-get-depressed/#1573f0cc3850, and Shane Snow, "The Fascinating Reason Many Billionaires Get Depressed," *Business Insider*, Sep. 26, 2014, http://www.businessinsider.com/psychology-of-success-why-billionaires-get-depressed-2014-9.

> Thus, the act of worship creates a store of real wealth which cannot be consumed by the workaday world. It sets up an area where calculation is thrown to the winds and goods are deliberately squandered, where usefulness is forgotten and generosity reigns. Such wastefulness is, we repeat, true wealth: the wealth of the feast time. And only in this feast time can leisure unfold and come to fruition.[27]

Freed from the calculus of cost and benefit, the person who worships experiences leisure as a gift in and of itself. Such a person need not treat all life as an arena of useful activity, for the natural state of life is itself enough of a gift. Given time and space, children will gravitate toward this kind of state; perhaps that is why Jesus suggested that the kingdom belongs to those who are like children (Matthew 19:14).

The opposite of leisure is frenetic, compulsive activity. Evagrius Ponticus described such activity as the result of being driven around by a demon, chasing desires that ultimately do not lead to happiness. He writes that "the demon of acedia...drives [a person] to desire other sites where he can more easily procure life's necessities, more readily find work and make a real success of himself."[28] Our concern, borne out through professional practice both in the classroom and the clinic, is that as a culture we are teaching young people how to work hard and play hard compulsively. To the extent that our message is that all activities must be ordered toward some other end—winning or working towards a scholarship, internship or job—we are forming young people in the habits of economic exigency but denying them the opportunity to experience real leisure.

There are, of course, some behavioral changes which can help restore a place for children's leisure: prioritizing "feast time," as Pieper put it, through family meals and other activities oriented toward interpersonal presence. Steering children away from screens toward active play is another strategy. Allowing children unscheduled time and even age-appropriate unrestricted space can help push back against the expectation that all activity be deemed "useful."

At the level of organizations, we recommend other changes. Organized sports, now occupying an outsized footprint in the American family's schedule, could seriously consider restoring Sabbath practice—leaving Sundays (to use the historical example) free. Coaches at every level ought to allow for free play even within the context of organized practices. Sports associations ought to reinforce existing rules that curtail parental involvement in organized games and consider more extensive training of parents and coaches in the goods of free play. Schools and athletic conferences could consider shortening

---

[27] Pieper, *Leisure the Basis of Culture*, 48.
[28] See Harvey D. Egan, *An Anthology of Christian Mysticism* (Collegeville: Liturgical Press, 1996), 49.

schedules, allowing for greater time between athletic seasons, and imposing stricter rules on organized training.

It is important to underscore that our concern is not organized sports per se. All of our children, and indeed many children everywhere, have experienced great benefits from sports. Our concern, rather, is that organized sports and other claims on the free time of children not be confused for the greater good of leisure, and that they be part of a more holistic approach to children's leisure time. If leisure is what we live for, and is so deeply related to happiness, it is an important responsibility of any civil society to protect encroachments on children's free play that arise from disordered attitudes towards utility. Instead, our concern is to protect children's free play, in order that they might develop a discerning approach to the proper balance between work and leisure that is constitutive of the good life.

Children's Right to Play

Mary M. Doyle Roche

NOVEMBER 2014 MARKED THE 25TH ANNIVERSARY of the United Nations *Convention on the Rights of the Child* (*C.R.C.*). Calling for a "culture of participation," Kirsten Sandberg, Chair of the UN Committee on the Rights of the Child noted, "The right of children to participate is wider than their right to be heard in matters affecting them. I am speaking about the right of all children to be active agents in the lives of communities at every level, whether it be in the family, in schools or in the broader community."[1] Recent work on children's moral agency and participation in social and family life has focused on children's roles as workers and consumers and their rights to be protected in these contexts. This work is urgent given the status of millions of the world's children who work in inhumane conditions that infringe upon the right to primary education and the exploitation of children's agency in privileged contexts by advertising media. Children's right to play, found in Article 31 of the *C.R.C.*, has received less attention in Christian ethics and could provide a lens through which to envision a more dynamic culture of participation for children that honors their dignity in the present as much as it values their potential future contributions as adults.

Many children of privilege play games and sports where the stakes are high for children, parents, communities, and corporations. These activities make children visible in their communities, but they may also constrain children's full participation in the common good because they frequently cater to adult desires and expectations. Many children and their parents also live in an environment saturated with commercial advertising that promises happiness with the acquisition of a new game or toy. Children living in poverty and working children often lack safe time and space for play. The right to play must respond to children as embodied, relational, developing, and spiritual persons; it must have some concrete measures that include time, space, and access to playthings, and it must have a broad network of guarantors. A culture of participation that welcomes children is enhanced by an ethical vision of their right to play that challenges cultural trends toward

---

[1] Kirsten Sandberg, Statement at the 69th General Assembly, High Level Session, November 20, 2014, www.ohchr.org/EN/NewsEvents/Pages/DisplayNews.aspx?NewsID=15327&LangID=E.

competition and consumption. Thinking about play as a form of participation in the common good and playfulness as a virtue may enhance child well-being *and* adult flourishing.

My argument begins with some working definitions and descriptions of play. The children's rights framework takes shape amidst a number of paradoxes in how we think about the nature and meaning of play, keeping them in creative tension. The *C.R.C.* rightly has its primary focus on the global picture and the situations of children in low income countries and countries marked by political instability and violent conflict. This essay focuses primarily on play in the United States, even though the ethical argument about play, participation, and the common good will have implications for thinking about play in global perspective. Even a focus on the U.S. context raises questions about play in resource poor communities and communities that struggle with high rates of crime and violence. The "signs of the times" with respect to play in the U.S. reveal an ambivalence about play on the part of adults, the domination of competitive consumerism in this sphere of children's lives, and structural injustices that impact who plays and who is left out.

Theological reflections on play within the Christian traditions have tended to focus more on God's playfulness, on Jesus as a player, or on *homo ludens* (the human person as one who plays) and less on the social ethical implications of play among children. A trend in contemporary Christian and secular spiritualities frequently advocates recapturing playfulness on the part of adults as an ingredient for "wholehearted" living and an antidote for the stresses of adult responsibilities. Pope Francis has encouraged, even admonished, parents to take time to play with their children both for the good of the children themselves and as a way to resist a culture of work that is dehumanizing and undermining family life.

What is missing in the ethical treatment is a consideration of play as a matter of Christian virtue for children and adults as well as an issue for social ethics. The *C.R.C.*'s "right to play" moves in this direction. Thinking about play through the lens of the common good tradition within Catholic Social Teaching, with its insistence on the connection between rights and responsibilities, the claims of solidarity, and the role of subsidiarity, opens a way to think about play very concretely as a form of participation for children and as a virtuous practice of resistance and transformation for all people.

DEFINITIONS AND DESCRIPTIONS: "THE OPPOSITE OF PLAY IS NOT WORK. IT'S DEPRESSION."[2]

Play according to one historian is "the spontaneous, joyous activity of children."[3] It is "a child's free, open, boundless, and self-controlled activity." Play is self-chosen and pleasurable. It can be "chaotic" and "transformative." Creative play is open-ended and more about the process than any particular activity or object of amusement. Play is an avenue of experimentation and exploration without real-world consequences in a "relaxed field." A working paper on the right to play prepared for the International Play Association (I.P.A.) describes two important roles for play, "As they play, children rearrange their worlds to make them either less scary or less boring."[4]

According to psychologists Dorothy and Jerome Singer, "Play, then, is an inherent capacity of children, but it is often also a set of behaviors adults expect of children, especially when they are relatively free of the immediate need to find food or avoid life-threatening danger."[5] These adult expectations can serve to enhance a commitment to children's play on the one hand, or they can restrict children's play on the other. I.P.A. researchers Stuart Lester and Wendy Russell note, "Play offers opportunities to move beyond existing ways of being, to transform structures and cross borders... and it appropriates, inverts and subverts adult cultural expectations of children. While adults may desire children's play to act as a socialisation process, at times it transgresses this, giving rise to adult concerns that play is disruptive, threatening or of no value, which leads to sanctions and prohibitions."[6] They also claim that children can play in most places.[7] Nevertheless, some environments are more conducive to play than others. Play requires time, space, and often partners and props, which may include but are not limited to commercial toys, play structures and playgrounds. The emphasis is on whether a space is hospitable to play more than on whether it contains particular objects.

Though descriptions tend to focus on freedom and open-endedness in play, play also includes games with rules that may be set and accepted by the players or may be made up and repeatedly reworked by

---

[2] James H. Evans, Jr., *Playing* (Minneapolis: Fortress Press, 2010), 57. Evans is citing play theorist Brian Sutton-Smith.
[3] Howard P. Chudacoff, *Children at Play: An American History* (New York: New York University Press, 2007), 1.
[4] Stuart Lester and Wendy Russell, "Children's Right to Play: An Examinations of the Importance of Play in the Lives of Children Worldwide," (Netherlands: Bernard van Leer Foundation, 2010), 10. The working paper is available at ipaworld.org/ipa-working-paper-on-childs-right-to-play/.
[5] Dorothy G. Singer and Jerome L. Singer, *The House of Make-Believe: Children's Play and the Developing Imagination* (Cambridge: Harvard University Press, 1990), 42.
[6] Lester and Russell, "Children's Right to Play," 10.
[7] Lester and Russell, "Children's Right to Play," 10.

players as the game goes along. *Playfulness* may be thought of as something akin to meta-play or playing with playing.[8] Players might know established rules, but half the fun is in bending and breaking them in new ways. Playfulness disrupts cultural dichotomies between work and play, school and play, and between childhood and adulthood. Play can happen in the context of work, education, and other mundane activities of daily living.

The list of what might be considered play for many scholars is deliberately expansive.[9] This expansiveness may allow us to consider the playful aspect of many activities performed by adults. It may also make it more difficult to assess whether children's right to play is being compromised or denied. Does the right to play require certain forms of play and exclude others? When is something that looks like play on the surface a mere imitation of play that is serving another end entirely, either for its participants or other often unseen actors? How do we tell the difference between play and ersatz play? The common criteria in the literature are *freedom* and *fun*.

CHILD'S PLAY: RIGHTS AND RHETORIC

Article 31 of the UN *Convention on the Rights of the Child* states,

> 1. States Parties recognize the right of the child to rest and leisure, to engage in play and recreational activities appropriate to the age of the child and to participate freely in cultural life and the arts.
>
> 2. States Parties shall respect and promote the right of the child to participate fully in cultural and artistic life and shall encourage the provision of appropriate and equal opportunities for cultural, artistic, recreational and leisure activity.[10]

This article appears between articles on children's right to participate in their cultural, linguistic and religious communities, especially if the children are members of minority communities, and their right to be protected from exploitative labor. Article 31 seeks to recognize, respect, and promote several interrelated but distinct basic needs: rest, leisure, play, recreation, cultural life, and the arts. Though the focus here is on play, this basic need depends, at least in part, on ready access to rest, leisure, culture and art.

Rights outlined in the *C.R.C.* fall into three general categories: *provision* rights (to food, shelter, healthcare, etc.), *protection* rights (from

---

[8] Brian Sutton-Smith, *The Ambiguity of Play* (Cambridge: Harvard University Press, 1997), 147-150.
[9] Sutton-Smith lists practices like daydreaming, hobbies, collections, listening to music, writing, art, gardening, watching movies, games and sports, playing tricks, etc.
[10] United Nations, *Convention on the Rights of the Child*, www.ohchr.org/ EN/ProfessionalInterest/Pages/CRC.aspx.

exploitative labor, conscription, trafficking, etc.), and *participation* rights (to be included in decisions that affect them, to exercise religious and cultural traditions, to affiliate, etc.). It is important to note that the *C.R.C.*'s vision is of interrelated and indivisible rights. Since they are indivisible, certain rights ought not be obtained at the expense of others. One right should not be sacrificed in pursuit of another. As we will see in some U.S. trends around practices like recess during school hours, eliminating play should not be a means to providing quality education and assuring future success in a highly competitive global marketplace. Play and recreation should not be considered luxuries that can be obtained only once other more basic rights are secured.

Play is a protection right in the sense that "Children's play can be seen as a self-protecting process that offers the possibility to enhance adaptive capabilities and resilience.... Play acts across several adaptive systems to contribute to health, well-being and resilience. These include: pleasure and enjoyment; emotion regulation; stress response systems; attachments; and learning and creativity."[11] The I.P.A. also maintains that the "persistent absence of play may disrupt emotion-regulation systems, which in turn will diminish children's physical, social and cognitive competence."[12] This language emphasizes the "adaptive value of play" and the desirable outcomes for children who have ready access to play experiences, rather than maintaining a strict "play is good in itself" approach. However, authors of the working paper insist, "Rather than simply being of value for becoming a better adult, play exists to enable a child to be a better child in their unique and complex environments, and thus enhance their chances of survival as a child.... Play enables children to try out their environments and develop a wide repertoire of responses to the situations they create."[13] These claims challenge the "deficit" model of childhood which focuses on what children lack and need to develop in order to mature and shifts toward the "asset" model which highlights the abilities that children have, as children, that they can bring to the challenges they face in the present.[14]

Play also figures among provision rights. According to the I.P.A. "Provision implies much more than providing play facilities. It requires wider consideration of children's rights to ensure that the social and physical environment can support children's ability to play. When children's rights to survival, development and well-being are infringed, this has an impact on their capacity to play."[15] Again, we see

---

[11] Lester and Russell, "Children's Right to Play," 11.
[12] Lester and Russell, "Children's Right to Play," 12.
[13] Lester and Russell, "Children's Right to Play," 26.
[14] Lester and Russell, "Children's Right to Play," 29.
[15] Lester and Russell, "Children's Right to Play," 12.

how interrelated children's rights are. When other basic needs are compromised, so too is children's play. Making provision for play is linked to multiple provisions but is often neglected in policy with respect to children's rights. Play facilities, like playgrounds and other props and equipment are only a piece of the puzzle. The notion that children can play anywhere, with anything, is an important corrective to some cultural assumptions about what "the right kind of play" requires, but it should not be used to deflect demands for concrete support and resources. As the I.P.A. claims, "Rather than requiring a specific designated location, a play space is created through children's shifting and dynamic interactions with each other and the materials and symbols present in any space; children's performance of play both takes and makes place."[16]

Play is also a participation right. According to Lester and Russell, play is "a primary form of participation, being interwoven into everyday life."[17] Children can combine work, education, and play. Play facilitates participation in social groups and may be an avenue to pursue a desire to be part of a community like a neighborhood or school. However, Lester and Russell also note, "Adults generally define the purpose and use of space and time; children usually find ways to play that appear within the cracks of this adult order." Play advocates are concerned about "the growing institutionalization of children's time and space, and an associated reduction in children's independent access to public space."[18] Playing in public spaces keeps children visible. Play that involves adults and children may provide insight into who children are as individuals, what frightens them, what gifts they might bring to the community, and how adults and children envision the world we live in together. Play in which children and adults are play partners is not the same thing as play organized and moderated by adults. Children remain the primary agents and directors of the activity.

Another framework that is used to distinguish among human rights is the distinction between economic rights (which correspond to the provision rights in the *C.R.C.*) and political rights (which correspond to the participation rights). Critical here is whether one considers rights primarily as claims that individuals or groups can make on the wider community for concrete support and resources or rights as immunities which protect the right's bearer from undue interference on the part of the state. The latter are in a sense, rights to be left alone to pursue religious practice, to affiliate with others, to voice opinions, etc. The right to play also sits within this latter category of immunities. Children's play rights advocates are clear, "play belongs to children."

---

[16] Lester and Russell, "Children's Right to Play," 25.
[17] Lester and Russell, "Children's Right to Play," 11.
[18] Lester and Russell, "Children's Right to Play," 11.

Ensuring children's right to play does imply that adults provide time and space for play and protect children from contexts that undermine this right. It may also imply that children ought to be left alone to play. This immunity from interference is limited, as other immunities are, by concern for children's health and safety (the "best interests of the child standard") and for the common good. Unless the safety of the children or the community is threatened, children should be left to play even when their play challenges or subverts adult expectations of the social order or about children's place in that order.

Turning again to the I.P.A. researchers, Lester and Russell, "Adults should be aware of the importance of play, and promote and protect the conditions that support it. Any intervention to promote play must acknowledge its characteristics and allow sufficient flexibility, unpredictability and security for children to play freely. However, children's play belongs to children; adults should not destroy children's own places for play through insensitive planning or the pursuit of other adult agendas, or by creating places and programs that segregate children and control their play." When adults control play, play is less free and may be less fun. Furthermore, "The urge to play represents a transforming rather than conforming stance... a belief in being able to change and have control over external conditions. In play, order (as a representation of dominant adult organization) is opposed, inverted and subverted."[19]

Play is at once in the "real" world and also beyond or "out of" this world. In play, other worlds can be created, new rules and relationships can be imagined. Psychologist Susan Linn reflects on wonder as an aspect of play that must be protected so that "children's unique way of seeing – whatever they notice about the world that the rest of us pass over" might alert adults to what is being taken for granted as the way the world works.[20] Leaving children alone to play implies that among adult responsibilities is resisting the urge to impose order on play and recognize that children may have a different lens on reality. That lens may be illuminating for the community. This is not to idealize children nor to deny that children can and do replicate the existing social order in their play— older children having power over younger, boys having power over girls, and a priority on winning when it comes to who "gets picked" first and last. However, the possibility exists that those who are powerless in their day-to-day lives can become powerful in play.

Advocates for children's right to play see play as both good in itself and good for the ways in which it advances children's health and well-

---

[19] Lester and Russell, "Children's Right to Play," 11.
[20] Susan Linn, *The Case for Make Believe: Saving Play in a Commercialized World* (New York: The New Press, 2008), 196.

being. As a right, play creates an obligation on the community to protect and promote that right by providing an environment that is conducive to play and playfulness. The rights and responsibilities of play are in a dynamic relationship in which children are the primary agents and through which they engage with their environment and participate in community.

SIGNS OF THE TIMES: ARE WE HAVING FUN YET?

U.S. culture is ambivalent about play. On the one hand, there is tremendous pressure on schools to perform in terms of high standardized test scores, and this has led to cuts in time for recess and physical education and funding for programs in the arts. In some communities, this pressure also requires more homework for students, and the ripple effect is less time for fun and play. If play is going to be squeezed into the schedule, the path of least resistance is play through electronic media.

On the other hand, the blogosphere is fraught with worry about children who no longer know how to play on their own, without commercial toys, without adult supervision and intervention. Even when the opportunity presents itself, children are playing less outside with flesh and blood friends and more on screens with others in the "virtual world." Some of this anxiety is warranted and some of it may be overblown, fueled by legitimate concerns about child health (in particular with rising rates of childhood obesity and diabetes) and by nostalgia for the ways that the adults of today remember (or imagine) playing as children.

Parental anxiety is also keeping children from various kinds of play. Some argue that parents have become overprotective and risk averse, hence the "helicopter" and "snow plow parent." Again, some of these fears are realistic responses to things like the mounting evidence that athletes in some sports (football is not alone) are more vulnerable to concussion and other forms of repeated head and brain trauma that may have lasting effects on a child's health and ability to learn.[21]

Other fears are linked to the environment. In *Our Kids: The American Dream in Crisis*, Robert Putnam (who we remember wanted us to be out bowling and bowling together[22]), notes that parents of privilege, though they harbor their own anxieties, tend to use "promotive"

---

[21] See American Academy of Pediatrics, "Sports-Related Concussion: Understanding the Risks, Signs & Symptoms," www.healthychildren.org/English/health-issues/injuries-emergencies/sports-injuries/Pages/Sports-Related-Concussion-Understanding-the-Risks-Signs-Symptoms.aspx.

[22] Robert D. Putnam, *Bowling Alone: The Collapse and Revival of American Community* (New York: Simon & Schuster, 2000).

strategies in raising their children. These strategies seek to nurture talents and expand opportunities for children (which may involve play, but may also involve less fun activities and programs). While promotive strategies can foster an environment for play, the emphasis tends to be on pursuing activities for the sake of future success and advantage. Putnam continues, "Impoverished parents, by contrast, use 'preventive' strategies, aimed at keeping their children safe in rough neighborhoods where dangers far outnumber opportunities."[23] This is not a personal moral failing on the part of either group of parents but rather a bellwether pointing to ways in which poverty and privilege, along with racism and other forms of discrimination, are undermining the ecology of play.

Children's play in the U.S. is also being influenced by the rise of social media, gaming apps, and other video games, many of which have violent content and are intended for adults (but marketed to appeal to children). It is beyond the scope of this essay to explore the complexity of electronic media's role in play and the common good, but according to Common Sense Media (a non-profit organization that rates various media including films, games, and apps), 8- to 12-year-olds average nearly six hours a day on entertainment media and for 13- to 18-year-olds the time increases to nine hours. They also note that though 45% of young people may use social media every day, only one third of them say that they enjoy it "a lot."[24] Are children having fun? Not so much. Do they feel free to play or not to play with social media when the fear of missing out compels children to keep devices near and on 24/7?

Another significant arena of play is organized sports including school teams, Little League, and Pop Warner. In suburban America, these teams are ubiquitous and life in many families and local communities revolves around sports. Practice and competition take a lot of time and a lot of driving. Sports can indeed enhance health and well-being. When combined with high academic expectations, they can also divert time from other activities, like family meals and sufficient rest that also enhance well-being. Though learning about cooperation through teamwork is a stated goal of many sports, competition is the dominant framework of relationships.

Play is good for children, and yet, even in the United States, many children do not have access to safe spaces for play, props like toys or other objects, and partners and teams. Many communities are not in a position to provide avenues for play, like recreation programs, camps, or organized sports. In communities with ample resources, play may

---

[23] Robert D. Putnam, *Our Kids: The American Dream in Crisis* (New York: Simon & Schuster, 2015), 121.
[24] Common Sense Media, "6 resolutions that every family with tweens and teens should make in 2016," www.commonsensemedia.org/.

lose some of the fun and freedom that are constitutive of play as children specialize in single sports, hobbies, and activities, and their "practice" becomes regimented preparation for competition.

In *The Case for Make Believe: Saving Play in a Commercialized World*, psychologist and founder of the Campaign for a Commercial Free Childhood Susan Linn argues that creative play is counter cultural and that the "dominant culture so strongly dictates against creative play that we have to take active steps – at home, in our communities, and at a policy level – to ensure its presence in children's lives."[25] According to the Toy Industry Association, the U.S. market in toys exceeded $20 billion dollars in 2016, with estimates that may reach as high as $26.5 billion.[26] Creative play on the other hand is not a "money-maker" because according to Linn, "the satisfactions gleaned from it rely more on the person playing than on what's being played with."[27] Creative play is a person-centered, though not individualistic, activity.

Many toys do enjoy a "halo" effect because they bear trusted brand names and advertise their educational and developmental benefits for even very young children (under the age of two).[28] Parents who resist commercialization may invest in more creative or "open-ended" toys like blocks, balls, or art supplies. Organizations like the Center for a New American Dream, whose motto is "more fun, less stuff," admit that these kinds of toys and playful experiences may not save money or make play any more affordable.[29] These halo toys and experiences may remain available only to parents who have the financial resources to access them. Even the sticks just waiting to be imagined into light sabers are more readily found in suburban locales.

For Linn, many commercial toys short-circuit creative imagination. Without imagination, we lose our capacity for meaning making and a sense of our deepest desires. The results are not inconsequential, "if we can't hang on to a sense of ourselves in the distractions of blinding glitter, deafening noise, and psychologically sophisticated come-ons – then we are less likely to know the difference between what we want and what we are told we want. We are less likely to question and unlikely to resist societal coercion, even if it is ultimately harmful to

---

[25] Linn, *The Case for Make Believe*, 202. Information on the Campaign for a Commercial Free Childhood can be found at www.commercialfreechildhood.org/.
[26] Toy Industry Association Inc., "Annual U.S. Sales Data," www.toyassociation.org/tia/industry_facts/salesdata/industry-facts/sales_data/sales_data.aspx?hkey=6381a73a-ce46-4caf-8bc1-72b99567df1e#.VowegK6rTEY.
[27] Linn, *The Case for Make Believe*, 3.
[28] Juliet B. Schor, *Born to Buy: The Commercialized Child and the New Consumer Culture* (New York: Scribner, 2004).
[29] The Center for a New American Dream, www.newdream.org/.

ourselves or other people. We may be good consumers but lousy citizens."[30] According to Linn, what adults must provide for children cannot be bought in a store: "time, space, and silence."[31] This is not to say that these "must haves" do not come at some cost.

In *Overwhelmed: How to Work, Love, and Play When No One Has the Time*, *Washington Post* journalist Brigid Schulte tackles time use research to try to make sense of what she names "time confetti" and life in the "overwhelm." Adults do not use time well and so fritter away time or attempt multitasking convinced that it is possible, even in the face of evidence that proves it is not. We have a culture of work that is at odds with our personal health and the health of our families. We have a culture of perfect parenting and family life that is draining rather than enriching our lives, particularly for women. Part of her proposal is re-envisioning the notion of leisure and committing time to it, which demands both individual and structural changes.

Schulte cites Mihaly Csikszentmihalyi, known for his theories about peak experiences he calls *flow*, "The popular assumption is that no skills are involved in enjoying free time, and that anybody can do it. Yet the evidence suggests the opposite: free time is more difficult to enjoy than work. Having leisure at one's disposal does not improve the quality of life unless one knows how to use it effectively, and it is by no means something one learns automatically."[32] Adults may accept that play comes naturally to children, but they also know that a playful spirit and playing well need to be nurtured. Implicit in this is that, without that nurturance, the ability to play may be lost. U.S. culture may advocate play for children, but the habits of nurturance seem to wane as children and adults age. What Csikszentmihalyi is suggesting is that adults need to relearn how to approach leisure. Adults need to relearn how to play.

Is play making a comeback? There has been pushback on the elimination of recess and physical education for children but not necessarily because they are good in themselves. The argument is more pragmatic and continues to build on adult desires and expectations. Recess and team sports are seen as antidotes to or vaccines for childhood obesity, illness, stress, and depression. Play is good for child health and may even be good for test scores, testing the assumption that in a high stakes testing environment recess and physical education, along with music and arts, must be sacrificed in order to improve test scores. Some argue that children who get out and move around a bit, who have access to activities that enrich their imaginations, who have team experiences that build self-esteem and a sense of belonging,

---

[30] Linn, *The Case for Make Believe*, 200.
[31] Linn, *The Case for Make Believe*, 204.
[32] Brigid Schulte, *Overwhelmed: How to Work, Love, and Play When No One Has the Time* (New York: Harper Collins, 2014).

may perform better academically and enjoy overall well-being that will reach into adulthood.[33] We might wonder that adults too might work better if they know how to, and have time for, play.

Are U.S. children free and having fun? Or are they working on their passing game, their jump shot? For themselves? For parents and coaches? For toy and media corporations? Are they playing? Sometimes. Our review of the signs of the times has revealed ambivalence, ambiguity, and even paradox in how we think about the nature, meaning, and goals of play. Play comes naturally but must also be taught. It is good in itself, just for the fun of it, but children should play because it leads to desirable outcomes. Play should be free and spontaneous, and yet children's play is frequently organized and moderated by adults.

THEOLOGICAL REFLECTIONS ON PLAY: "CHRIST PLAYS IN TEN THOUSAND PLACES"[34]

Theological reflections on play have tended to arise in the context of systematic theology (how God plays or is playful) or spirituality (how playfulness is a mark of life lived in the spirit or how the practice of liturgical worship might be playful). In *God and Games*, David Miller noted that like discourse on play in other disciplines including sociology, anthropology, and psychology, theologians attempt two different projects, either "to analyze accurately the serious (i.e., cultic and sacred) aspects of man's play" or "to analyze the playful aspects of man's serious activity, a task whose purpose is best fulfilled when the dichotomies of sacred and secular, serious and nonserious, etc., are transcended in a unified scheme of human meaning." There are, he claimed, "theories that attribute to the play of children a serious function" and "theories that attribute a playful function to the seriousness of adults."[35]

The more things change, the more they stay the same. In an introduction to Hugo Rahner's 1967 *Man at Play*, Walter Ong, S.J., noted, "Play should interest our contemporary world more than perhaps it does. Not only in the United States, but all over the world man today is much concerned with freedom, and the world of play is the world of freedom itself – of activity for its own sake, of spontaneity, of pure realization. Today, however, we seldom associate freedom with

---

[33] April Brown, "Why Recess and Physical Education are Making a Comeback," PBS Newshour, www.pbs.org/newshour/updates/why-recess-amp-physical-education-are-making-a-comeback/#.VoWY8-8iKQk.email.
[34] Gerard Manley Hopkins, "As Kingfishers Catch Fire." The complete poem can be read at www.poetryfoundation.org/poem/173654.
[35] David L. Miller, *God and Games: Toward a Theology of Play* (New York: Harper and Row, 1970), 22 and 37.

play."[36] Part of his concern was that play was considered "inconsequential" and beneath adults, "childish" rather than "childlike." Nearly fifty years ago, Ong and Rahner sensed that an appreciation of the role of play and playfulness was losing ground, though the concern seems less about the impact of this trend on children, but rather on adults, who, so desirous of freedom in many other aspects of their lives, were not cultivating a habit of play that could be a touchstone for the experience of authentic human freedom. Freedom is serious business. Freedom is for adults.

Rahner turned to Thomas Aquinas to inspire his investigation of the human person at play and play as central to the Christian life of virtue, "Therefore unmitigated seriousness betokens a lack of virtue because it wholly despises play, which is as necessary for a good human life as rest is."[37] Rahner continues, "It is this humane and Christian philosophy of man at play that is my subject here, and for us men and women of today some knowledge of it is a healing necessity, trapped as we are on the hopelessly wrong road of idiotic earnestness, or on the senseless one of exclusive preoccupation with the things of this world."[38] He sees in children at play the human person's "deep-seated longing for a free, unfettered, eager harmony between body and soul."[39] Play is an "anticipation of heavenly joy" and a "playing Church" is made up of "those who have found gladness in Christ."[40]

Play for Rahner is free and unfettered activity that allows the person to more readily experience God's glory. Yet, he also relies on the language of virtue, recalling *eutrapelia*, which for Aristotle was characterized by wit in conversation, a sort of mean of playfulness that kept one from being a stick in the mud on the one hand and a clown on the other. Rahner observed that the virtue "has led a miserable existence in the standard books of moral theology, scantily adorned with the same quotations that Aquinas knew, tired and reduced to a virtuous neutral attitude, upholding the mean in recreational play and joking."[41] Clearly play had lost some of its playfulness. Perhaps Rahner's insight might lead us to something more like "re-creational" play that does not observe a mean in terms of the amount of a particular kind activity, but rather becomes ever deeper, ever more free. The playful person, guided by prudence (imposing reason on play), then would know

---

[36] Walter Ong, "Introduction," in Hugo Rahner, *Man at Play* (New York: Herder and Herder, 1967), ix.
[37] Rahner, *Man at Play*, 2, citing Thomas Aquinas, Commentary on Aristotle's Nicomachean Ethics, 4, 16, 854.
[38] Rahner, *Man at Play*, 3.
[39] Rahner, *Man at Play*, 7.
[40] Rahner, *Man at Play*, 8 and 51.
[41] Rahner, *Man at Play*, 91. For more on eutrapelia, see John Morreall, *Comic Relief: A Comprehensive Philosophy of Humor* (Oxford: Wiley-Blackwell, 2009).

when to play more and when to play less, but perhaps more importantly how to infuse freedom and openness into all aspects of life.

Jürgen Moltmann would continue the theological conversation in his 1972 *Theology of Play*. He was also concerned about the inability of adults to immerse themselves in leisure and thereby "play the game of the new creation" in the freedom opened to us by the Resurrection. Without play and imagination, he claims, "the new obedience deteriorates into legalism" and "Christian living would become a matter of watching out for the things one is not allowed to do."[42] This latter point resonates with Rahner's comment about the manuals of moral theology and more recent endeavors to reunite moral theology and spirituality with attention to virtue ethics.[43]

Moltmann sees in adult leisure the tendency to "replay the very same things we have endured in our work and business, only without coercion and necessity." He continues, "In fact, most of our compensating and relaxing sociability reflects our work in society and occurs in conjunction with it.... We cannot *turn off* after all and are unable to make ourselves talk about something entirely different."[44] Moltmann paints a picture of work and leisure remarkably similar to twenty-first century assessments, long before phones, and tablets, and laptops became extensions of ourselves. It is not merely their existence that has caused work to bleed into leisure and family time. They are the prostheses of the moment, devices that we are using to replace something that is missing or injured.[45] What is that missing or injured thing? Perhaps it is the spirit of playfulness and the virtuous habit of play animated by the offer of freedom in Christ, "The steps leading from a reproduction of the working world during leisure to the production of new conditions in leisure are difficult but must be attempted if we are to live our freedom actually."[46]

James Keenan's retrieval of virtue ethics is instructive for how to think about play ethically. Keenan outlines three important keys to Aquinas' view of moral action: first, every act is a moral act; second, we become the things that we do; and third, the moral life requires a proactive plan.[47] As the Christian sets out a plan of action, she asks herself three questions. Who am I? Who do I want to become? How will I get there? As person-centered and goal oriented, virtue ethics

---

[42] Jürgen Moltmann, *Theology of Play* (New York: Harper and Row, 1972), 32 and 43.
[43] See James F. Keenan, *Moral Wisdom: Lessons and Texts from the Catholic Tradition,* Second Edition (Lanham, MD: Rowman & Littlefield, 2010).
[44] Moltmann, *Theology of Play*, 69.
[45] For definitions of "prostheses," see Merriam Webster, www.merriam-webster.com/dictionary/prostheses.
[46] Moltmann, *Theology of Play*, 69.
[47] James F. Keenan, "Ten Reasons Why Thomas Aquinas is Important for Ethics Today," *New Blackfriars*, 75, no. 884 (1994): 354-363.

has called Christians to be just, faithful, and self-caring people. In this schema, playfulness too would be a virtue, and might be viewed as an auxiliary virtue like temperance and fortitude, a virtue that helps us in our striving to care well for ourselves, to be faithful to particular others, and to be just toward all people. Playfulness might keep us from burnout, might deepen physical and emotional intimacy, and provide the creative imagination needed to continue to challenge unjust social structures, particularly those that have excluded children from the practices of play.

Playing is a moral act; it shapes who we are and helps us envision who we want to be. While play is free, open, spontaneous, it also requires planning, particularly on the part of adults – but not over-planning. Adults need to plan time, space, and silence for children's play. They have to think well about how to respect, protect, and promote play for the children for whom they bear particular responsibility and for other people's children. They need to plan time, space, and silence for their own play. This means that they must also have a habit of paying attention to children, and taking the child's eye view. Paying attention includes but is not limited to supervising children. It is also being willing to be a play partner.

This is only possible if adults can play a bit themselves and model play that is free, fun, and also fair. Susan Linn admits, "Remembering to play with our children, and hanging on to our own playfulness in the throes of raising them, can be difficult."[48] It is made more difficult when we think of playfulness primarily as a feeling that we have sometimes, or we don't, or a face that we need to put on as we make abrupt shifts between work and home. Like virtue, play is person-centered and requires habits that exercise the spark of playfulness in freedom that play theorists and theologians alike suggest is present in all people.

Play is then an element of personal moral striving for all people, but is of particular importance for children as children. Play is also a profoundly social practice, in part because people play not only in solitude but also with others. Play is also social because it relies on social structures and the mediating institutions of social life to make play possible. Play and playfulness are among the "conditions of social living" that make the flourishing of individuals and communities more readily accessible. It is on this point that the common good tradition within Catholic social teaching can provide direction.[49] The common good requires broad participation from all people, including children, who do not merely draw on a community's resources but who also contribute important assets. The common good requires that people

---

[48] Linn, *The Case for Make Believe*, 203.
[49] Thomas Massaro, *Living Justice: Catholic Social Teaching in Action, The Classroom Edition* (Lanham: Rowman & Littlefield, 2008), 84-87 and 89-91.

pursue goals beyond their own self-interest and share the risks and burdens required to meet the community's needs, especially of its poorest and most vulnerable members. Children are counted among the most vulnerable, but again, this is not their only place. The common good requires the just distribution of the fruits of common endeavor. The common good is best secured when guided by the principle of subsidiarity. Multiple sectors of society, at various levels of organization, can contribute – from the family to the school and church, from local business to global private industry, from local, to state, and national governments and international bodies. However, larger and more distant institutions take their lead from the smaller and more local ones. Adults take their lead from the children.

With regard to play, and the right to play in particular, this insistence on participation is crucial. The right to play creates an obligation, a responsibility on the part of others to help secure it when persons cannot do this on their own. Adults have a responsibility to promote and protect this right in various ways – as parents, teachers, neighbors, ministers, voters, worshippers, and as people who work in the public and private sectors. This is a mark of intergenerational solidarity as much as a commitment to education is. They have a responsibility to protect and promote play for all children especially children in resource poor regions and for particular groups of children who might be excluded from play due to racism, sexism, or discrimination against persons with disabling conditions.

Children have responsibilities too. While they rely on adults for time, space, and silence, they also create and re-create time and space, roles and relationships. They make noise that can be disruptive and joyful, chaotic and transformative. They have a growing responsibility to make play possible for others, just as adults do. A Christian vision of play would mean that children's play would need to become ever more inclusive and welcoming. Adults can model this practice for children in their interactions with others and in basic practices like sharing. However, children can also be models of solidarity for adults especially in creative play as they adapt to welcome new players.

A "playground," the time and space and silence for play, is a common good. It may be protected and provided by adults, but it is received as and transformed into something new by children. It is not time and space and silence set apart from life but is happening in the midst of life, in every sphere. It happens in homes among families, in communities and schools among friends and strangers, at work among colleagues, and in church communities as well. Worship and ministry can be playful for everyone in a "relaxed field" where everyone can dare to envision new life in Christ.

Taking Children and Childhood "Playfully"

In recent years Christian ethicists have been taking childhood "more seriously" as a subject of critical intellectual inquiry, and children "more seriously" as moral agents who contribute to their families and communities. Scholars in the fields of psychology, sociology, anthropology, history, and education have long been taking play "seriously" as a vital ingredient for child well-being and growth. Corporations involved in the multi-billion-dollar toy industry in the U.S. certainly take play very seriously. Increasingly, adults are taking play more seriously as a way to cope with stress. Unfortunately, some of this attention has resulted in play becoming one more thing on the checklist of things to do, do well, and do better than someone else. We work at playing.

I have argued that Christians must take play seriously as a right of children and, indeed, a human right, albeit one that adults have a particular responsibility for respecting, protecting and promoting. Play is an important avenue of children's engagement with the world around them and participation in the common good of their communities. The I.P.A. researchers caution, "A common feature of adult rationality of play is the drive to imbue childhood with some significance for the future. Yet, this future perspective, and its utopian message of hope, needs to be balanced with an appreciation of children's own sense of hope in their current and near future."[50] As participation in the common good, it also is a way to engage in the process of world-making or what Christians might call kingdom-making. Play is both an "already" and "not yet" activity. Play has the potential to be both a sign of a future world transformed by God's love, justice, and mercy as well as an embodied instantiation of that world here and now.

As a virtue, playfulness and play require practice. It is less about what we have (material goods or advantage) and more about who we are, what we do, and with whom. If we catch glimpses of the kingdom in children and in those who welcome them, might we expand reflection on this insight to include not only children's innocence, vulnerability, and low social status but their play and playfulness as well? Even, and perhaps especially, when their play is transgressive and transformative of social norms and expectations? Could we take children and childhood more playfully? I do not intend the shift from "seriousness" to "playfulness" to suggest trivializing the concerns of children or the very real demands that caring for children entails. Rather, cultivating a habit of playfulness and being attuned to the very practical play requirements of time, space, silence, props, and partners could open a way to imagine and re-create new, more welcoming, more just, and more compassionate ways of living.

---

[50] Lester and Russell, "Children's Right to Play," 15.

REVIEW ESSAY

Exclusion, Fragmentation, and Theft: A Survey and Synthesis of Moral Approaches to Economic Inequality

David Cloutier

IN HIS 2015 BOOK *OUR KIDS* SOCIOLOGIST Robert Putnam strikingly captures the differences between today's society and that of 1950s postwar America through a series of powerful vignettes that exemplify broader data. Beginning with his own hometown of Port Clinton, Ohio, Putnam depicts the place in the 1950s as "a passable embodiment of the American Dream, a place that offered decent opportunity for all the kids in town, whatever their background."[1] Even taking account of the realities of race and gender discrimination, Putnam explains that "the children of manual workers and of professionals came from similar homes and mixed unselfconsciously in schools and neighborhoods, in scout troops and church groups."[2] While there were certainly inequalities, Putnam's overall claim is that equality of opportunity for kids from very different backgrounds was quite strong. However, in today's Port Clinton, we see "a split-screen American nightmare, a community in which kids from the wrong side of the tracks that bisect the town can barely imagine the future that awaits the kids from the right side of the tracks."[3] He suggests that "the opportunity gap has widened dramatically, partly because affluent kids now enjoy more advantages than affluent kids then, but mostly because poor kids now are in much worse shape than their counterparts then."[4] His book goes on to depicts these two Americas in many other locales, and in the aggregate through a long series of what he calls "scissor graphs," measuring the divergence between rich and poor kids in terms of everything from household income to "Goodnight Moon time" (the time spent on developmental activities

---

[1] Robert Putnam, *Our Kids: The American Dream in Crisis* (New York: Simon & Schuster, 2015), 1.
[2] Putnam, *Our Kids*, 7.
[3] Putnam, *Our Kids*, 1.
[4] Putnam, *Our Kids*, 29.

of parents with their children, in contrast to "diaper time" spent meeting basic physical needs).[5] Interestingly, some (not all) of the data he cites indicates that poor children have not necessarily lost absolute ground, but they have lost relative ground – that is, the gap between what upper-income, educated kids receive and what poorer kids receive has widened. In his conclusion, Putnam strongly argues that we ought to distinguish between equality of outcomes and equality of opportunity, noting that agreement on the latter ideal polls a society-wide acceptance "that is virtually never reached in contentious contemporary America."[6]

Putnam's study captures well the complexity of the issues gathered under the heading "inequality." His measures range across income, wealth, education, among others. Moreover, his story is but one national slice of a larger global picture, in which it is increasingly intertwined. Thus, his study displays the challenges seen across the literature: that "inequality" is multi-faceted phenomenon that arises in many ways and must be addressed in many ways. But the study also demonstrates that the problem *must* be addressed. Pope Francis, among many others, has insisted that ignoring the problem is not an option, and it would be difficult to read Putnam's vignettes and not conclude that something is very wrong. But what is the "something"? And from the standpoint of Christian ethics, how might the responsibilities for action – both personal and structural – be named?

In this essay, I will draw on existing literature in both economics and Christian ethics to indicate the range of explanations and responsibilities proposed, and then suggest a synthetic constructive approach that more carefully identifies three types of inequality which differentiate requirements of justice and guide the exercise of prudence. I will begin by focusing on the wide variety of measures and explanations of rising inequality, and then explain several existing approaches in Christian ethics to the overall problem. I will then synthesize these approaches and suggest that the framework of analyzing the "moral ecology of markets" helpfully sorts the moral concerns raised by different elements of inequality in developed economies. This differentiation allows the insights of Christian ethics to operate more precisely and effectively in proposing the responsibilities Christians have in responding to the problem.

A word about the limits of this essay. When discussing "inequality," the essay mainly restricts itself to the phenomenon of economic inequality in developed economies, particularly though not exclusively in the United States. In so doing, it artificially distinguishes this phenomenon from concerns about political inequality, as well as the inequalities of systems of gender, race, and other identity groupings.

---

[5] Putnam, *Our Kids*, 126.
[6] Putnam, *Our Kids*, 241.

A pure separation is obviously not possible – indeed, we will see that one main line of thought suggests economic inequality is a problem precisely insofar as affects equal political participation, and as we already saw in Putnam, discrimination against groups of persons must be attended to. But these (real) phenomena will only be treated in this essay insofar as they are related to economic inequality. Also, the essay ignores the urgent problems of human use of the environment. I take it as a given that the current economic use of the planet's natural resources is not sustainable in the long run, and that in fact this may make all the debates over inequality appear epiphenomenal to the deeper problem that the entire scale of the present economy may not continue. However, there is respectable debate about the relationship of long-term sustainability to the question of purely "economic" growth; while I myself am more inclined to believe that there are "limits to growth," it is also possible that economic growth can (though not necessarily) generate more sustainable ways of using resources overall. In any case, like the questions of race and gender, a full engagement with the environmental questions would be a whole other essay, and so I simply note the encompassing challenge here. Finally, the paper does not directly engage the complicated issue of global inequality. The issue of whether global inequality is rising or falling is debated vigorously, though what is generally not debated is that the effects of increased trade and technology have reduced extreme poverty by a lot in the past couple decades.[7] As Roser and Ortiz-Ospina summarize a great deal of long-term data and suggest plausibly that "global inequality increased for two centuries and is now falling," at least in aggregate terms.[8] Yet the difficulties in measuring such matters – already a challenge in a national context – are exponentially greater at the global level. Albino Barrera notes in his study, those on different sides of the globalization debate often employ incommensurable measures, or even "employ the same statistics but use them differently to arrive at diametrically opposed conclusions" about poverty and inequality.[9] The global question would require a separate essay.

---

[7] Tyler Cowen, "Income Inequality Is not Rising Globally. It's Falling," *New York Times*, July 20, 2014, www.nytimes.com/2014/07/20/upshot/income-inequality-is-not-rising-globally-its-falling-.html. On the decline in global extreme poverty, see the very balanced report by the Pew Foundation: Rakesh Kochhar, "A Global Middle Class Is More Promise than Reality: From 2001 to 2011, Nearly 700 Million Step Out of Poverty, but Most Only Barely"; www.pewglobal.org/2015/07/08/a-global-middle-class-is-more-promise-than-reality/.

[8] Max Roser and Esteban Ortiz-Ospina, "Income Inequality"; ourworldindata.org/income-inequality/. The article pulls together citations and data from many authors, and the site is sponsored by Oxford.

[9] Albino Barrera, OP, *Globalization and Economic Ethics* (New York: Palgrave MacMillan, 2007), 12.

NAMING THE INEQUALITY PROBLEM: MEASUREMENTS AND TRENDS

Rising concern about economic inequality is not a phenomenon of the past five or ten years. Douglas Hicks, in his book-length study, quotes a 1999 conference suggesting "inequality is back on the agenda."[10] But this implies that the concern had faded. In the postwar decades, the political success of "economic growthmanship" combined with a grand sense of American optimism had made economic success for all seem like a real possibility.[11] Even progressive economists like John Kenneth Galbraith stated that "few things are more evident in modern social history than the decline of interest in inequality as an economic issue," insofar as in "advanced" countries, "increased production is an alternative to redistribution" and "the great solvent of the tensions associated with inequality."[12] Galbraith notes that large-scale redistribution was not the initial object of Lyndon Baines Johnson's War on Poverty; it aimed at aid to "that small percentage of people who would not benefit from growth."[13] The Kuznets curve became widely accepted as a "stylized fact" in economics: it stated that when industrializing, countries experienced an increase in inequality, which is then followed by a decline in inequality.[14]

From today's perspective, that period appears as exceptional. Peter Lindert and Jeffery Williamson, in their definitive history of American inequality, call it the "Great Levelling," which was followed by a "second great rise of American inequality."[15] Why did this happen? The literature displays a wide variety of explanations. One recent study lists the following factors in rising inequality: technological change, international trade, financialization, immigration, the expanding size of markets, decreases in tax progressivity, the loss of union power, and changes in social norms for top earners.[16] Lindert and Williamson

---

[10] Douglas Hicks, *Inequality and Christian Ethics* (New York: Cambridge University Press, 2000), 3.

[11] For an illuminating history of this period, see Robert M. Collins, *More: The Politics of Economic Growth in Postwar America* (New York: Oxford University Press, 2000).

[12] Galbraith, *The Affluent Society*, in *The Affluent Society and Other Writings, 1952-1967* (New York: Library of America, 2010), 419, 428.

[13] Galbraith, *Affluent Society*, 419; Hicks, *Inequality*, 6-7.

[14] Simon Kuznets, "Economic Growth and Income Inequality," *American Economic Review* 45 (1955), 1-28. Branko Milanovic, *Global Inequality: A New Approach for the Age of Globalization* (Cambridge: Harvard University Press, 2016), revives this idea, but in cyclical terms, renaming the rising and falling of inequality in terms of "Kuznets waves." Depressingly, the countervailing forces that produce a change and decline in inequality are often violence born of exploitation and stagnation.

[15] Peter Lindert and Jeffrey Williamson, *Unequal Gains: America Growth and Inequality since 1700* (Princeton: Princeton University Press, 2016), 11-12.

[16] Uri Dadush, Kemal Dervi, Sarah Puritz Milsom, and Bennett Stancil, *Inequality in America* (Washington: Brookings Institution Press, 2012), 2.

highlight in particular the pressures on labor, pressured from "below" by increasing immigration, from "beyond" by globalization, and from "within" by automation and a decline in the previous American leadership in education.[17] Joseph Stiglitz champions the central role of financialization, which he consistently portrays as a sophisticated form of "rent-seeking," leveraging market power and profits to gain monopolistic power or favors from government, rather than by taking "innovation-driving risks," which were the source of the real growth in the prior era.[18] Other writers highlight non-economic factors, such as the increase in contextual competition in society or the changes in family structure that have increasingly diverged along economic lines.[19]

This complex set of contributing factors is difficult to resolve causally, not least because measuring what is meant by "inequality" is no simple task. For example, conservative economists often suggest that the appropriate measure is differences in consumption, not income – as Gregory Mankiw reports from 2006 data, the richest fifth of households may average 15 times the before-tax income of the lowest fifth, but the actual per person consumption gap is only 2.1 times.[20] But William Bole critiques this position as "the We Got Stuff school of thought," suggesting that even Adam Smith recognizes that material deprivation is relative to social custom, and so absolute poverty isn't the only moral concern.[21] Moreover, the simple consumption approach underestimates the advantages reaped by the ability of wealthier people to save and thus avoid scarcity traps that have quite adverse effects on the poor.[22]

The most well-known measure of inequality, the Gini coefficient, represents the extent to which the overall distribution of incomes deviates from perfect equality. It is useful as a comparative measure across space and time, but as with many overall scoreboard numbers in economics, an overreliance on it can significantly distort analysis. Most importantly, the Gini coefficient cannot tell us anything about why the inequality is widening, nor what an "ideal" ratio would be.

---

[17] Lindert and Williamson, *Unequal Gains*, 227-239.
[18] Joseph Stiglitz, *The Great Divide* (New York: Norton, 2015), 420-421.
[19] On the rise in relative deprivation, see Robert Frank, *Falling Behind: How Rising Inequality Harms the Middle Class* (Berkeley, CA: University of California Press, 2007). On family effects, see an overview of studies in Jason Deparle, "Economic Inequality and the Changing Family," *New York Times*, July 14, 2012, economix.blogs.nytimes.com/2012/07/14/economic-inequality-and-the-changing-family/.
[20] N. Gregory Mankiw, *Principles of Economics*, 5th edition (Mason, OH: South-western/Cengage Learning, 2009), 440.
[21] William Bole, "Relative Poverty: The Indignity of Gross Inequality," *Christian Century* 128, no. 26, December 27, 2011, 10-11.
[22] On how this lack of a cushion takes up bandwidth and leads to poor decision-making, see Sendhil Mullainathan and Eldar Shafit, *Scarcity: Why Having Too Little Means So Much* (New York: Times/Henry Holt, 2013).

The easiest example is that, while the United States has always been more unequal (i.e. had a higher Gini coefficient) than many European countries, the overall income level of the United States –at the median and even to some extent below it, as well as above it – has also been higher. As Peter Hill argues in an essay that represents a standard view, "wealth creation is the most effective anti-poverty measure available."[23] Attempts to redistribute broadly founder, Hill says, because they lack the ability to distinguish effectively between "meritorious" inequalities and those deemed excessive, and then tend to create their own inequalities based on the corruption of authorities in charge of redistribution.[24]

Two other ways of measuring inequality are more useful in understanding the complexity of the phenomenon. One is the relative ratio of returns to labor and capital in an economy, and the distribution of these returns across the population. Economists seem to agree that trends in these areas contributed to declining inequality in the postwar era and subsequent increasing inequality since the 1970s. Anthony Atkinson's recent book shows that across many developed economies, the relative share of national income paid out in wages increased through the 1970's, and then reversed by the 2000s.[25] In general, more of the national income paid out in wages tends to reduce inequality, although Atkinson cautions that this is not entirely the case if more of the population shares in capital returns (e.g., mutual funds, increases in home ownership) and if wage dispersion is increasing (as is the case post-1980 in most places).[26] Atkinson's overall project suggests that various postwar social policies served to mitigate some economic factors in the earlier period, but then failed to keep up in the later part. For example, a decline in workforce participation because of demographic change was offset by generous social pensions and unemployment insurance (therefore, reducing inequality earlier in the period), but these were "unable to keep up" as benefits were reduced and eligibility tightened later in the period.[27] Thus, Atkinson's study, while

---

[23] The world list of countries ranked by Gini illustrates this: Japan is worse than India, the UK and Canada are side by side with Croatia and Bangladesh. See the CIA World Factbook, "Country Comparison: Distribution of Family Income." www.cia.gov/library/publications/the-world-factbook/rankorder/2172rank.html. See Peter J. Hill, "Creating and Redistributing Wealth: Whose Responsibility?" in *Wealth, Poverty, and Human Destiny*, ed. Doug Bandow and David L. Schindler (Wilmington, DE: ISI Books, 2003), 1-17.
[24] Hill, "Creating," 8.
[25] Anthony Atkinson, *Inequality: What Can be Done* (Cambridge: Harvard University Press, 2015), 68-70.
[26] Atkinson, *Inequality*, 70-74. Wage and capital dispersion helps those outside the 1%, but in both cases, it can widen the gaps lower down the income scale, as we will see later.
[27] Atkinson, *Inequality*, 65-67.

not ignoring the often-cited issues of technological change and globalization, suggests that no single "exogenous" change such as this should be cited without looking at the overall structural context of economic returns to labor and capital within which the change is taking place.

Another helpful common measure of inequality is the gap between broad segments of household income. For example, the 90/10 ratio measures the relationship between those at the 90th percentile of household income versus those at the 10th percentile. Other such ratios are also available (e.g. 80/20, 50/10, etc.). For example, Atkinson plots wage dispersion based on the 90/50 ratio, showing a rise in US wage dispersion from under 160% in the early 1950's (the full-time worker at the 90th percentile made 160% of what the median full-time worker made) to over 210% by 1990.[28] This measurement seems to give us more precision in understanding how inequality has evolved over time.

Attention to the change of the various bands over time offers further illumination. A Brookings Institution study broke down income over time into 6-percentile brackets, and charted how much each bracket contributed to overall inequality.[29] The results suggest, first and foremost, that the highest contributions come at the 6-12 percentiles and the 90-96 percentiles – the very bottom and the very top. These contribute over 30% of the overall inequality, with the 12-18 band contributing about another 10%. Second, these figures have remained surprisingly constant over the past few decades. The report's authors note:

> Our findings suggest that income gaps across the broad middle of the distribution—from about a quarter to three-quarters of the way up—account for about as much of top-bottom income inequality today as they did 40 years ago. The action is at the ends. ... while much of the political rhetoric is focused on inequality at the top, a large chunk of overall top-bottom inequality is due to gaps at the very bottom—the 24/6 gap or even the 12/6 gap.

This conclusion is made even clearer by detailed Census Bureau data that chart the raw income at deciles over time. The 80/50 ratio level is up slightly from the 1970s, from around 1.5 to around 2, but is pretty much steady since the 1990s. But in terms of (inflation-adjusted) dollars, income is flat at 10th and 20th percentiles since the 1970s, and the median is barely better, going from 48-50,000 in the

---

[28] Atkinson, *Inequality*, 73.
[29] Richard V. Reeves and Emily Cuddy, "Stretchy Ends: The Shape of Income Inequality," Brookings Institution report (July 9, 2015); https://www.brookings.edu/research/stretchy-ends-the-shape-of-income-inequality/.

early 1970s to 53-54 in 2013-14. Yet those at the 80th percentile experience an over 30% increase (83.5 (1976) to 112), and those at the 90th percentile do even better, a nearly 50% increase (107 to 157.5). As Richard Reeves summarizes this succinctly in his recent book, the gap between the bottom fifth and the middle fifth has not widened at all since 1979.[30]

How might ethicists take the above complexity seriously, without losing the forest in the trees? As these numbers help clarify, the economic description of inequality can be said to have three related dimensions, at least in advanced economies at this time in history. One is at the very top, and another at the very bottom of the income scale. Both groups are not only small, but have particular characteristics not prevalent at any of the middle levels (e.g., 25th, 50th, or even 90th percentile). Yet in the broad middle, there is also a distinctive change, not between those in the middle and those lower down, but between those in the middle and those in what we might typically call the "upper-middle." At the income levels of the 80th and 90th percentiles, we are not talking about hedge-fund managers or music superstars. We are talking higher-level managers and many professionals (from lawyers and doctors to engineers and computer programmers). While there is significant action at the very ends, a lot of inequality is still about things happening in parts of the middle. I will return to these three dimensions of the economic problem after examining the constructs theological ethics has used in analyzing inequality.

EXCLUSION, FRAGMENTATION, AND THEFT: THREE THEOLOGICAL ACCOUNTS OF THE PROBLEM OF INEQUALITY

The first question to be engaged is whether inequality is an ethical concern at all: there is little material in the biblical tradition that is directly concerned with inequality in a complex, global system. One may think of the common ownership of the early Jerusalem community depicted in Acts 2 and 4 as an ideal, but few strands of the Christian tradition have made this normative. There is simply too much evidence elsewhere in scripture that a broader understanding of sharing and generosity is the general principle for handling possessions.[31] The scriptural tradition here aligns with typical secular analyses. For example, Atkinson's book begins with the usual claim that he is "not aiming for total equality," but rather is seeking to "reduce inequality

---

[30] Richard V. Reeves, *Dream Hoarders* (Washington: Brookings Institution Press, 2017), 6.
[31] For authoritative overviews, see Luke Timothy Johnson, *Sharing Possessions: What Faith Demands*, 2nd ed. (Grand Rapids: Eerdmans, 2011); Sondra Ely Wheeler, *Wealth as Peril and Obligation: The New Testament on Possessions* (Grand Rapids: Eerdmans, 1995); and Craig Blomberg, *Neither Poverty Nor Riches: A Biblical Theology of Possessions* (Downers Grove, IL: IVP, 1999).

below its current level, in the belief that the present level is excessive."[32] Atkinson's moral claim is founded on defining "excessive"; he recognizes that it ultimately means "unjust," and seeks to use a combination of John Rawls and Amartya Sen to ground his claim (briefly), before moving on to the economic dynamics. But his book is really meant for those who already share his presuppositions that current inequality is unjust, and want to understand how it got that way and what to do about it. Fortunately, the Christian tradition allows for much more detail in grounding the injustice of inequality, understood with more precision than merely "excessive."

The Bible implies a preference for economic structures that discourage extreme inequalities, a concern that has then been further specified in modern Catholic social teaching. The more detailed norms of the Old Testament community evidence a far-sighted concern for avoiding economic extremes. As Clive and Cara Beed argue, in a comprehensive survey of the biblical material, the Mosaic law aims at "a relatively egalitarian society" in various ways.[33] Walter Brueggemann summarizes "no coveting" as the core narrative of the Old Testament when dealing with money and possessions; Sabbath-keeping and various injunctions on behalf of the neighbor limit any "acquisitive system" and are "regulations for refusing the endless propulsion of wanting and taking."[34] Most significantly, its restrictions on usury and land accumulation go a long way toward minimizing extremes of both wealth and poverty in a subsistence agricultural society. Even God's skepticism over Israel's desire for a king addresses inequality: the king will "take the best of your fields, vineyards, and olive groves" and "tithe your crops" to support his retinue, and even take "your best oxen and your asses, and use them to do his work" (1 Sm 8:14-16).

Modern Catholic social teaching has also shown this moderate egalitarian tendency by avoiding what Pius XI terms the "twin rocks of shipwreck" of "individualism and collectivism," via the "twofold character of ownership" that insists on an individual right to property subject to obligatory use for social good *(Quadragesimo Anno*, nos. 45-46). Pius begins to explain the universal destination of goods, which now functions as the foundational principle of modern Catholic teaching on money and possessions (*Catechism*, nos. 2401-2403). All property has a "social mortgage."[35] The most stringent application of

---

[32] Atkinson, *Inequality*, 9.
[33] Clive and Cara Beed, "Recent Christian Interpretations of Material Poverty and Inequality in the Developed World," *Journal of Markets and Morality* 16 (2013), 407-427, here 419.
[34] Walter Brueggemann, *Money and Possessions* (Louisville: WJKP, 2016), 17-25.
[35] *Sollicitudo Rei Socialis*, no. 42. Douglas Hicks, *Money Enough: Everyday Practices for Living Faithfully in the Global Economy* (San Francisco: Jossey-Bass, 2010), 74, in discussing this idea, notes that even John Locke's concept of private property assumes that "enough and as good" is left over for everyone else.

this ideal has been in the small but influential literature of "distributists," who have maintained that widespread small proprietorship is the appropriate Christian vision for an economy.[36] However, the development of a clear (if ignored) teaching on just wages as the key means of supporting dignity and "an equitable distribution of income" should be understood as an analogous distributional standard in a society less centered on small proprietorship (CSDC, nos. 302-303).

These broad principles rule out a purely individualist account of the economy, which has no moral concern for equitable distribution, and also a strongly socialist account that deprives agents of their distributional rights and responsibilities. But that leaves a good deal unspecified. In the existing literature, three models help specify (in related though distinct ways) the ethical problems of economic inequality: exclusion, fragmentation, and theft.

Douglas Hicks's book-length study relies on a combination of Niebuhrian theocentrism and liberationist preferential option for the poor to ground a relationship between egalitarian universalism and partiality. The combination of Niebuhr's insistence on our radical equality before God and liberationism's call to preference for the poor in light of a vision of the eschatological Kingdom of God makes sense of why Christians should be concerned about equality, not simply poverty. These claims about creation and eschatology reveal a profound equality of persons, toward which we ought to strive in the present. This "moral-theological vision" is "one of the principal contributions that Christian ethical perspectives make in public discourse," since "theological language and imagery can move people to action."[37]

But might this not lead to pure equality approach, like the Acts community? In his analysis of particulars, Hicks relies on Sen, thus paying special attention to how levels of material inequality are problematic not simply in themselves, but instrumentally. Solidarity involves "a genuine sense of stake" in society, and material adequacy must be relative to social standards, because "a person's well-being is at least partially a function of one's position relative to others in such basic functionings."[38] In following Sen, Hicks adopts a model which I will call, drawing on Willis Jenkins, the "inequality as exclusion" model.[39] The assumption here is that, at some point, a certain level of inequality hinders the development of personal dignity, understood not simply in base, material terms, but in terms of social participation.

---

[36] For a recent account, see John Medaille, *Toward a Truly Free Market* (Wilmington, DE: ISI Books, 2010).
[37] Hicks, *Inequality*, 233.
[38] Hicks, *Inequality*, 171, 193.
[39] Willis Jenkins, "Is Plutocracy Sinful?" *Anglican Theological Review* 98, no. 1 (2016), 33-50, here 44. Jenkins claims that the exclusion model is dominant in Catholic social thought, but I would suggest that at various times, CST emphasizes either exclusion or fragmentation.

Many criticisms of inequality (dating back to Rousseau and Marx) have sought to identify the crucial problem for inequality as one of distorting social power. Hicks' volume also relies on Michael Walzer, who in one piece, highlights inequality as undermining the system of "countervailing power" necessary for ongoing democracy.[40] Thus, morally unacceptable inequality exists not when there is *any* difference, but when the difference is of a sort that leads some to be left out. Citing an earlier article by Dennis McCann, as well as Walzer, Andrew Yuengert nicely specifies this: "Inequality is not morally offensive, as long as those at the bottom have a dignified standard of living," which is not merely about material dearth, but involves not being "shut out from social groups and from the legal and democratic process."[41]

The "exclusion" view is most obvious in less-developed countries, where the poor live in shanty-towns on the edge of vast cities, denied even basic water and sewer services or functioning schools, and may possess no political rights at all, victims of endemic political corruption. Compared to such situations, the U.S. system, even at its worst, mostly avoids these problems.[42] One may cite instances like the appalling 2015-16 water crisis in the city of Flint, Michigan, but it is precisely the ordinary functioning of U.S. water systems, even for the poor, that brought so much attention (and aid) to people in Flint – attention and aid that surely the poor in other countries would have welcomed. As for politics, while their particular concerns are often given more lip-service than genuine long-term attention, constituencies of the poor and disadvantaged do play a vital role in both U.S. political parties. Some say economically and culturally marginalized white voters played a role in lifting the anti-establishment campaign of Donald Trump to the presidency.[43] And others argue that the failure of poor

---

[40] Hicks, *Inequality*, 10.

[41] Andrew Yuengert, "What is Sustainable Prosperity for All?" in *The True Wealth of Nations: Catholic Social Thought and Economic Life*, ed. Daniel Finn (New York: Oxford University Press, 2010), 37-62, here 53-54.

[42] For a careful and balanced look at how Pope Francis's discussions arise from a context of exclusion that differs from most advanced countries, see Andrew Yuengert, "Pope Francis, His Predecessors, and the Market," *Independent Review* 21 (2017), 347-360.

[43] There is considerable controversy over how to parse "economic" versus "cultural" factors in determining why some votes swung Trump's way. See for example, German Lopez, "Survey: the poor, white working class was, if anything, more likely than the rich to vote for Clinton," www.vox.com/policy-and-politics/2017/5/9/15592634/trump-clinton-racism-economy-prri-survey. But the article detailing the survey results is much more nuanced than the headline. For more information, see Nicholas Carnes and Noam Lupo, "It's Time to Bust the Myth: Most Trump voters were not working-class," Washington Post, www.washingtonpost.com/news/monkey-cage/ wp/2017 /06/05/its-time-to-bust-the-myth-most-trump-voters-were-not-working-class/?utm_term=.a1482544c26b. Carnes and Lupo rightly argue that, on the basis of sheer numbers, Trump received a majority of his votes from others. But which votes

urban African-Americans to turn out in 2016 (compared to the prior elections of Barack Obama) was crucial to the outcome.[44] While neither Obama nor Trump may have done or do what they promised their constituencies, the continued political relevance of poorer populations is at least enough to suggest that they are not simply "excluded" from an elite process.

Unfortunately, the fact that the U.S. mostly does not suffer from the exclusion that ensues from extreme economic inequality can be used as a way of dismissing inequality as a problem. Thus, it is worth distinguishing a second, no less important way of approaching the moral contours of the problem: the "inequality as fragmentation" model. The problem is not so much that some specific group of people are discarded; instead, economic inequality leads to the breakdown of the social cohesion necessary for the flourishing of all, especially in terms of projects that require social cooperation seeking common goods.

This view is well-represented by Kate Ward and Kenneth Himes, who survey the landscape of inequality research, summarizing the concerns in terms of how inequality retards economic growth, leads to political exclusion, corrodes shared civic standards, and affects social mobility.[45] Obviously, this approach includes the first, but Ward and Himes intentionally go beyond it. They cite other works that hew quite formally to the "exclusion" view, but argue that Catholic ethics requires *more* than this.[46] They characterize the problem in terms of an inadequate social vision of solidarity. As St. John Paul II famously defined it, solidarity means "we are all really responsible for all" (*Sollicitudo Rei Socialis*, no. 38). I call this approach "inequality as fragmentation" because it names the problem not simply in terms of those excluded, but as a deeper misunderstanding of human flourishing for all, failing to root it in the common good. In deploying a similar approach to inequality, Albino Barrera notes the development of papal social encyclicals toward a "solidarism" as "the deep theory undergirding postconciliar egalitarianism," which is analogous to the idea that the peace of social "harmony" or "concord" is more than just the

---

swung the election? My point is simply to indicate that many voters who suffer from increasing inequality – for example, those who live in rural areas of Ohio and Pennsylvania – are not excluded from the political process, but in fact may be among the most powerful swing voters, in part because of the structural realities of U.S. presidential elections. Their relative power would be genuinely diminished by a structural change, such as the direct popular vote election of the president.

[44] On this, see Reid Wilson, "Voter Turnout Dipped in 2016"; thehill.com/homenews/campaign/332970-voter-turnout-dipped-in-2016-led-by-decline-among-blacks.

[45] Kate Ward and Kenneth Himes, "Growing Apart: The Rise of Inequality," *Theological Studies* 75 (2014), 118-132.

[46] Ward and Himes, "Growing Apart," 126.

absence of war.[47] As well illustrated by Putnam's vignettes, the core problem here isn't simply this or that exclusion experienced by the poor, but the "coming apart" of the community as a whole, especially in terms of a shared conviction about all children of the community as "our kids." On this reading, Catholic social teaching relies on "the tacit intuition or vision that undergirds a conception of justice" which is "communitarian and gives high priority to solidarity" – a vision ultimately reliant on a vision of "humanity as one family."[48]

This model is more applicable to advanced economies not facing much outright exclusion, but raises trickier questions for specification. Ward and Himes recommend a "moral norm of relative equality" designed to hold inequalities "within a range defined by moral limits."[49] What are the "relative equality" and "moral limits" required? Catholic economist Anthony Annett, also stressing solidarity, helpfully adding some specifications. In a lengthy, detailed response to conservative economist Arthur Brooks, Annett does not dispute Brooks's familiar claim that the poor of today "own devices and enjoy conveniences that would have astonished the richest robber baron of a century ago."[50] But, he goes on to argue, "the real problem with inequality is that it severs the sense of shared purpose necessary for the realization of the common good."[51] It is not simply about whether someone can individually get on the Internet or not, but whether they can participate well in the "commons" of society. This goes beyond the obvious forms of exclusion cited previously. Annett notes that "people in more unequal societies trust each other less, fear each other more, participate less in community life, and are more prone to violence."[52] This erosion of social trust "harms productivity" on sheer economic grounds, and also "reduces the likelihood of growth-enhancing investments" by the society. Lest one associate such mistrust only with the extreme inequality present in more corrupt "crony capitalist" states, Annett persuasively highlights the recent failures in the U.S. context to solve the major problems of health care and environmental sustainability.[53] Both items are inherently common-good problems, requiring cooperative solutions; in both cases, there is a relatively robust consensus that

---

[47] Albino Barrera, *Modern Catholic Social Documents and Political Economy* (Washington: Georgetown University Press, 2001), 40-43. Like Ward and Himes, Barrera points back to Drew Christiansen, SJ, "On Relative Equality: Catholic Egalitarianism After Vatican II," *Theological Studies* 45 (1984), 651-75.
[48] Ward and Himes, "Growing Apart," 131.
[49] Ward and Himes, "Growing Apart," 132.
[50] Anthony Annett, "This Economy Kills," *Commonweal* 144, no. 11 (June 16, 2017), 21-25, here 23.
[51] Annett, "This Economy Kills," 24.
[52] Annett, "This Economy Kills," citing evidence from Richard Wilkinson and Kate Pickett, *The Spirit Level* (New York: Penguin, 2010).
[53] Annett, "This Economy Kills," 25.

business-as-usual must be changed – for example, everyone seems to agree that the U.S. health care system is broken and too expensive.[54] Yet there is an inability to achieve even a moderate compromise; one wonders how the taken-for-granted achievements of Medicare and the Clean Air Act would have fared in today's more unequal economic terrain. By implication, the fragmentation of the society then harms not just the poor (though it often harms them relatively more acutely), but everyone, because the social capital necessary to work together across diverse interests to achieve necessarily-shared solutions is no longer available. Thus, by specifying more precisely the linkages between a sense of solidarity and particular economic outcomes, Annett further clarifies the moral problems with economic inequality understood as fragmentation.

But these two models do not exhaust the problem. Annett's article also notes the tendency toward "corporate rent-seeking" in more unequal economies, in which the wealthy find it easier or more attractive "to extract rather than create wealth." This comment reminds us that not all economic activity is created equal, in terms of what might be called its "invisible hand," shared-benefit qualities. To account for this aspect of inequality, a third model is needed, "inequality as theft," when "wealth accumulation has become so excessive that it causes harm."[55]

This view, which he rightly associates with ancient Christian writers, often is thought to be anachronistic today, as it seems to rely on a zero-sum world. But as I have argued partially in *The Vice of Luxury*, it is incorrect to assume that modern economics portrays all market activities as a matter of self-interest conducing to common benefit.[56] Some self-seeking economic activity really does benefit both the wealth-seeker and the society as a whole, but some does not. Zero-sum conflicts continue to exist all across the economy.[57] The failure to make this distinction is the key error of strongly pro-market approaches that favor "wealth creation." As an example, Hill is right to point out that flat-footed redistributionists commit the "fallacy" of believing "wealth is a zero-sum game."[58] Yet he commits the opposite error, assuming that economic growth is simply synonymous with wealth creation, and ignoring the spaces in the economy where zero-sum conflicts do exist. Such zero-sum conflicts become even more tempting for the wealthy and damaging to the poor in light of recent authoritative studies that indicate the unusual productivity growth of

---

[54] However, there is real disagreement about whether health care should be viewed as an entitlement for all, as is, e.g., K-12 education.
[55] Jenkins, "Is Plutocracy Sinful?" 47.
[56] David Cloutier, *The Vice of Luxury: Economic Excess in a Consumer Age* (Washington: Georgetown University Press, 2015), 160-169.
[57] Dadush et. al., *Inequality*, 35-38.
[58] Hill, "Creating and Distributing," 3.

the period 1870-1970 was due to a series of "one-time-only" advances that cannot be repeated.[59] As productivity growth has lessened, the demand for more extractive forms of wealth appropriation almost inevitably grows – unless the wealthy simply refuse them.

For Jenkins, the point is not to identify exactly where this happens, but rather to combat the "interior disciplines of imagination" that undergird and legitimate "plutocratic politics."[60] The fact that *some* people do become rich by efficiently providing goods and services that the society wants is falsely transformed into a truth that *all* people who are rich benefit the society in this way. While Jenkins is right to highlight this ideological point, it is worth noting that economists have long had tools that would assist the ethicist in identifying more precisely instances of economic activity that might be best characterized as "theft." The issue is not simply that the difference "causes harm," as Jenkins says – that's true of all three models – but that the harm is morally specifiable as theft.

SYNTHESIZING THE APPROACHES TO INEQUALITY: WHAT DOES JUSTICE REQUIRE?

The above survey indicates that the phenomenon of economic inequality itself, as well as the ethical approaches to the phenomenon, are complex. Some ethical studies refrain from much specification, preferring to offer general warnings of potential moral violations. Meanwhile, most economic texts are laden with policy proposals. This dynamic can produce an unhelpful back-and-forth among ethicists in which each side accuses the other of failures in prudential judgment about this or that situation or proposal. While some amount of prudence is obviously required, the demands of justice need clarification. Eventually, one might develop guidelines for just and unjust inequality, much like the just war tradition. The synthetic portion of this essay can be seen as a step in this direction.

In applying these three ethical accounts of the problem of inequality, it is helpful to return to the three areas of inequality displayed in economic measures. The first is the poorest of the poor. Some studies have documented a rise in "extreme poverty" in recent decades.[61] However, this rise should be differentiated from the relative *success* of anti-poverty measures for the majority of the population in advanced economies, even the United States. In an impressive pair of detailed articles, Christopher Jencks takes a 50-year-view of War on Poverty programs, and suggests that the programs have actually been

---

[59] Robert J. Gordon, *The Rise and Fall of American Growth: The U.S. Standard of Living Since the Civil War* (Princeton: Princeton University Press, 2016).
[60] Jenkins, "Is Plutocracy Sinful?" 39.
[61] See especially Kathryn Edin and H. Luke Shaffer, *$2 A Day: Living on Almost Nothing in America* (Boston: Houghton Mifflin Harcourt, 2015).

quite successful in overcoming much of the deprivation experienced by the poor. He critiques the official poverty measure (which suggests almost no change since 1970) for omissions and distortions, and suggests the actual measure (as of 2013) is more likely 5-6%.[62] He also notes correctly that this finding tends to be politically inconvenient for both conservatives (who would have to admit that the government programs of the last decades have achieved a lot of success) and liberals (who fear admitting success will undermine continuing efforts to expand programs). A further, extremely detailed study suggests that the official poverty measure fails to reflect the success of anti-poverty programs of various sorts, especially in sustaining consumption levels for the poor. By their calculations, a properly adjusted measure of poverty suggests a steep and pretty consistent decline from consumption poverty over 25% in the mid-1960's to under 5% today.[63]

Nevertheless, extreme poverty remains a concern, even if it is for only a small segment of the population. The problem of extreme poverty can easily be connected to the "inequality as exclusion" approach. There is a widespread consensus that Christians bear ethical responsibility for neighbors who are suffering from a bare lack of basic needs. Even the aforementioned "We Got Stuff school of thought" would have to recognize that, at least for this segment of the population, there is still basic material deprivation, which also spills over into the ability to participate in the economy and the community. The disagreement as to how to meet those needs is real, but few are heartless enough to suggest a cold refusal allowing people to die of starvation, freeze to death, or perish outside hospital ER rooms without urgent care. Insofar as affluent economies are still unable to reach this 5%, there is a clear lapse in moral responsibility. Notably, extreme poverty also overlaps with some obvious issues – such as addictions and mental illness – that are not directly involved in any of the market economy arguments about inequality causation.[64] Better to differentiate and target this problem specifically. Insofar as the society simply fails to care for these households, we have an example of "inequality as exclusion."

A second distinguishable application concerns the rise of the extremely rich – the problem of the 1%. Like the problem of extreme poverty, extreme wealth involves only a tiny sliver of the overall population, and one which presents some unique challenges. But unlike those in extreme poverty, the extremely wealthy exercise a great deal of economic and political power over the whole system. Therefore, the

---

[62] See Christopher Jencks, "The War on Poverty: Was It Lost?" *New York Review of Books*, April 2, 2015, 82-85.
[63] Bruce D. Meyer and James X. Sullivan, "Winning the War: Poverty From the Great Society to the Great Recession," NBER Working Paper No. 18718, January 2013; www.nber.org/papers/w18718.pdf.
[64] Obviously such issues do involve access to adequate health care, which is part of the larger economic picture, albeit a very complicated one in the U.S.

problem of extreme wealth is more impactful on overall inequality, even if their numbers are small.

The crucial moral argument involves the prudent application of "inequality as theft," by making some distinctions among the top group. In explaining the "increased skewness at the top," economists Robert Gordon and Ian Dew-Becker introduce "a three-way distinction between superstars in the sports and entertainment industries, high-paid lawyers and investment bankers who do not have the audience-magnifying properties of superstars, and the controversial additional category of CEOs and other top corporate managers."[65] These groups function differently. The authors attributes much of the increase in "superstar" pay and in pay to prestigious law and banking firms to market forces, amplified by technological developments. In principle, these individuals are genuinely earning their very high rates of pay, at least in terms of securing their income by putting their services in a competitive marketplace. It would be difficult to characterize this as theft.

But Gordon and Dew-Becker go on to ask, "Why is there any need to distinguish between CEOs and our broadly defined set of superstars? The primary distinction is that CEOs are not paid like superstars by multiplying a ticket price times numbers of tickets sold (or for investment bankers the price per deal times the number of deals). Rather, CEOs, through compensation committees and inbreeding of boards of directors, have a unique ability to control their own compensation."[66] Thus, Gordon and Dew-Becker imply what others have also argued: that CEO pay in particular is ethically suspect, because they are not simply earning their incomes through productivity in market competition. In a genuine sense, the problem of insular pay systems for CEO's involves outright unjust appropriation of proceeds of a business, proceeds which might go to stockholders – or perhaps better, to workers. Moral argument that the rich "take" unjustly from others is most effective if it is accurately targeted.

Other activities that amplify the wealth of the 1% might also be classifiable as theft. Three are worth naming. First, there is the maintenance of quasi-monopolies. Stiglitz in particular highlights examples, such as the credit card industry, where (even apart from usurious interest rates) outsized profits are made by charging far more than a service requires to provide.[67] Atkinson also suggests that the oft-cited factor of technological change may "be biased in favor of capital,"

---

[65] Robert J. Gordon and Ian Dew-Becker, "Controversies about the Rise of American Inequality: A Survey," NBER Working Paper no. 13982 (2008), 19, www.nber.org/papers/w13982.
[66] Gordon & Dew-Becker, "Controversies," 28.
[67] Joseph Stiglitz, "Monopoly's New Era," *Project Syndicate*, May 13, 2016; www.project-syndicate.org/commentary/high-monopoly-profits-persist-in-markets-by-joseph-e--stiglitz-2016-05?barrier=accessreg. See also Stiglitz, *Great Divide*.

insofar as it enables a small number of large firms to control technology and attain uncompetitively-high profit levels.[68] Second, the payment of manifestly unjust wages in otherwise-profitable companies is clearly named by the Catholic Catechism as a form of theft (*Catechism*, no. 2409). In these cases, guidelines for prudence should be developed; I will further comment on the role of such guidelines below.

A third set of activities which should be carefully scrutinized are those of finance. At the upper end, studies agree that much of the rise of inequality is due to the increasing financialization of the economy, which has led to explosive growth in capital gains.[69] Most people accept the need for a functioning financial and banking system in advanced economies. But as Keynes famously quipped, "It is usually agreed that casinos should, in the public interest, be inaccessible and expensive. And perhaps the same is true of stock exchanges."[70] In the United States, we now do neither. Thus, to address inequality, Lindert and Williamson support much tighter regulation of the financial industry, which not only would limit returns at the top, but more importantly would help those at the bottom by "the prevention of unemployment caused by financial busts."[71] As Deaton points out, financial services may "play an important role in financing innovation," but "some highly profitable financial activities are of little benefit to the population as a whole, and may even threaten the stability of the financial system."[72]

The question of how and when finance becomes theft is a difficult one, but in his recent book, Alasdair MacIntyre offers an interesting argument on this point. MacIntyre suggests most moral disagreements in a community offer "opportunities for learning," but that some disagreements require engaging in conflict when the opponents are "enemies of any rationally defensible conception of civil and political order."[73] Who might these be? MacIntyre cites national ratios of CEO-to-worker pay – perhaps a bit too facilely – but then suggests the reasons these agents are enemies of the order is because they "immunize themselves from risk" while making decisions that "expose the weakest and most vulnerable to risk" and make them and their children "pay

---

[68] Atkinson, *Inequality*, 96.
[69] Dadush et. al., *Inequality*, 17.
[70] John Maynard Keynes, *The General Theory of Employment, Interest, and Money* (Boston: Harcourt, 1964; orig. 1936), 159.
[71] Lindert and Williamson, *Unequal Gains*, 260.
[72] Angus Deaton, *The Great Escape: Health, Wealth, and the Origins of Inequality* (Princeton: Princeton University Press, 2013), 209. In his discussion of top incomes, he similarly distinguishes between superstars/innovators and the problems of CEO pay and financialization.
[73] Alasdair MacIntyre, *Ethics in the Conflicts of Modernity* (New York: Cambridge University Press, 2016), 219-220.

the cost." In so doing, they seek to appropriate *gains* to themselves, but inflict *losses* on others. For MacIntyre, this makes them necessarily enemies of "the common goods of family, workplace, and school." The description here – which could then be further specified by economists – may not apply to every capitalist institution at every point in time, but insofar as the intention of their actions is to maximize personal gain and socialize loss, the gains may be understood as theft. In all of the above instances, ethical and economic critique substantially converge and enhance one another.

The problem of extreme wealth in today's world has a few indirect effects that are less easily characterizable as theft. Instead, they contribute to the complex and pervasive problem of "inequality as fragmentation," spilling over into the problems of inequality in the 90+% portion of the income scale. For example, geographically, extreme wealth has an interesting set of effects. The largest extremes in current inequality tend to emerge in the so-called "global cities," which for various reasons concentrate a great deal of high-earning talent in finance, technology, and education.[74] These "post-industrial production sites" tellingly display among the highest Gini coefficients in the United States: New York City and San Francisco, rather than the Rust Belt.[75] These are often quite "progressive" places, concerned about inequality, and yet are great engines for generating it.[76] Ironically, by concentrating this wealth, these are also the places where demand, even for medium-skill manual work, is relatively high, and to which some economists suggest the citizens of places like Port Clinton should move. Putnam's Port Clinton vignettes do not involve the 1%, but of course part of Port Clinton's problem has been the erosion of work at adequate wages by the corporate and financial centralizations of globalization. Putnam's poor kids also suffer from a constant squeeze placed on public services that depend upon increasingly geographically-based funding disparities. It would be hard to overlook the

---

[74] See Saskia Sassen, *The Global City* (Princeton: Princeton University Press, 1991).
[75] See "Income Inequality in the U.S. by state, metropolitan area, and county"; www.epi.org/publication/income-inequality-in-the-us/. The study also indicates that small regions which include highly-desirable resort and retirement areas (Florida, Nevada, parts of the Mountain West) also have very high inequalities. By contrast, the states among the lowest in inequality were, regardless of region or even politics, those which lacked major cities or celebrity destinations (Iowa, Nebraska, Vermont, Maine, West Virginia, etc.) – strikingly, the lowest 10 states have a total of zero professional sports franchises in the four major sports. For full data on every US county, see the graphs available through the St. Louis Federal Reserve site: fred.stlouisfed.org/search?st=income+quintiles.
[76] The originator of the notion of the "creative class," Richard Florida, has recently highlighted the serious problems generated by these cities. See *The New Urban Crisis: How Our Cities Are Increasing Inequality, Deepening Segregation, and Failing the Middle Class and What We Can Do About It* (New York: Basic Books, 2017).

fact that the very rich faced extremely high levels of national taxation throughout the period of the Great Levelling – much higher than they do today. Besides marking the coming of the perpetual budget deficit, many other babies went out with the bath water of "eliminating government waste," from adequate infrastructure spending to Putnam's frequently-highlighted example of free participation in character-building school sports.

Unfortunately, the above claims are not limited to the 1%, but arise among a much broader section of the upper-middle class, who may not command large flows of wealth individually, but who nevertheless enjoy disproportionately the collective benefits of global cities, key tax breaks, and the like. This is an area in which ethics is most needed and least developed: the increasing division between two segments of the population, both of which are far larger than the extreme rich or extreme poor. This is the "place" where most of us live; the concern about "inequality as fragmentation" best accounts for its moral challenges. If some of the 1% are thieves, and some of the extremely poor are simply excluded from basic human dignity, the much larger group in the middle faces serious challenges in the actual structures of social solidarity. We need more precision about this. What actions are fragmenting the fabric, and what responsibilities do agents in those social locations bear?

This is a very difficult conversation, because it often involves actions that seem ordinary and innocent, but are nevertheless aspects of the problem. Consider first the example of increasingly expensive housing, particularly in areas with the most well-educated and prosperous populations. When (as some economists suggest) the solution to dying rural towns is that people should move to where the jobs are, one of the prime objections made is that adequate, safe housing in these areas is unaffordable.[77] Moreover, within those areas, differentials in school districts and commuting convenience (both of which contribute to quality parenting) are subject to intense competition, bidding up prices in what Robert Frank calls "expenditure cascades." Finally, those already present in the existing market and older workers benefit greatly from these expenditure cascades and often resist efforts that would in fact create more "affordable housing" – since that means they won't make as much money from their house. City planners have coined the acronym BANANAs for these folks: build absolutely nothing anywhere near anything. And once someone squeezes into these markets, they "go bananas," because the last thing one desires is for inflated housing prices to decrease.

---

[77] On this debate, see Rod Dreher, "Why Don't Poor People Move?" *The American Conservative*, December 12, 2016, www.theamericanconservative.com/dreher/why-dont-poor-people-move/. Dreher's article also makes a deeper cultural point about social belonging that is relevant but complicated.

A second example involves the protection of salaries and benefits by older workers at the expense of younger ones. For example, many cities and some corporations face pension crises due to what can only seem today like exorbitant promises, and the refusal of older workers to sacrifice some of these benefits has generally had the effect of either squeezing or altogether eliminating younger workers.[78] An example that might hit closer to home is the wage earned by senior professors at struggling educational institutions, which not only makes getting an academic job harder but deprives those younger faculty (who are often raising children and trying to compete in the aforementioned housing markets) of the compensation they genuinely need.

Finally, consider the challenging role of family formation choices and immigration in the fragmentation. Some studies have indicated about a third of the overall inequality increase since the 1970's has to do with changing marriage patterns – on the one hand, the impoverishing increase in single-parent families and on the other, the enriching increase in "assortative mating" in which high-income individuals are more and more likely to marry other high-income individuals.[79] To be sure, some of this change may be understood more as effect than cause: studies in particular indicate that the rise of single-parenting is in part due to the disappearance of good-paying jobs for less-educated men, such that the women who opt not to marry may be making a better economic choice.[80] As Andrew Cherlin notes, for many blue-collar women, the loss of stable, economically-attractive marriage partners makes children "the reward they know they can get."[81] Regardless of blame, there is clearly a cycle here that contributes significantly to rising inequality, just as there is a cycle in which two high-income professionals are in quite a commanding position to bid up housing prices.

Immigration raises further complications. Economists of all stripes acknowledge that the unusual character of the midcentury labor market was in part due to a strong tightening of immigration quotas in the 1930's through the 1970's. As Lindert and Williamson note about the Great Levelling, low-education immigrants fell from 21% of the labor force at the beginning of the period to 5.4% in 1970 – a number that

---

[78] The example of my birth state, Illinois, is the most extreme: see Matt Egan, "How Illinois Became America's Most Messed-Up State," CNN, July 1, 2017, money.cnn.com/2017/06/29/investing/illinois-budget-crisis-downgrade/index.html.
[79] See the report on studies in Aparna Mathur, "The Biggest Reason for Income Inequality is Single Parenthood," American Enterprise Institute, November 19, 2014, www.aei.org/publication/biggest-reason-income-inequality-single-parenthood/.
[80] Emily Badger offers a response in the *Washington Post*, April 10, 2014, www.washingtonpost.com/news/wonk/wp/2014/04/10/the-relationship-between-single-mothers-and-poverty-is-not-as-simple-as-it-seems/?utm_term=.b7f1ca6e0f88.
[81] Andrew Cherlin, *The Marriage-Go-Round* (New York: Knopf, 2009), 165.

rose back up to 15% by 2005.[82] Some studies suggest that this rise of immigration contributes only a little to the *overall* picture of inequality.[83] However, others point out that, while this is true, the impact of immigration is not felt as an "average" across all workers, but rather on *particular groups of workers* – more precisely, low-skilled workers.[84] While the evidence is complex, it may be the case that immigration is actually most challenging to *earlier* immigrants who work in immigrant-heavy sectors, increasing the competition between older and newer arrivals and pushing down overall wages in the sector.[85] But who benefits? Again, it is the upper-middle class who depend on immigrant labor to produce the goods and services to support their lifestyles.

These examples all involve facing up to the fact that inequality is not simply about the very rich and the very poor. Crucially, it is about individual choices and structures in the "middle" of the economy. But a recognition of the complexity here seems to make identifying moral responsibilities extremely difficult. Are we faced with a proportionalist trade-off between immigrants rightly searching for a better life and native-born workers also seeking to hold onto that life? Do we recommend that the highly educated start rethinking their marriage choices in order to spread the wealth around? Do we force senior workers to take pay cuts? All these options seem problematic, both practically and on moral grounds.

Yet there are important and underappreciated resources for addressing the economic factors that drive this fragmentation. In *Dream Hoarders*, Richard Reeves suggests that the "obsession" with the 1% "allows the upper middle class to convince ourselves we are in the same boat as the rest of America; but it is not true."[86] As noted earlier, those in the top quintile of income account for virtually all of the inequality rise since 1979, and "for each extra dollar going to the 'upper class,' two dollars went to the upper middle class."[87] These gains added to their relative advantages in relation to the median. Much of this relative gain is explained by economists as "skill-biased technical

---

[82] Lindert & Williamson, *Unequal Gains*, 232.
[83] David Card, "Immigration and Inequality," NBER Working Paper no. 14683, 2009, www.nber.org/papers/w14683.
[84] Steven Camerota, "Unskilled Workers Lose Out to Immigrants," *New York Times*, January 6, 2015, www.nytimes.com/roomfordebate/2015/01/06/do-immigrants-take-jobs-from-american-born-workers/unskilled-workers-lose-out-to-immigrants. See also Pamela Constable, "The Majority of Undocumented Immigrants Work in Low-Skill Jobs," *Washington Post*, March 26, 2015, www.washingtonpost.com/local/majority-of-undocumented-immigrants-work-in-low-skill-jobs-report-finds/2015/03/26/dada9f2a-d3bc-11e4-a62f-ee745911a4ff_story.html?utm_term=.9b0dfbdd7358.
[85] Gordon and Dew-Becker, "Controversies," 14-15.
[86] Reeves, *Dream Hoarders*, 3-4.
[87] Reeves, *Dream Hoarders*, 24.

progress"—that is, as technology progresses, the premium attached to developing greater skills is greater.[88] But Reeves argues that many of these advantages come from a fierce defense of systems of privilege that protect advantages, from exclusionary zoning laws to preferential tax treatment for housing wealth and college savings to the ability to use the extra wealth to support children in expensive cities if they take the many "unpaid internships" that are such a crucial advantage in landing jobs in the professional class.[89] He even notes how the practice of "merit aid" at mid-tier colleges means that it is much more advantageous for such schools to offer $5000 "scholarships" to four average (but wealthy) students – and then get the rest of their tuition money – than to offer one $20,000 scholarship to an above-average but poor student.[90] The sum total of all these practices is what Reeves calls "opportunity hoarding" by the upper middle class, especially in order to pass on this position to their children. In short, Reeves suggests that it's not the super-rich that stand in the way of struggle working-class people trying to help their children make it; it's the upper-middle class, who push up housing prices, have extra dollars to spend for test prep, and in general are able to use their extra funds to maintain their position.

The heart of this problem—and in a way, the real reason the Kuznets hypothesis is not sustained over the long run – is this phenomenon of economic positionality, or "positional competition." It has been identified clearly at least since Fred Hirsch's landmark *The Social Limits to Growth*. That book, developed in partial response to the early 1970's "limits to growth" concern about natural resources, argues a twofold thesis. First, as economies become more affluent, more and more of the population participates in the market for "positional goods" – that is, goods and services whose characteristics include a relative, positional aspect. "In a poor society," Hirsch writes, "the consumption of the mass of the population is concentrated on basic material goods," and "the positional sector is uncrowded" – in such a situation, the (vain) competitions of the rich do have spillover benefits to the larger population, as Adam Smith saw.[91] They do end up converting the excess wealth of the rich into the basic necessities of the poor. But once "demand for luxuries becomes more extensively diffused throughout the population," the competition for such goods increases,

---

[88] Deaton, *Great Escape*, 191-193.
[89] Interestingly, the very pro-market Peter Hill ("Creating and Distributing," 15) also notes this, saying "once redistributive programs are put in place, they are likely to result in transfers from the well-off to those in the middle rather than a transfer of resources from the rich to the poor."
[90] Reeves, *Dream Hoarders*, 89-91.
[91] This is the original meaning of Smith's reference to the "invisible hand" in *The Theory of Moral Sentiments* (part IV, chapter 1) (New York: Oxford University Press, 1976), 184.

and with this increased competition, their price.[92] But unlike basic commodity goods, the positional elements are inherently zero-sum, and so these resources are bid up in the aforementioned "expenditure cascades." While the price for raw computing power plummets, so that everyone can have a computer, other prices skyrocket. These costs soak up real resources of the society – they are, as Frank dubs them, smart for one (since, for example, you want to help your child succeed) but dumb for all (everyone makes the same expenditure, and so all the spending is devoted to holding position).[93] Thus, to use Reeves's example, as more and more families have enough excess income to compete with the very wealthy for schooling positionality, the previously uncrowded field of both private schools and desirable public districts becomes crowded further "down the grades." The effect is to limit access to "the most prestigious" schools, both because they become more and more expensive and (perhaps more importantly) the competition intensifies.

One might chide people for "keeping up with the Joneses," but as Frank argues, examples like college or housing aren't totally a product of Veblenian leisure-class envy and status competition (although they are sometimes). Instead, they are simply a matter of an increasingly wealthy upper-middle class using its excess income for its highest priorities. They *are* in fact smart for one – but they only remain smart insofar as the opportunities *are not available to all*. Thus, Hirsch's second, more damning prediction: because of the nature of positional goods, "what the wealthy have today can no longer be delivered to the rest of us tomorrow; yet as we individually grow richer, that is what we expect."[94] Hence, as the society grows richer, the need for cooperation in managing the commons and for moderate forms of redistribution—that is, for solidarity—actually becomes *harder*… because the resources that need to be shared are the ones the upper-middle class are using to help their own children. Reeves illustrates this by the Obama administration's attempt to remove the tax-free "529 savings plans" for college, which disproportionately provide a tax benefit for

---

[92] Fred Hirsch, *The Social Limits to Growth* (Cambridge: Harvard University Press, 1976), 66.

[93] Robert H. Frank, *Luxury Fever* (New York: Free Press, 1999), 146-158, gives a range of examples of this phenomenon, from the use of high heels to the costs of advertising to the use of steroids in sports to the SAT test prep industry. In each case, an individual behavior that seeks a positional advantage is nullified when everyone engages in the behavior, and so resources are burned up with no advantage gain. Frank contrasts this sort of competition with non-positional competition, which increases overall productivity, by developing new methods of production, more efficient uses of resources, and the like. Non-positional competition is smart for one AND smart for all. A relevant example for professors explains this contrast further: college degrees function both as a differentiating credential and as an investment in the development of human skills and abilities. The former function is positional; the latter is not.

[94] Hirsch, *Social Limits*, 67.

the wealthy (the ones with more funds to save).[95] The shelving of this attempt was due, according to Reeves, to the efforts of Democrats from wealthy suburban districts whose constituents counted on this tax break and saw it as a win-win – savings for them, and a better chance for college for their child. The group to whom the tax break mattered most were those families for whom a $60,000 a year college tuition bill could be managed if they saved along the way – but of course they were the ones who *had* the excess to save in the first place.[96] For families making just over $100,000, this was the tax break that enabled them to keep up with the increasing positional pressures imposed by the heightened competition for the most elite schools. Presumably, working class families wouldn't have cared – because they saved very little in these accounts.

While some aspects of upper-middle class life are positional in this indirect sense, where a genuine good is sought but in collectively-wasteful ways, others are positional in a more "keeping up with the Joneses" sense: they are expectations that come to be expected as "ordinary," even though in past times, they would certainly have been seen as something pretty much reserved for the rich. As Deaton points out, the trajectory of US economic growth over the past six decades meant that roughly "each generation would have double the living standards of its parents," a pace which "would have astonished our ancestors."[97] Things like routine foreign travel, eating out regularly with children, even the practice of buying 8-10 custom-tailored business shirts a year sound (at least to my ears) like practices of the very wealthy, but are clearly understood as routine among many "upper-middles."[98] These sorts of extravagant practices not only make people in the upper-middle "feel" like they are "just getting by" (and so are less open to, say, the removal of preferential tax treatment), but also

---

[95] Reeves, *Dream Hoarders*, 136-137.
[96] The advantage accruing to the top 20% because of the tax code is enormous. The cap on payroll taxes makes them regressive starting just about at the top quintile. And in total, the deductions for mortgage interest and property taxes save the top 20% nearly $70 billion, while the middle *40%* get less than $30 billion out of it. The bottom 40%? Virtually nothing. See "Who Benefits from Asset-building Tax Subsidies"; www.urban.org/research/publication/who-benefits-asset-building-tax-subsidies (referenced in Reeves, *Dream Hoarders*, 105).
[97] Deaton, *Great Escape*, 170.
[98] Neil Irwin – apparently unwittingly – reveals the shirt-buying habits of journalists in "The Amazon-Walmart Showdown That Explains the Modern Economy," *New York Times*, June 16, 2017: "I used to buy my dress shirts from a Hong Kong tailor. They fit perfectly, but ordering required an awkward meeting with a visiting salesman in a hotel suite. They took six weeks to arrive, and they cost around $120 each, which adds up fast when you need to buy eight or 10 a year to keep up with wear and tear. Then several years ago I realized that a company called Bonobos was making shirts that fit me nearly as well, that were often sold three for $220, or $73 each, and that would arrive in two days." www.nytimes.com/2017/06/16/upshot/the-amazon-walmart-showdown-that-explains-the-modern-economy.html.

set presumed standards for lifestyle choices that the middle class simply can't meet. A recent commentary by David Brooks on the fragmenting effects of such cultural standards (building on Reeves' book) is remarkable, not least for the tone-deaf reactions from upper middles.[99] My father rose through the hotel ranks to a management position, but eating out meant Denny's on occasion, vacation meant driving to Wisconsin, and his dress shirts were not consumed at that rate. Both the systemic and the standard-of-living versions of positional goods exacerbate inequality "in the middle." They undermine a more robust sense of social solidarity by embroiling the relatively wealthy upper-middles in spending patterns that require the rich to feel like they are not "really" rich.[100] These are all examples of "inequality as fragmentation," ways the upper middle class acts that sacrifice its ability to exercise real solidarity with those who are barely getting by.

INEQUALITY AND THE MORAL ECOLOGY OF THE MARKET

By correlating the three theological construals of the problem of inequality with three distinguishable aspects of the economic phenomenon of inequality, we are able to bring more clarity and precision to specific moral responsibilities. We can go even further in doing so by analyzing these three aspects of inequality in terms of Daniel Finn's proposal that issues of markets and justice involve attention to the "moral ecology of markets." The four aspects of Finn's moral ecology speak further to specific demands of justice in the three different areas.

Finn's framework highlights the insufficiency of arguing over individual self-interest and greed when trying to understand and evaluate economic actions in market economies. He develops the framework to overcome the tendency for economic ethics to reach an impasse between those who argue that markets are fundamentally "amoral" and those who argue that markets are inherently morally suspect because they form agents who act simply in terms of self-interest. The problem, Finn notes, is that "we cannot assess markets, or even comprehend them, in isolation."[101] We should resist asking the question "Are markets just?" Instead, we should recognize that individual exercises of self-interest in markets can be beneficial or harmful based on four elements of the context – or "moral ecology" – within which

---

[99] See David Brooks, "How We Are Ruining America," *New York Times*, July 11, 2017, www.nytimes.com/2017/07/11/opinion/how-we-are-ruining-America.html?_r=0. On the reaction, see Rod Dreher, "When is a Sandwich Not Just a Sandwich?" www.theamericanconservative.com/dreher/sandwich-david-brooks-culture-class/.

[100] Atkinson, *Inequality*, 38, relates key studies of how higher-income professional consistently underestimate where they are located in the income scale.

[101] Daniel K. Finn, *The Moral Ecology of Markets: Assessing Claims about Markets and Justice* (New York: Cambridge University Press, 2006).

the exchange takes place.[102] The first is the basic recognition that while markets involve free exchanges, these exchanges always exist within social structures with restrictions – "fences" – which limit the arena of free exchange. Thus, some moral debate is really about where to put the fences. Second, all markets exist in a larger context where "the provision of essential goods and services" is required, to facilitate market transactions themselves (e.g. a fair court system for upholding contracts), as well as to manage provision for those who are unable to do so through the market (e.g. children and the elderly). The provision of comprehensive education, for example, makes children expensive, but ultimately also supports the market with an educated and trained workforce. Some moral debate is about how these essentials are provided, and whether some are unable to receive them. Thirdly, markets depend on "the morality of individuals and groups." For example, one economist begins his introductory textbook by suggesting the key differential between advanced and less developed economies is simply trust – the ability, with low transaction costs, to carry out various exchanges with strangers both facilitating and necessitated by a widespread division of labor.[103] Finn notes as well that Ayn Rand's morally-libertarian novels make "almost no reference" to the labor of love that is the rearing of children, and its obvious importance for flourishing markets.[104] Fourthly, Finn notes the importance of "a vibrant civil society," in significant part because its associations "are critically important for the appropriate resolution of the first three elements of the moral ecology of markets" – serving as places to cultivate civic virtues, mediating decision-making processes about market "fences," and supporting various public-spirited ways to provide essential goods in cases where markets do not do so.[105]

How might looking at the present state of the market's moral ecology help us further specify the demands of justice to address problems of inequality? While the correspondence is not exact, one can see ways in which the problems in each of our three areas of economic inequality involve different elements of Finn's moral ecology. Perhaps most obviously, those who suffer from extreme poverty and experience outright exclusion are lacking in their access to essential goods and services. Somehow the market has failed to deliver for this group, in the sense that they are unable to generate enough market income to meet their most basic needs. There is a moral responsibility in justice to

---

[102] Finn, *Moral Ecology*, 111-112, offers a very vivid comparison of the consumer facing two cans – one dented, one not – and two rugs – one cheap, one not – and explains how in one case the self-interested decision produces a chain of beneficial effects, whereas in the other it produces a chain of effects that entrench injustice.
[103] Partha Dasgupta, *Economics: A Very Short Introduction* (Oxford University Press, 2007), 30-47.
[104] Finn, *Moral Ecology*, 132.
[105] Finn, *Moral Ecology*, 138-39.

address this problem.[106] No one, whatever their own moral flaws, "deserves" to starve. Prudence, then, is required to develop a better understanding of what exactly is happening in these cases in our society, and what actions are needed that would best help, especially because access to ordinary economic exchange is key to dignified social participation.

For those at the top of the income structure, the preeminent concern of the moral ecology should be about "fences." The problems of unfair oligopolistic profits, unjust wages, and problematic financial-sector activities all can and must be addressed through regulations. For example, the rules and regulations of the finance sector must be tightened. Whatever the personal greediness of very rich people, much of what goes on in global finance involves large institutional investing, sovereign wealth funds, and various other impersonal entities. And the same is true for multinational corporations and their stocks. To personalize these decisions (tempting as it is) is to return to an age of overlords or robber barons that is not objectively characteristic of today's financial sector. Perhaps the very existence of these large impersonal entities is the problem, but already we are in the land of Finn's "fences," since the size and scope of corporations themselves are a creation of law. Arguments about "breaking up" corporations or banks are arguments about the right placement of fences. The same is true about international currency markets, the key to the dream of John Maynard Keynes for the world economy emerging from World War II.[107] It is a mistake to think that one can simply do *without* such systems – the question is always about how to structure the systems, and most often this involves making rules about what is allowed and what is not allowed.

When Pope Francis suggests that the financial crisis reveals "a new idolatry of money" in which "the worship of the ancient golden calf has returned in a new and ruthless guise in… the dictatorship of an impersonal economy lacking a truly human purpose," he says in high relief what has been said perennially by the popes: that business and finance should serve people, and not the other way around (*Evangelii Gaudium*, no. 55). While it might sound as if Francis is simply criticizing individual attitudes, he astutely goes on to note how this idolatrous system rejects any "control" by those "charged with vigilance for the common good" (no. 56). Rejecting control is unjust because it results in theft, most vividly thought of as the true target of the

---

[106] Though, as Finn has suggested elsewhere, this is best understood simply in terms of the longstanding Christian commitment to addressing poverty and offering to all basic human dignity.

[107] Benn Steil, *The Battle of Bretton Woods: John Maynard Keynes, Harry Dexter White, and the Making of a New World Order* (Princeton: Princeton University Press, 2014).

longstanding prohibition against usury, actions which result in the transfer of wealth from the poor to the rich with no real good produced.[108] Charles Clark and David Zalewski conclude that addressing financialization "will require innovative thinking on how incentives can channel the profit motive so that wealth creation is tied to well-being promotion. It will require a change in social attitudes so that long run sustainable economic progress is promoted and not the bonus culture of winning the lottery. And it will require regulations and regulators that are on equal footing with the firms they are regulating."[109] While there is a moral dimension to these steps ("social attitudes"), proper incentive structures and regulation – that is, *fences* to block kinds of theft – are key.[110]

What about the problem of the growing split in the middle of the economy? What does justice require? In terms of Finn's framework, we must recognize that some of the factors – such as technological innovation and even global trade – are simply outcomes of markets. Yes, they depend to an extent on fences and can prompt responses involving the (re)distribution of essential benefits. But these problems in the middle are far less straightforward than the first two. This is in part because their causation is simply a lot more complex. But it is also because the typical solutions proposed have a very difficult time hitting the mark. Take two examples. One reaction to global competition has a long history: protectionist policies. And one reaction to increasingly divergent compensation is to impose various sorts of minimum requirements across the board on employers – most prominently, a minimum wage. It is telling that, on both of these issues, economists across the ideological spectrum are at best muted in their support for these inventions, but often enough are vocal in explaining how – though they *seem* beneficial – they actually impose substantial overall costs in the long run, sometimes on the very people they are designed to help. Protectionist policies seem to help workers, but they may in fact most benefit domestic companies who are shielded from competition and therefore become inefficient. Across-the-board minimum wage policies may simply produce inflation. Both policies may induce employers to speed up the process of automation, eliminating exactly the lowest-skilled positions. None of these arguments produce moral absolutes one way or the other – trade is always regulated and should be fair, some minimum wage and working conditions level is agreed

---

[108] Charles M.A. Clark and David A. Zalewski make this comparison to usury, as well as a more detailed argument explaining the problems and possibilities of financialization. See "Rethinking Finance in Light of Catholic Social Thought," *Journal of Catholic Social Thought* 12 (2015): 19-44.
[109] Clark and Zalewski, *Rethinking Finance*, 44.
[110] An additional crucial fence, noted especially by Lindert and Williamson, *Unequal Gains*, 259, is the inheritance tax on family fortunes, which they rightly understand to be a moral imperative for America's anti-hereditary-class identity.

to by virtually everyone. But prudence requires us to recognize that, when addressing the "Our Kids" problem of the growing gap between a poor low-skill class and an increasingly-wealthy "creative class," these typical solutions aren't moral slam dunks.

Finn's framework proves particularly helpful by directing attention to the other two elements of the market's moral ecology – too often overlooked, and in fact absolutely central to controlling this problem in more precise ways that move toward real social solidarity. Virtually every analysis of this problem calls attention to the breakdown of civil society institutions that used to exist, and most importantly, to institutions that would provide a space for members of both classes to come together and solve problems collectively.[111]

Where should the attention to civil society be directed? Here there is an interesting comparison of two recent comprehensive studies of inequality. In Anthony Atkinson's volume, he proposes a series of solutions, a number of which aim to increase the "countervailing power" for workers in the marketplace—most notably, a better framework for unions and a "voluntary pay code" developed out of a "national conversation."[112] On the other hand, Lindert and Williamson's study insists most strongly on the importance of educating labor to be more skilled. They caution against equating this proposal to more spending on education, since, they say, such increases in recent decades have not improved performance; however, it must involve "more learning," insofar as the US workforce once (but no longer) was the most educated and genuinely skillful in the world.[113] Both schools and unions are elements of civil society – and perhaps both are needed to address the gap in the middle. While this is a matter of prudence, not justice, given the current structure of U.S. society, one might suggest that Williamson and Lindert's education track is a more viable and worthwhile path in the long run. Barrera's detailed analysis of the proportionally-rising importance of the role of human capital in a knowledge economy establishes this on Catholic grounds.[114] This approach takes seriously another element that is highlighted in Barrera's work: the importance of what he calls "market-driven redistribution," as opposed to an abstract, after-the-fact redistribution. Reinforced by Finn's moral ecology, Barrera suggests that much more attention should be paid to "before-market" interventions that insure "universal access" to a mar-

---

[111] For competing examples, see Brian Alexander's narrative of Anchor Hocking's gradual departure from Lancaster, Ohio (*Glass House* [Boston: St. Martin's Press, 2017]) and Beth Macy's description of Bassett Furniture's remaining in Bassett, Virginia (*Factory Man* [New York: Little Brown, 2014]).
[112] Atkinson, *Inequality*, 115-154.
[113] Lindert and Williamson, *Unequal Gains*, 258-259.
[114] See Barrera, *Globalization*.

ket whose demands now may require "higher entry cost" and "intensified socialization."[115] For instance, a recent article gives a heartening example of a rural community college system in South Dakota that has partnered very effectively with local industry to increase training for workers and place them immediately into higher-skilled manufacturing jobs already present regionally.[116]

But it is also important to address the morality of individuals and groups, and this in two ways, corresponding to the two sides of this problem. On the one hand, the crucial role of the broken family structure is not denied, even by more liberal observers.[117] What those observers do typically deny is that the government can do much about this. They may be right, but this is exactly why Finn includes the morality of individuals and groups in the moral ecology of an economy. What would be unjust, in this case, is to ignore this problem or pretend it doesn't exist. As Nicholas Barr notes, a major challenge being faced by all welfare states is "the possibility that the strategic design of the welfare state is based, at least in part, on a past social order with stable, two-parent families, with high levels of employment, and where most jobs were full-time and relatively stable."[118] But it is also important to avoid a "closed household" approach to family life, where this issue is reduced to exerting individual will to "save marriage." As most eloquently seen in the work of David McCarthy and Julie Hanlon Rubio, communities – especially church communities – must bring families who are challenged into networks of support, care, and genuine mutual sharing.[119] Of course, some moral commitments could also result in more family-friendly structures, such as paid parental leave. If advocates for norms of familial responsibility as a response to economic inequality want to be taken seriously, then they ought at the same time to insist on the simultaneous responsibilities of community and business to make room for personal commitment.

On the other hand, the earlier discussion of the increasing "positional" economy suggests a crucial moral blind spot on the part of the wealthy: their inability to retain modest standards of ordinary life that would keep them closer to their fellow workers, reduce the economic competition for some critical goods and services, free up economic resources for investment in common goods that would benefit and bring together both groups, and set realistic and realizable standards

---

[115] Barrera, *Modern Catholic Social Documents*, 177-223.
[116] Josh Sanburn, "The Case for Community College," *Time*, June 1, 2017, time.com/4800811/the-case-for-community-college/.
[117] See, for example, Putnam, *Our Kids*, 244-251.
[118] Nicholas Barr, *Economics of the Welfare State*, 4th ed. (New York: Oxford University Press, 2004), 14.
[119] See David Matzko McCarthy, *Sex and Love in the Home: A Theology of the Household* (London: SPCK, 2001) and Julie Hanlon Rubio, *Family Ethics: Practices for Christians* (Washington: Georgetown University Press, 2010).

of "social inclusion" and "success" for those who make less. This is why I have argued for the importance of reviving a shared sense of the vice of luxury, especially a critique that is not simply aimed at the very wealthy. As with questions of family structure, it is not easy to legislate solutions to address this problem (though some might help).[120] So again, Finn's inclusion of the morality of individuals and groups as a key element for "regulating" markets morally is essential. Solidarity simply can't happen if the ordinary lifestyle gap is in practice too wide. In my study of the vice of luxury, I emphasize the fact that wealthier members of the society can think more thoroughly about how they spend their money, so that it becomes a means of both financial support of and personal solidarity with those who are providing them with whatever they are buying, instead of merely more European travel, tailored shirts, and Uber-driven mobility. This is a crucial element of realizing Pope Benedict's insistence that even market transactions themselves must be infused with "quotas of gratuitousness and communion" *(Caritas in Veritate*, no. 39).

CONCLUSION

Moral arguments about economic inequality are widespread but often imprecise. In this essay, I have drawn on both economic literature and theological studies to develop a differentiated account of the demands of justice in addressing the very complex problem of rising inequality in advanced societies. By differentiating three types of injustice in inequality, and by connecting those accounts to specific economic factors of the problem, we are able to name the problem at different "places" in the society more precisely. We are especially able to see that a significant part of the problem of inequality is not a matter of the very poor or the very rich. Finally, by looking at these different areas through the lens of the market's "moral ecology," we are able to name – not exactly, but with increasing precision – the responsibilities of justice that must be undertaken if we are to build a genuinely human and grace-filled economy. That economy may not give everyone everything that they want, but it will do a better job at giving people what they deserve, and just as importantly, binding us closer together in solidarity in our pursuit of common goods. Ⓜ

---

[120] In particular, different overall measures of economic success and an emphasis on Pigouvian consumption taxes would help; see Cloutier, *Vice of Luxury*, 166-169.

Contributors

David Cloutier is associate professor of theology at The Catholic University of America in Washington, DC. He is the author of several books, including *The Vice of Luxury* (Georgetown University Press, 2015) and *Walking God's Earth: The Environment and Catholic Faith* (Liturgical Press, 2014), as well as the co-editor (with Jana Bennett) of a forthcoming collection of essays on the seven deadly sins and the sacrament of reconciliation. He blogs at catholicmoraltheology.com.

Kari-Shane Davis Zimmerman is Associate Professor of Theology at the College of Saint Benedict/Saint John's University (MN). She teaches undergraduate courses in Catholic theology, Christian ethics, sexual ethics, economic ethics, and feminist ethics. Dr. Davis Zimmerman has published articles in *Horizons*, *Heythrop Journal*, and the *Journal of Catholic Social Thought*. She is married with three children.

Craig A. Ford, Jr., is a doctoral candidate in theological ethics at Boston College. His research is principally at the intersection of queer theory and the natural law tradition, and his dissertation is entitled "Foundations of a Queer Natural Law." Before living in Boston, Craig received his M.A.R from Yale Divinity School and his B.A. in Philosophy and Theology from the University of Notre Dame.

Jason King is Professor of Theology at St. Vincent College in Latrobe, PA. His *Faith with Benefits: Hookup Culture on Catholic Campuses* was published by Oxford University Press in 2017.

Marcus Mescher is an Assistant Professor of Christian Ethics at Xavier University. He has contributed essays to the *Journal of Catholic Social Thought* and the *Annual Volume of the College Theology Society* and chapters to *Green Discipleship, 2010Boston: The Changing Contours of World Mission and Christianity*, and the forthcoming *T&T Clark Companion to Christian Ethics*. He is currently working on his book manuscript *The Ethics of Encounter: Christian Neighbor Love as a Practice of Solidarity*.

Timothy P. Muldoon is a theologian, professor, and author/editor of twelve books, with particular interests in Ignatian spirituality and ecclesiology. He has taught at Boston College for over a decade. **Suzanne M. Muldoon** is a counselor and educator who has worked in clinical and academic settings. Together they are the parents of three teens and the authors of three books, the most recent of which is *Reclaiming Family Time: A Guide to Slowing Down and Savoring the Gift of One Another* (The Word Among Us Press, 2017).

Mary M. Doyle Roche is Associate Professor of Religious Studies at the College of the Holy Cross in Worcester, MA. She is the author of *Children, Consumerism, and the Common Good* (Lexington, 2009) and *Schools of Solidarity: Families and Catholic Social Teaching* (Liturgical, 2015).

Cristina L. H. Traina is Professor and Chair of Religious Studies at Northwestern University and 2017 President of the Society of Christian Ethics. She currently writes on issues of children's moral agency in work, migration, and consumer settings.

STUDENT INTERNS

Sydney D. Johnson, C'19, majoring in Philosophy with minors in History and Spanish, is from Lincoln, NE.

Molly K. Kennedy, C'18, is from Bethlehem, PA and is earning a double major in English and Communication.

Articles available to view
or download at:

www.msmary.edu/jmt

The

Journal of Moral Theology

is proudly sponsored by
The College of Liberal Arts
at
Mount St. Mary's University

With special thanks to
Sr. Mary Katherine Birge, S.S.J.,
Fr. James M. Forker Professor
of Catholic Social Teaching
and
Fr. James Donohue, C.R.,
Knott Professor of Theology

BIOETHICS & BEING HUMAN

Conference June 21-23, 2018

on the campus of
Trinity International University
Deerfield, IL USA

PLENARY SPEAKERS

Christina Bieber Lake, PhD
Wheaton College

Read Mercer Schuchardt, PhD
Wheaton College

C. Christopher Hook, MD
Mayo Clinic

Michael Sleasman, PhD
The Center for Bioethics & Human Dignity

Paul Scherz, PhD, PhD
Catholic University of America

Pia de Solenni, SThD
Roman Catholic Diocese of Orange

Warren Kinghorn, MD, ThD
Duke Divinity School
Duke University Medical School

Morse Tan, JD
NIU College of Law

Stephen Williams, PhD
Union Theological College

Join us for our 25th annual summer conference, as we explore anew our individual and common humanity in light of the ever-evolving developments in medicine, science, and technology. Plenary speakers will address being and remaining human in an age of science and technology, genetics, neuroscience & the BRAIN Initiative; bioethics in literature and pop culture; human rights & dignity; and theological examinations of contentment, human flourishing, particularity, and embodiment as they relate to bioethics.

Engage more personally in workshops and parallel sessions on a wide spectrum of perennial and emerging issues in contemporary bioethics relevant to professional practice, public policy, scholarship, the classroom, and making moral decisions in everyday life.

REGISTER

FOR EARLY BIRD PRICING BY MARCH 15
www.cbhd.org/conf2018

THE CENTER FOR
BIOETHICS
& HUMAN DIGNITY
TRINITY INTERNATIONAL UNIVERSITY

In Partnership with:

www.ingramcontent.com/pod-product-compliance
Lightning Source LLC
Chambersburg PA
CBHW071457150426
43191CB00008B/1376